POWER SPEECH

THE QUICKEST ROUTE TO BUSINESS AND PERSONAL SUCCESS

ROY ALEXANDER

With a foreword by Stewart Granger

amacom
AMERICAN MANAGEMENT ASSOCIATION

This book is available at a special
discount when ordered in bulk quantities.
For information, contact Special Sales Department,
AMACOM, a division of American Management Association,
135 West 50th Street, New York, NY 10020.

Library of Congress Cataloging-in-Publication Data

Alexander, Roy, 1925-
    Power speech.

    Bibliography: p.
    Includes index.
    1. Public speaking. 2. Success. I. Title.
PN4121.A45   1986   808.5'1   85-48214
ISBN 0-8144-5829-7

Printing number

10 9 8 7 6 5 4 3 2 1

To **Connie Jason:**
*Her professional standards have
enriched this book.
Her personal
speech enriches society.*

Other Books by Roy Alexander

Climbing the Corporate Matterhorn
  (with James A. Newman)

Direct Salesman's Handbook

Secrets of Closing Sales (with Charles B. Roth)

Nothing Is Impossible

Foreword

When filming the classic *King Solomon's Mines* with the talented Deborah Kerr, I was struck by the deftness of the screenwriter's dialogue—an inspiration to the cast. Later, critics hailed us for our "impressive, subtle, real-life performances."

In another movie, which will remain nameless, actors were flayed by critics for "pedestrian performances." Yet in the two movies, performers and director were equally competent. But the dialogue? As Hamlet warned us: "Aye, there's the rub."

These contrasts prove, once again, the power of *content* in speech. You must start with good content before delivery techniques mean much. That's why I'm delighted with this book. Roy Alexander takes us down dual roads—content *and* presentation—in revealing the wonders of power speech.

And what a wealth of instruction and information you'll find here! If I, a seasoned screen and stage performer, can learn from this book—as most certainly I have—there's something here for you, too.

I'm particularly impressed by the author's comingling of education and instruction—each making the other more memorable. *Power Speech* is a prime example of instruction that's compelling to read and re-read.

Shakespeare, that master of the spoken word, was fascinated by great men who changed history with speech. Henry V, born a king, was handsome, brave, clever. But we remember most his exhortation on the eve of Agincourt, as Shakespeare imagined it:

> Once more into the breach, dear friends, once more;
> Or close the wall up with English dead . . .
> I see you stand like greyhounds in the slips
> Straining upon the start. The game's afoot,
> Follow this spirit; and join this charge
> Cry: God for Harry! England! and Saint George!

Evaluate other headliners moving across the world stage. They are, without exception, adroit users of power speech.

Julius Caesar invaded Gaul. (There's a role I've always yearned to play!) In 47 B.C., after the decisive battle of Zella, he reported back to imperial Rome: *Veni, Vedi, Vici.* "I came. I saw. I conquered." Today I doubt if school boys and girls know much about the battle of Zella. But we will always remember what Caesar said there.

In the 1860s, Abraham Lincoln reunited America. One of his greatest weapons was power speech. Yet although his words at Gettysburg are immortal, Lincoln himself had no idea of his word power: "The world will little note nor long remember what we say here. But it can never forget what they did here."

During the 1940s, Winston Churchill stood as a bulwark against Nazism. That small, rotund figure, who did not cast a Lincolnesque shadow, unleashed speech that moved millions: "We shall fight on the beaches. We shall fight on the landing grounds. We shall fight in the fields and in the streets and in the hills. We shall never surrender." Churchill's words strengthened the free world's resolve when we stood with our backs to the wall.

In the 1960s, John F. Kennedy—young, handsome, confident—challenged Americans: "Ask not what your country can do for *you;* ask what *you* can do for your country." Powerful and unforgettable.

Now you aren't conquering Gaul, reuniting a fractured nation, standing alone against the Nazi hordes, or making your inaugural speech to a new generation. But your objectives in business and personal success are important to you and to society. Enhance your opportunities by learning and using power speech, a tool proved effective over the ages.

To speak better, I say: "Once more into this book, dear friends, once more." Power speech can be your career victory at Agincourt.

Stewart Granger
Hollywood, California

Acknowledgments

Basic acknowledgment, of course, must go to the thousands of speakers—all good in some ways, a favored few excellent in many ways—who inspired this book.

In a more personal sense, I'm indebted to two gifted speech teachers—Elizabeth Welch and Dorothy M. Crane—who taught me about quality and expression at a formative stage (otherwise you and I could not be holding this conversation now).

I've been influenced by professional performers (George C. Scott, Hal Holbrook, Jason Robards) who have served as models for distinctive speech. My instructors in humor in speech are Donald P. Horton in New York and Jack Wright in Newport News, Virginia.

In the arena, I've been guided by the extemporaneous platform abilities of Walter H. Johnson, Jr. and by the one-on-one command presence of Lee Stanley.

In giving this book its form, Arthur Schwartz, the diligent literary agent, suffered with me through conception and Eva Weiss, the talented copy editor, aided considerably in delivery of the final product. During gestation the expert word processing of Linda Sullivan and Evril Thompson, either of whom could meet tight deadlines in translating the Rosetta Stone, made all the difference. The wry and perceptive margin notes of McAllister Upshaw put excess wordage to shameful flight.

At this point, it is customary to thank dozens of other contributors—while carefully absolving them all of blame for errors. That's hogwash. We're all in this together, fellows and gals, and if gaucheries have crept in, share and share alike!

Roy Alexander
New York City

Mend your speech a little, lest you may mar your fortunes.

—Shakespeare

Before a man speaks, it is always safe to assume he's a fool. After he speaks, it is seldom necessary to assume.

—H. L. Mencken

Thy speech betrayeth thee.

—Matthew 26:79

Contents

Prologue:
Where Can I Get
That Talking Job?

In the frenzied era of World War II, people called Newport News, Virginia, a boomtown in boomtime. My father and 19,000 others worked there in the nation's largest shipyard. Families like ours had voluntarily uprooted themselves from everywhere to come to Virginia to build aircraft carriers that were widely hailed as critical in the war against Germany and Japan.

With a 14-year-old's chronic quest for walking-around money, I too began to look for work to finance local recreation—not that there was much of it. A popular diversion was going to the main drag to push into one of four crowded movie theaters. (Today no one remembers Ann Corio in *Swamp Woman*. But back then it ran for four weeks!)

Another choice: sitting on the back (never the seat) of a wooden bench in front of Montfalcone's candy store nursing a grape soda and watching schools of sex-starved sailors wash by—an eddy of humanity backing and filling on Washington Avenue.

Limited though these choices were, I felt the high schooler's characteristic need to join the herd, so I applied for work at Pender's Meat Market on Jefferson Avenue across the street from a giant wall poster that warned: "Loose lips sink ships."

As he looked me over, I could tell the manager thought I was too young. Sure enough, he asked:

"How old are you?"

Right away, I saw this as a trick question.

"How old do I need to be to work?"

"Sixteen," he said.

"That's funny," I said. "I just turned 16."

So after school and on Saturdays, I toiled in a butcher's apron under a large sign that said: "Lucky Strike Green has gone to war." We collected ration points for meat and accepted fats for wartime salvage—except on our busiest day. I put a sign in the window that said: "Ladies, please do not bring your fat cans here Saturdays!" Moments of humor aside, the job was hard and the hours long. Back in the stockroom where we washed the meat trays, depression-era graffiti remained on the wall: "Hoover is my shepherd—and I want."

Our market was one of several hundred throughout the mid-South operated by the giant Colonial Stores chain. Unfortunately, we had to be ready for inspection at any time. George R. McLeod, Colonial Stores' supervisor, turned up twice a week on the average—but never let us know in advance. In our blue-collar customer crowd, Mr. Mac stood out with his knife-creased business suit and cowhide briefcase.

But the thing that really intrigued me about him was the astounding fact that Mr. Mac didn't *do* any work—he just talked! He'd tell us how other stores used this or that technique to bolster sales. "Put the price tag at the back of the hamburger tray so the customers can see it." Or, "You should order neck bones. They sell well in this area." Or, "Why don't you try more of that green garnish paper in the case? It makes the meat look fresher."

Although we all felt we worked harder than Mr. Mac, we certainly got paid less than he did. After his second visit, Mr. Mac's talent hit me— he didn't *need* to work with his hands; he was paid for *talking*. Mr. Mac, as they said in those days, was in like Flynn.

"How can *I* get a talking job?" I wondered.

The next summer, I signed on as waiter for the Orkney Springs Hotel in the fertile Shenandoah Valley of Virginia—a region made famous by Stonewall Jackson's foot cavalry during "the late unpleasantness between the states."

Few of the waiters were experienced—but we soon learned how to bring trays of food from the kitchen into the American Plan dining room.

Each waiter got room and board and $30 a month salary plus tips— which, in my case, worked out to $25 a week. That seemed all right until several of us began playing poker each evening on the pantry maid's salad table. I particularly enjoyed card-jousting with Stanhope Bittler, a waiter unusually susceptible to psychological warfare.

"I can always beat you at draw poker with deuces wild," I told him. He believed me (what you *say* to your opponent can be more important than the cards you hold). Game after game he dropped out too soon and transferred the tips he made during the day to his night depositary—

me. After several weeks of being steadily creamed, Bittler fought back by bragging: "I'm still ahead because I make $50 a week in tips!" Suddenly the money I was winning from Bittler and others lost its allure. How Bittler could make twice what I did in tips riled me.

From then on, I carefully watched Bittler as he worked the dining room, determined to find out how he did it. It sure wasn't the food. Each guest got largely the same fare, perhaps with a few variations in desserts and salads. I was so eager to walk by his tables that one day I spilled six plates of soup and stopped all dinner action for ten minutes. But my diligence paid off and I found out his secret—it was the way he talked to his guests.

Bittler learned the guests' names right away and then used their names in conversation. He remembered guests' likes and dislikes and counseled them on what not to order. He told vivid stories, often about his own experiences, and at times portrayed himself as the goat.

Another victory for power speech. I didn't call it that at the time, but I got the message.

Later that summer, I fell hard for a 19-year-old brunette guest at the hotel. I suppose she thought that at 15 I was "too young," for she soon became attracted to another guest who could recite the famous poem "The Face on the Barroom Floor" at the slightest encouragement. Again, I got the message: Power speech is as valuable "in the courts of Venus as on the fields of Mars," as Gilbert and Sullivan related in *Patience*.

Fortunately for me, after two years in Newport News, we returned to our native western North Carolina. It was there that I started studying speech—in a mountain society that has long revered oral history. The society was close to its Anglo-Saxon beginnings. The Anglo-Saxons did not think it enough to be a warrior—you had to be an orator as well. Honored was he who could "unlock the word hoard," in their phrase. (Mountain authors have drawn on this word-of-mouth lore to good advantage—the most famous example is Thomas Wolfe's *Look Homeward, Angel.*)

As the first of three sons born to William Roy and Ruth Upshaw Alexander, I grew up in Cane Creek Valley—ten miles from Asheville, North Carolina. Two of my childhood memories remain etched in my mind: the depths of the Great Depression and the height of the Great Smoky Mountains around me. I could no more imagine flat land than I could picture prosperity. To me the world was a mountain range, and all its people were flat—broke.

When I was quite young, my mother, a schoolteacher, started me off chasing words by reading aloud—animal stories by Thornton W. Burgess were my favorite. She was a woman who saw education as the key to "brainwork," as opposed to "handwork," and she wanted me to get on the right side of the ledger early on. "Some men work with their hands," she told me. "This is a fine thing. But others work with their minds. Education allows you to work with your mind."

Her side of the family included a Methodist bishop in Atlanta, two governors of Georgia, and uncle Asa G. Candler, who founded the Coca-Cola Company. As politicians, entrepreneurs, and churchmen, they were, of course, powerful speakers. So was her father, J. B. Upshaw, a cotton broker—effective on the telephone in one-on-one deals buying cotton.

I took my mother's advice seriously. When I ran out of reading at the local school library, I went to Asheville's City Library and returned with shopping bags full of books. Naturally, this mystified my boyhood contemporaries, who followed me along the street, baseball bats in hand, shouting: "I bet he's a reader."

When I got to high school, I encountered a gifted speech teacher, Miss Elizabeth Welch, who changed my life. I didn't realize it, but at that time I spoke in an unnaturally high voice. Miss Welch recorded my speech so I could hear it. I was horrified. She gave me breathing and relaxation exercises, and her technique—coupled with my determination—wrought a powerful change. I've never forgotten her help. Nothing would have been the same without her.

In non-academic ways my father exerted a telling influence on me as well. His common sense allowed him to see amusement in bleak situations—including his own. He went broke in the auto repair business early in the booming 1920s, before the Great Depression. ("The rest of the country didn't go bust until 1929," he recalled wryly.) Later, as a deputy sheriff, it was his own particular talent to know hundreds of people throughout Buncombe County, calling them by name and talking in a pleasing manner about their families and fortunes. This created respect.

In fact, I saw it demonstrated again and again that the movers and shakers in our Appalachian society—the prosperous retailer, the lawyer, the country philosopher, the preacher—were formidable wordsmiths. Often the evidence for this came in humor. My grandfather, William Cruser Alexander, was one of the first in the community to buy a car—a Model T Ford.

"Before I got a car," he told us, "I had no idea why there were so many automobiles on the road. *After* I got one, I found out—they were all on the way to the repair shop to get the car worked on."

What it amounted to: Good talkers were prized by a mountain race that had not, until recent years, been skilled in reading and writing. These folks—like the blind person who acquires greater hearing and touch in compensation for a disability—placed immeasurable value on descriptive story-telling.

They spoke the language that the first colonists had brought to America. In many ways, mountain talk echoed characteristics of Elizabethan English in its vocabulary, its grammar, and, above all, its vitality—slangy, hasty, playful, and often insulting.

And when it came to oral *history*, believe me, these people had plenty to talk about. From the hill pockets of Wales, the wild moors of Ireland, the highlands of Scotland, my ancestors settled in Appalachian valleys under the shadow of peaks higher than any in eastern America. The early settlers developed a capacity to endure recurring plagues of smallpox and malaria, uncounted Indian raids, and natural accidents common to frontier life. Proud and cantankerous, this Appalachian race hewed to a life as relentlessly as pine roots growing through granite.

My regular diet of folklore paved the way for my appearances in school and community folk plays. There, my passion for speech flowered and threw me headlong into better theater productions: first a summer session in dramatics at the University of North Carolina, then a coveted apprenticeship in a summer theater in Holyoke, Massachusetts.

At summer's end, with high hopes fueled in part by ambition and in part by naïveté, I left Holyoke—drawn inexorably to New York. After all, that's where The Theater is.

I was 18 at the time, and I discovered then, as I had before, that effective talkers were paid more. I arrived in Manhattan with $13 in my pocket. Celebrating my first visit to Times Square, I promptly spent every cent. At 46th and Broadway—where the money ran out—I started job hunting.

My first stop was the Globe Theater. "Sure, we've got a job," the Globe chief of service said. "Usher on night side. Twenty-five dollars a week."

"I'm your man," I said. Then I noticed another Globe employee—in finery to shame a rear admiral—standing in front of the theater chanting, "Going in now for immediate seating. We have immediate seating at this time."

"How much does *he* make?" I inquired.

"The barker?" the Globe chief asked. "Thirty a week. He gets more for talking so good."

"For five dollars more, I can talk better," I said. "Can you put me down for the next opening as barker?"

In two weeks, I was out front. Because I had learned how to use my voice (speaking from the diaphragm to avoid strain), my verbal pyro-technics got better with each performance. One day, a movie-goer asked me: "Are you studying for the Metropolitan Opera?" I thanked him for the compliment.

After becoming aware that power speech paid better, I noticed that all speech had two parts: *style* and *content*. I assumed that style could be self-taught, but content, I felt, required formal education. This meant college. College on $30 a week simply wasn't possible, so I joined the Army in order to go to college via the GI Bill.

The original bill expired on October 5, and I signed up on October 4—at the Times Square recruiting station near the Globe. Sartorially, it was a painful demotion: an opulent barker's uniform traded for olive drab.

At Fort Dix, New Jersey, I was put to work as a clerk-typist in battalion headquarters. I didn't like the job or the pecking order. (When the major laughed, the captain laughed, then the lieutenant, then the sergeant-major, and—only then—could I laugh. By that time, it wasn't funny.) One day a fellow GI passed along a cryptic latrine rumor: "Public relations office at post headquarters is looking for people."

"What's public relations?" I asked.

"Damned if I know," the GI gossip whispered. "But it sounds like it might get you into town often."

Since getting into town was every soldier's beau ideal, I applied. I could see myself talking about Army life to high-school career-counsel-ing sessions.

"What makes you think you can do it?" the officer in charge asked. "We have experienced men to pick from."

I was candid. "I know something about people," I said. "I've worked in the theater—I know how to present things. I wrote plays and poetry in high school. I'll work harder than most. Give me a chance and you'll see."

"Start today," the officer said. Later he admitted my presentation edged out a couple of rivals.

I never did get to speak at high schools. But I soon re-learned the lesson I'd picked up as a waiter—the power of an individual's name. My Army assignment was writing hometown press releases:

> Private John Jones, son of Mr. & Mrs. H. P. Jones, of 21 Maple Lane, Anytown, U.S.A., has arrived at Fort Dix, New Jersey, where he will . . .

We sent those press releases all over the country, and many were published because local names make news. Even newspapers that cut our material drastically often ended up with a single-sentence headline: JONES AT DIX. The point is, they didn't cut the local name.

"If names are this powerful," I figured, "the habit of referring to people by name—and always attaching the right name to the right face—must be powerful, indeed." I converted this valuable lesson to speech.

After the Army, my GI Bill in hand, I enrolled at Northwestern University in suburban Chicago. There I started a new round of part-time jobs: helper in a metal shop, night watchman on a construction site. In the meantime I kept asking, "Where's that talking job?"

The first summer at Northwestern a far-reaching event occurred—I joined a crew of magazine salesmen selling subscriptions house-to-house. But I'd go days without getting an order. My colleague Bob Hawkins, a veteran salesman, set me straight. "Look," he advised, "you've got to get yourself across first. Make them want to listen to you. Then talk about the product. It won't work any other way."

I got the point—and put it to work. My sales volume soon ranked in the crew's upper 25 percent. When I returned to Northwestern at the end of the summer, I had money in my pocket and one more power speech lesson in my head.

The next summer, I made a presentation of my campus work to an old-line electrical products manufacturer—and got the job. The next year, I applied for a public-relations job with a large Chicago-based mobile-home manufacturer. "What can you do for us?" the marketing vice president asked. I remembered the Army.

"You've got a convention coming up," I said. "We'll send out home-town releases on each dealer attending."

I got the job.

My boss believed in the root-hog-or-die non-training approach: "No indoctrination. If you do well, fine, if not, we'll get someone else." I plunged in. Since I didn't know I couldn't do the job, I did it—up to and including loaning a mobile home for Phil Harris (a popular bandleader of the time) to use as backstage dressing room at the Illinois State Fair. When in Chicago, which was most of the time, I finished my final year at Northwestern via evening classes.

When I started on my next job, as editor of *Specialty Salesman* magazine, I deployed public speaking as an added cutting edge. I found it valuable to represent the magazine as a speaker at conventions.

This impressed advertisers and helped me get a salary increase. Once again, power speech paid better. Speech also kept my name before other employers—including the Philip Lesly Company, a Chicago-based public-relations firm with an expanding New York office. In an interview, I made the president a verbal presentation about my New York experience and my interest in going back there. He signed me on. In a few years, I was supervising a staff of 18 in the famed Time-Life Building in New York.

In 1962, I formed my own public relations firm, The Alexander Company, a few blocks east of—and 16 years after—my first New York job at the Globe Theater. Power speech had taken me this far. Why get off the winning horse?

To make sure my new company became known quickly, I launched a round of public-speaking appearances. I have never stopped.

WRAPPING IT UP

Because of my early story-telling heritage and dozens of clutch-hitting experiences with speech, I'm a dedicated advocate of power speech. I believe:

- If you don't ask, you don't get.
- If you ask right, you get more.
- Striving to be understood is not enough. You must make sure you're not *mis*understood.
- If anything can be misunderstood, it will be.
- When in doubt, talk it out. Better to be repetitious than vague.
- Speak to express, not to impress. In the long haul, what you say will be impressive.

I see speech as decisive in society, and I'm determined to show you the how and why of power speech—in dozens of valuable business and professional situations. You can literally use power speech to talk your way to uncommon success. Let's get on with it and you'll see how.

PART I

Power Speech: Why It's Vital to You

1

You Are What You Say

That popular Friday night TV show *Washington Week in Review* invited David Rogers, a *Wall Street Journal* reporter, as a panelist. He joined regulars Charles Corddry, Jack Nelson, Haines Johnson, and Paul Duke, the moderator.

To me, Rogers appeared to be en route to the guillotine. In his opening statement, he logged in six *yuh nos* and eight *uhs*. He swallowed his words and didn't project his voice out where the viewer could get at it.

Not only were his fellow panelists concerned for him (Paul Duke's normal composure was near the edge) but the home viewers felt embarrassed for him. We all breathed easier when the show rolled to end credits.

That same day, in New York, I heard a Boston banker speak to a press conference, representing an association of 40 banks. Unlike David Rogers, the banker was confident—but maybe he shouldn't have been. He pronounced dais as DY-us rather than DAY-us. He said *boutique* as BOW-teek, not the preferred BOO-teek. He talked about being INNA-restered instead of IN-trest-ed. Knowledgeable people in the audience winced.

These two unrelated incidents—and hundreds like them—prove each day the vital importance of power speech in modern society. When your speech is shabby, you get demerits—despite expertise in your own field.

David Rogers is a rising star in Washington journalism; he's a respected reporter and a talented writer. He won the Raymond Ciapper Award for his congressional coverage in 1984. Does he get credit for his stature with *Washington Week* viewers? Not at all.

The banker was elevated to association office by his peers (a notably hard-nosed lot). Did he reflect these credentials at the New York media event? Not with his pronunciation gaucheries. Listeners started waiting for the next gaffe.

Portrait of two professionals getting lower grades than professionalism alone indicates. But that's just the problem: Your professionalism doesn't stand alone. Your credentials are linked securely to your speech—as incontrovertibly as two mountain climbers inching up the slope together. Each depends on the other for life itself. If one falters, both plunge into the abyss.

You *are* the way you sound. The B student in life who sounds like a C student will get a final grade of C. The B student who sounds like an A student often gets an A. Effective speech can upgrade your professional status. Tawdry speech can drag you down.

Which one's for you? It's your choice. Power speech is available. It is learnable. Will you take the time and invest the effort to acquire this vital asset? You'd better, because your competitors—for better jobs and higher prestige—*will!* Listen to Daniel Webster: "If all my possessions were taken from me with one exception, I would choose to keep the power of speech, for with it I would soon regain all the rest."

Why You Are the Way You Sound

For starters, power speech is based on standard American English—not on what linguists call substandard. Substandard is the speech of uneducated groups—punkers, mountaineers, dock-wallopers, migrant field hands, people with no interest in "book learning," people not interested in changing their ways. A person unimproved from such a background who wants to become an office worker or a manager will certainly need to lose substandard speech.

If you're reading this book, you're beyond the substandard stage. But most people are more hampered by speech they think is *right* than by willful disregard of speech they know is *wrong*.

In this book I plan to shed new light on both the content and presentation of your speech, so you will avoid unwittingly making a poor impression. The Boston banker, for example, assumed his pronunciations correct. Otherwise, being bright and accomplished, he would have changed them. I'll teach you to use speech as a tool for personal and business advancement.

Charlton Heston once said the actor has three (and only three) assets—voice, body, and personality. But what powerful tools when employed correctly! With voice tone, stage presence, and body language, the skilled thespian moves his audience to laughter or tears—transports you to another time and place or into another person's psyche.

The unusually effective performer (recall Hal Holbrook as *Mark Twain Tonight* on the stage or George C. Scott as *Patton* on the screen) can play the audience the way a musician plays an instrument.

Power speakers, who are also performers, use classic techniques again and again. You can master those techniques until they become second nature. Soon effective speaking becomes a reflex. In time, power speech emerges—almost automatically—as an always-available tool. It's there when needed, at the right time, in the right way.

Once you become aware, too, you'll find the world awash in poor speech. Los Angeles talk maven Lillian Glass says we spend 80 percent of our lives communicating—and much of it poorly. Once you can tell good from bad, you'll see what high cards you hold with power speech.

Did you miss out on the long-awaited promotion? Was it your breath? No. But it could have been your breath*less*ness. The way you speak—exhaling profusely like Marilyn Monroe, for example—can make or break you in the corporate world.

"Women have a lot of problems in the corporate world when it comes to communicating," Glass explained in an interview in *USA Today.* "Many have such little-girl voices it's difficult to take them seriously."

How to improve? Cut out the *ahs, ums,* and *buts,* Glass says, keep your chin off your chest, "flow out your tones," be enthusiastic, and learn to listen.

As a child, you learned to talk. You've been at it ever since. But with most of us, the development of speaking and listening has been remarkably haphazard. You've learned from parents, relatives, playmates, schoolteachers, street urchins.

You've been influenced by movies and TV and radio, by reading ranging from comic books to classics. When you analyze this verbal mulligan stew, it's not surprising that some of your speaking habits are poor, some are good, and others are in between.

In most cases, they all sound familiar to you. In this book, you'll learn to take regular inventories of your oral communication and then to retain and capitalize on the effective techniques, improve indifferent habits, and unlearn and replace the clinkers.

Speech: Key to Personal Influence

Power speech allows you to influence other people, to get them to follow your ideas and your directions. Without exception, the influential ones are effective "me-to-you" speakers.

Napoleon knew and lived this credo. His biographer, Emil Ludwig, said that half of what Napoleon achieved, he achieved through the power of words.

While at the Pyramids, Napoleon said to his army: "Soldiers, 40 centuries are looking down on you! I will lead you into the most fertile plains of the world. There you will find flourishing cities, teeming provinces."

In another campaign, he said: "You will return to your homes, and your neighbors will point you out to one another saying, 'He was with the army in Italy.' "

The Corsican who conquered most of the world unlimbered verbal artillery to match his field guns. Speech, properly produced and applied, wins battles.

Man is a word animal. Speech conveys our thoughts. We need to talk. It gives us confidence, relieves our tensions, makes way for good human relations. Speech is the main connector between people.

The Importance of Word Wealth

Career-climbing is a competition between you and many other upward-strivers, and, as Napoleon said, "God is on the side of the big battalions." The big battalions, in the career fray, are *words*. Adroitly and properly deployed.

If you're an average speaker, you know and use about 20,000 words. A real word genius might know 50,000. If we count recognition vocabulary (words you recognize but don't normally use), the number for an average speaker rises to above 40,000. In a week of polite superficial conversation, you probably use only 2,000 of the words in your inventory. Experts say that about 35 words make up 50 percent of your everyday conversation, so you generally use only a small part of what's stored away. You draw on your larger inventory only occasionally. That means the career-climber with stored-up *word wealth* starts with a cutting edge in the battle for position, prestige, and social acclaim.

Why is word wealth so vital? Words are the bricks that build your thoughts and feelings, desires and dislikes, hopes and fears, business and pleasure—everything, indeed, that makes up you. You'll probably never develop a vocabulary that can meet every need that arises on every occasion, but the more words you know, the closer you will come to saying precisely what you want to say.

Besides clarity, a large vocabulatory provides variety, the basis for discrimination. You choose from a large number of tools. A hammer won't do when a saw is called for, and a nail file is inadequate when you need a rasp.

A varied vocabulary makes you more interesting, helps you avoid the dullness of repetition. Your speech demands attention. The interesting person is more likely to be persuasive. People endure dullards with secret distaste—wondering how soon they can escape. Clearly, a versatile vocabulary is part of the winner's arsenal.

Thomas Wolfe reveled in words with glory and gusto (perhaps more than anyone since Shakespeare or Rabelais). Upon seeing a shabby man lying on a subway bench, Wolfe commented on the fellow's sterility of speech. "Poor, dismal, ugly, sterile, shabby little man," Wolfe wrote in "Death the Proud Brother,"

> with your little scrabble of harsh oaths, and cries, and stale constricted words, your pitiful little designs and feeble purposes. . . . Joy, glory, and magnificence were here for you upon this earth, but you scrabbled along the pavements rattling a few stale words like gravel in your throat, and would have none of them.

Caliban, the half-human monster in Shakespeare's *The Tempest*, furiously denies he owes any gratitude to his master, the magician Prospero. Caliban asks what Prospero has ever done for him. Prospero passes over the many benefits he has conferred on the wretched creature to stress only one: He has taught Caliban to speak.

> [I] . . . took pains to make thee speak . . .
> When thou didst not, savage,
> Know thine own meaning, but wouldst gabble like
> A thing most brutish, I endow'd thy purposes
> With words that made them known.

We all begin as Calibans. We do not know our own purposes until we endow them with words. Indeed, we do not know ourselves. Developing your vocabulary gives you pleasure that comes with increased power. Even greater pleasure comes with increased knowledge of yourself. You begin to appreciate expression as an art. You feel the advantages and rewards of commanding words to do your bidding. You're pleased to produce or hear effective speech just as you're happy to see a forward pass completed, or a long putt holed, or a dance step gracefully executed. Adroit wordage is to the mind what successful actions are to the body.

A larger vocabulary will help you create and articulate ideas. More sophisticated ideas will help you add to your word inventory. And the cycle continues.

Says Dr. Bergen Evans in *The Word-A-Day Vocabulary Builder:*

> Words cannot be separated from ideas. They interact. The words we use are so associated with our experiences—and what the experiences mean to us—that they cannot be separated. The idea comes up from our subconscious clothed in words. It can't come any other way.
>
> We don't know how words are stored in our minds, but there does seem to be a sort of filing system—controlled by a perverse if not downright wacky file clerk. Everyone has tried to remember a word and been unable to. Sometimes it is a common word, one that we know we know. Yet it won't come when we want it. It can be almost a form of torture trying to recall it. Then usually some time later (when it's no longer useful to us) the word comes to mind readily.[1]

An ample vocabulary helps your mind conduct associative search. With a generous supply of words on file, you can call up a host of synonyms, which increases your chances of retrieving the desired word. Words have subtle and complex associations, and the mind's ability to sort through and categorize stored information can make the most spectacular computer seem like a simple gadget.

The ability to increase vocabulary throughout life is a sure reflection of intellectual progress. Trying to force a small vocabulary to serve an intelligent person's needs is nearly impossible.

Words provide a chief means of adjusting to difficult situations in life. The better your control over words, the more successful your adjustment.

Attend these lines from Isaiah:

> So shall my word be that goeth forth out of my mouth: it shall not return unto me void, but it shall accomplish that which I please, and it shall prosper in the thing whereto I sent it.

What Speech Says About You

In the performing arts, speech is an invaluable shorthand for giving the audience a quick fix on a character's background and destiny. In the film *An Officer and a Gentleman,* Debra Winger tells Richard Gere: "And I don't think you have what it takes to be no officer." Her double negative instantly establishes her factory-girl background.

In *On the Waterfront,* Marlon Brando tells Rod Steiger: "Cholly, Cholly. You shuda looked after me, Cholly. I couda been a contendah! Instead I got a one-way ticket to Palookaville." This portrait-speech, coupled with Brando's marbles-in-the mouth delivery, tells us everything about the past and probable future of longshoreman Terry Malloy.

Novelist John O'Hara put all his chips on dialog as an indicator of character. His precinct cop picks up the telephone to say: "Wukkan I do fya?" When his teenage girl from Bryn Mawr or Wellesley says: "Robert didn't come with she or I," her grammatical error tells us about her breathless need to appear grown-up.

If such speech shorthand is widely accepted as telegraphic about a fictional character, why should real life be different? It isn't, of course. In England, speech has always been *the* class establisher. A member of the laboring class can say *bloody* every other breath, but the proper person does not utter the word except under the most dire circumstances. The dropped *h* in *'otel* is an indelible sign of lowness and would be perceived as an unspeakable lapse coming from respectable middle-class lips.

In America, a much less structured society, the rules are not as clear-cut. But the negative effect of poor speech is just as devastating.

They Toil Not, Neither Do They Spin

What about the horrible examples—the celebrities who violate the principles of good speech, yet laugh all the way to the bank as they bombard our eardrums with their gaucheries? Unfortunately, the modern TV-driven society can support a few general celebrities who exist, and indeed climb ever higher, by following one outrageous principle: "I'm famous and in demand; therefore, I will continue to rise in power and status."

Thus we suffer the egregious gutter New York accent of Howard Cosell ("the struc-cha of spo-ats"), the speech impediment of Barbara Walters (enough to spur rejection at any 258-watt radio station in the republic), or, until recently, the raspy-precious tones of the late Truman Capote, a talented writer who, in a sane vocal society, wouldn't have been placed in front of a microphone.

As syndicated columnist Sidney Harris said: "A personality is not a person of importance, prominence, renown, or notoriety," but "a performer who can neither sing, dance, act, nor tell jokes with more than average proficiency but manages to combine these mediocrities into a highly profitable public package."

Mercifully, there's a limit to human suffering. Society will tolerate only a handful of such no-talents at any given time. If you'd like to petition for a General Celebrity slot (the odds are not nearly as good as winning the lottery on a $1 ticket), go right ahead. Don't bother to read further. Just be an outlandish personality and wait for lightning to strike.

If, on the other hand, you'd like to increase your opportunities by planning carefully and working hard, hang in there—better speech will help.

The Evolution of English

In the search for quicker, more direct communication, the human mind is always going to break or ignore current rules. That's how language evolves. Shakespeare used *pneumonia* to mean *head cold*. He used *nice* to mean *lascivious*.

Young people on both sides of the Atlantic are often the innovators. In the United States *ex* is short for *excellent*. In Britain, an achievement is *dead brill,* as in *brilliant.* It was ever thus, much to the distress of conservatives.

For every innovative change, there is a traditionalist standing ready to cry "foul!" Thomas Jefferson drew brickbats for coining the verb *belittle.* Groaned a Londoner: "Freely, good sir, will we forgive all your attacks, impotent as they are illiberal, upon our national character; but for the future—oh spare, we beseech you, our mother tongue!"

Today the distinction between *who* and *whom* is disappearing: *Who* is being used before verbs and *whom* after verbs, regardless of whether subject or object is called for. The distinction between *fewer* and *less* is disappearing. *Loan* is used more and more as a verb instead of *lend.*

The most noticeable changes are new words. Hundreds of thousands enter the English language, while relatively few drop out. Old English had 50,000 to 60,000 words. We still use about 70 percent of them. By Shakespeare's day, another 80,000 to 90,000 words had been added, and we still use about 75 percent of those. Words do fade away, of course, but very slowly. *Gadzooks (God's hooks)* is no longer in active use. But many other words, equally old, are.

Yet 1,200 years ago, the beginnings of the language were confined to a few seafaring tribes inhabiting the coast of present-day Denmark and Holland. England's original inhabitants were Celts, and their language survives in Gaelic, still spoken in parts of Ireland.

For 400 years (beginning with Julius Caesar in 55 B.C.), the Romans ruled England while the natives stubbornly continued to speak Celtic. In 410 A.D., Rome's Britannic legions withdrew. Soon afterward bands of seafaring robbers (Angles, Saxons, Jutes, Norsemen) began to invade the British Isles.

By 800 A.D., the Celtic language had been pushed back into the mountains of Wales and Scotland. The land's chief speech became a combination of the languages of Germanic tribes—called Anglo-Saxon (Old English). This poetic language was much like its modern cousin, German.

England was invaded again in 1066 by William of Normandy. Norman was a form of French, which, in turn, came from Latin. The Norman conquerors went right on speaking French, while the conquered Anglo-Saxons kept their language. The conquerors (as conquerors do) lived in ease, leaving the hard work to the conquered. Modern English language reflects that arrangement. The names for live animals (which need caring for) are Old English: *cow*, *sheep*, *swine*. But the words for the food they become are Norman French: *beef*, *mutton*, *pork*. *Work* is Old English, but *leisure* is French.

For all its leisure advantages Norman French did not replace Old English. Two hundred years after the Norman Conquest, English (Angle-ish) conquered its conquerors. It emerged once again as the language of all the people.

In England, London was headquarters for church and state and commerce. And since learned lawyers, courtiers, and captains were headquartered there, the London dialect came to be accepted as the "normal" way of speaking.

In the Tudor period (1485–1603), the theater made great poetry as common a diversion as TV sitcoms are today. Many great speeches in Shakespeare's plays are dramatically inappropriate and historically improbable. But that didn't matter—the Elizabethan audience demanded rolling words. The whole age was drunk on words.

The Challenge of Learning English

English is the most widely used language in world history. More people speak it than speak any other (if you agree that various forms of Chinese are separate tongues).

English's astoundingly rich vocabulary makes it enormously flexible, capable of expressing the finest shades of meaning. It is rich in synonyms—a language of unusual range and subtlety. Yet the chaos of English spelling and pronunciation can frighten the bravest and brightest foreign students. An old bit of doggerel advises:

> Beware of *heard*, a dreadful word
> That looks like *beard* and sounds like *bird*,
> And *dead*: It's said like *bed*, not *bead*—
> For goodness' sake, don't call it *deed!*

The words *tough, bough, cough, dough,* and *through* show English at its most perverse—five uses of *ough*, five separate pronunciations.

Forty percent of modern English words are of Old English origin. The rest are borrowed. From Spanish come words like *cannibal, cigar, mosquito, tornado,* and *vanilla.* From Turkish: *coffee, turban, kiosk, caviar.* From Hindi: *guru, pundit, thug, jungle, shampoo, loot, pajamas.* From African tongues: *boogie-woogie, gumbo, jazz, okra, tango, voodoo, zombie.*

In English, word order is crucial. Phrases can be arranged and rearranged like putty, turning nouns into verbs, verbs into nouns, nouns into adjectives. You can, for example, plan a table or table a plan, book a place or place a book, lift a thumb or thumb a lift.

"French is widely viewed as more beautiful, musical, pleasant, rhythmic, refined, intimate, pure, soothing, graceful, tender, and lovely," declared linguistics authority Joshua Fishman in an article in *U.S. News & World Report.* "But English is viewed as richer, more precise, more logical, more sophisticated. English is less loved but more used."

The American Language Today

Millions use English as a second language. And although English may be the toast of Paris and Peking, back home in River City there's trouble, trouble, trouble. The shortcomings of U.S. schools, waves of immigrants, and addiction to TV are all taking a toll on our linguistic skills. The verbal scores of college-bound high-school seniors on the Scholastic Aptitude Test fell from an average of 466 in 1967 to 424 in 1981 and had risen only two points by 1985.

A survey by the National Opinion Research Center shows that the language ability of the U.S. population has dropped ever since the 1950s. Doubly worrisome: The ranks of the illiterate and marginally literate are swelling at the very time that rapid technological change makes proficiency with words and concepts more and more important.

Today, many college graduates have a weaker command of language than their parents do.

"In its short lifetime, television has become the major stumbling block to literacy in America," says Jim Trelease, author of *The Read-Aloud Handbook.* This problem, alarming sociologically, has a personal impact on the man or woman determined to master power speech: Effective speech is now much more in demand and will be much more highly rewarded.

Politics: To Persuade Is to Succeed

Throughout the ages, the ability to speak effectively has been a prerequisite for leadership. Men and women who make impressions on society have been unusual speakers. (Clothed speakers, evidently. Mark Twain warned us that "Naked people have very little influence on society.") Demosthenes, an ancient Greek orator, said: "As a vessel is known by the sound, whether it be cracked or not, so men are proved by their speeches whether they be wise or foolish."

A leader must stimulate and motivate using emotion and power. Good speakers influence followers far beyond the content of words alone (Hitler and Mussolini were prime examples). In American history, the great influencers were competent pulpit clergymen or political leaders: Daniel Webster, Patrick Henry, James Madison, and scores of others. Their persuasive tongues and memorable thoughts helped forge a nation.

The White House has always given speech top priority. Each president since Franklin D. Roosevelt has retained speech writers and often retained coaches on delivery. Says Anatole Broyard in *The New York Times:* "Language plays a subtler part than we suppose in politics. One of the reasons the American electorate twice voted for Ronald Reagan may have been a nostalgia for the rhythms of human speech, no matter what he was saying."

Agrees speech coach Dorothy Sarnoff: "All through history, people have been more quickly perceived and accepted as leaders if they could speak persuasively. The superb quality of Reagan's speechmaking, refined through the years before he took office, has had tremendous impact on the nation."

Reagan's speech is a White House upside. On the downside, Nicholas Gage (in *The Wall Street Journal*) tagged unfavorable speech as instrumental in retiring Lyndon B. Johnson:

Now it can be told. Here's why President Johnson decided not to run for reelection. It wasn't because of war or peace. It wasn't because of tax increases or gold drains. Rather, it was because his voice had become so grating to so many ears that his popularity had fallen dangerously low. He no longer sounded like a President.

The more people heard his voice the less secure they felt about him. The man just doesn't sound sincere.

In 1984, I recall a CBS News anchorman calling Jesse Jackson "the foremost orator in American politics. The awesome power of his speeches is envied by his competitors. He makes the language work for him."

New York Governor Mario Cuomo's speech to the San Francisco convention catapulted him into the national ring. As Roberta Entner of Rutgers University wrote to *The New York Times:* "After his address at the Democratic Convention, Mario Cuomo became a serious candidate for President in 1988. Speech preparation, like letter writing, has become a dying art. It is time to encourage and foster an appreciation for speech communication in our schools."

On TV call-in shows, Cuomo is quiet, confident, concerned, sincere. In taking issue with a caller, he's more likable when disagreeing with someone than most politicians are when they're agreeing. "May I tell you something—with respect?" he asked one violent caller. "I disagree with you. Set the record straight for yourself."

This TV-age politician is quite a contrast to Al Smith, a politician from the stump-speaker era. Smith used to shout: "Let's look at the record." Cuomo's style is keyed to your living room—Smith's was for the Tammany Hall rally.

Anyone who doubts the importance of speech in swaying political audiences need only look at the 1984 furor over Geraldine Ferraro. As a congresswoman, her New York accent was accepted without comment. As a candidate for vice president, her speech attracted attention. *The New York Daily News* headlined in pure Gothamese: TO HEAH HUH IS TO KNOW HUH.

And the *Daily News'* Stuart Marques pointed out that New Yorkers say "berl the erl" and "I sawr huh." Although Ferraro doesn't go that far, she does say *daughta* and *supporta*. Further, she uses expressions such as "stand on line" for "stand in line" and "I'm here for ten years" for "I've been here for ten years." During the campaign the question was not how would New Yorkers respond, but how would Ferraro's speech play in Peoria.

Ferraro took the comment seriously and got a voice coach. Media consultant Ray Strother recommended that Ferraro moderate her New

York accent. "It sounds perfectly natural in the Northeast," he observes, "but when you get to the West and South it sounds abrupt."

"I'm trying to learn not to say *lemme*," Ferraro told an Oregon audience (conscious of how different her voice sounded to voters there). "I've got to say *let me*."

People advised Ferraro to stop swallowing words and drop "I gotta tell you" and "Can we talk?"

Voters are more critical of a woman, Strother said in the *People* magazine article: "When the candidate is female, they talk about the issues, but they also talk about her style of dress and her family relationships and concern themselves with things that would never come up in discussions of male candidates." That close scrutiny most assuredly includes speech.

Part of Ferraro's baptism by fire included learning to cope with intimacy-seeking TV talk-show hosts. And in all the land, no interviewer seeks more intimacy than Phil Donahue. Ferraro, in a vibrant red dress, went before Donahue's seven million viewers.

When Donahue asked whether she had wept upon reading a newspaper report about her family, Ferraro coolly replied: "Does it make any difference to anyone whether or not I cried? There are certain things, Phil, that are personal." Veteran observers say she passed the Donahue test with good grades.

In the same campaign, Joan Mondale got high marks for speech and grace. *New York Times* reporter Maureen Dowd described Joan Mondale's delivery as "a soft voice that lingers on certain syllables, leaving the impression of *italics*." Earlier, Betty Ford won plaudits for sincerity and candor—an enormous asset to Jerry Ford's campaign.

Some analysts trace Walter Mondale's rousing 1984 defeat to the contrast between his and Reagan's speaking styles. Certainly in one area—his concession speech on election night—Mondale proved conclusively that lack of restraint can be lethal.

In the first part of his speech, Mondale won the nation over completely—defeated or no. Then he threw most of his gain away by over-talking. The winning part of his concession:

Thank you very much.

A few minutes ago I called the President of the United States and congratulated him on his victory re-election as President of the United States. He has won. We are all Americans. He is our President, and we honor him tonight.

Again tonight, the American people, in town halls, in homes, in fire houses, in libraries, chose the occupant of the most powerful office on earth. Their choice was made peacefully, with dignity and with majesty, and although I would have rather won, tonight we rejoice in our democracy, we rejoice in the freedom of a wonderful people, and we accept their verdict. I thank the people of America for hearing my case.

I have traveled this nation, I believe, more than any living American, and wherever I've gone, the American people have heard me out. They've listened to me. They've treated me fairly. They've lifted my spirits and they've added to my strength, and if there is one thing I'm certain of, it is that this is a magnificent nation, with the finest people on earth. I thank, above all, my family. How lucky I am. Joan has campaigned with class all over this nation. And we're very, very proud of our kids—Ted and Eleanor, Jane and William. Everywhere they went they got us support.

And I thank Geraldine Ferraro. We're very proud of Gerry—very proud of Gerry.

We didn't win, but we made history, and that fight has just begun.

Mondale held four aces at this point. He should've raked in his chips and gone home a winner. But he didn't. In this second part, he lost most of what he'd gained:

And once again, here I am in Minnesota. In over 24 years, never once have the people of Minnesota turned me down. They voted tonight. Minnesotans, this is a special state—a remarkable state with a special spirit. And time and time again in the past, Minnesota has led the way for our nation, and I think you did it again tonight.

And I want to especially thank my staff—Jim Johnson and the whole crew, my workers and my volunteers all over this country. What a special group of Americans they are. I know what you sacrificed for me and my country, and I want to say a special word to my young supporters this evening.

I know how you feel because I've been there myself. Do not despair. This fight didn't end tonight. It began tonight. I have been around for a while, and I have noticed in the seeds of most every victory are to be found the seeds of defeat, and in every defeat are to be found the seeds of victory. Let us fight on. Let us fight on.

My loss tonight does not in any way diminish the worth or the importance of our struggle. The America we want to build is just as important tomorrow as it was yesterday. Let us continue. Let us continue to seek an America that is just and fair. Tonight, tonight especially, I think of the poor, the unemployed, the elderly, the handicapped, the helpless and the sad, and they need us more than ever tonight.

Let us fight for jobs and fairness. Let us fight for these kids and make certain they've had the best education that any generation ever had. Let us fight for our environment and protect our air, our water, and our land. And while we must keep America strong, let's use that strength to keep the peace, to reflect our values and to control these weapons before they destroy us all. That has been my fight. That has been our fight in this campaign. And we must fight for those goals with all of our heart in the future.

I am honored—I am honored by Minnesota, by all the people of this country that have permitted me to wage this fight. What an honor it is. And I'm at peace with the knowledge that I gave it everything I've got.

I am confident that history will judge us honorably. So tonight let us be determined to fight on. Good night and God bless you and God bless America. Thank you very much. Thank you. Thank you very much.

Too much! A good lesson: In power speech, *less is often more.*

Reagan, on the other hand, was a clutch-hitter when it counted. During the Reagan-Mondale debate, when queried on the age issue, Reagan turned on his familiar grin and pointed out he'd made a decision earlier not to use "my opponent's age and lack of experience as an issue" in the campaign. Bingo!

Said *Time:* "Once again The Gipper was up to the task." *New York Times* essayist Bill Safire said: "Walter Mondale lost the debate because he wasn't listening." Another vital power speech lesson: Listen.

In today's media coverage, candidates are evaluated as *performers.* You too are a performer, every time you open your mouth to speak.

Executive Success Requires Power Speech

Let's say you're interested in a management career. You've got the education and experience credentials, and now your eye is on a top job. You've got lots of company. Come to think of it, that's the problem. A great many competitors have credentials that look a lot like yours.

Style is vital, too. When you are trying to convince someone—when logic is important—it usually boils down to how you come across rather than how good your argument is. As good trial lawyers know, *how* you plead your case is vital.

A *New York Times* article noted that businesswomen are seeking out speech classes. Maureen Cullinane, a Manhattan fashion designer, believes her business depends on how well she communicates with buyers and customers. Cullinane, who is just under 5 feet tall, sought out Manhattan speech teacher Lily Lodge. "I'm short," the designer said, "and I want to generate a presence. I also want to deliver a message that makes me sound intelligent."

One way a woman can attain credibility, Lodge pointed out, is by lowering a shrill, high-pitched voice. "When a woman meeting with men has a squeaky little voice, nothing she says is going to be taken seriously," Lodge said. A woman with a southern drawl is also going to lack authority, she said, "because whatever she says might sound flirty and sexy, even if she doesn't mean it to be."

Many successful women attribute achievements to their speaking skills. Jo Foxworth, who owns an advertising agency in Manhattan and is author of *Boss Lady,* first became fascinated with public speaking as she listened to Baptist ministers during her Mississippi childhood. After she moved to New York, she decided she wanted to rid herself of her southern accent. "They [the speech instructors] stuck a cork between my teeth," she said.

Speech and Corporate Power

As Fred Glass, former chairman of the New York Port Authority, sees it: "The higher you climb, the more exposed your assets." And the more important your speech. Speech, in fact, is a direct key to corporate power, reports John T. Malloy, savant of personal success. In *Marketing Times,* Malloy said that upper-middle-class patterns, absolutely essential to power, announce you as a member of an elite group. Lower-middle-class speech is effective only with lower-middle-class listeners.

He noted that power people use simple declarative sentences—usually without modifiers. Women are more apt to use weakening modifiers ("I think" or "Don't we all believe").

Low tones are the mark of power. Lower your voice tone to increase respect. Many women, Malloy said, have high-pitched voices when they are excited. And although a man can occasionally shout to make a point, women usually cannot get away with it. The male power voice is slow, almost solemn. The female voice is icy, steely, and precise.

In learning business speech, be willing to start at the bottom (something MBAs are under fire for not doing these days). You're not seeking the top executive slot on opening day. Far from it. Heed the advice of Earl D. Brodie, San Francisco business consultant: "Don't hesitate to go to work at the lowest possible level of production or sales. Recognize your need to learn the nuts and bolts, the nitty-gritty, of how the company produces, sells, makes money. If you have a choice, head for the sales department first. Get out on the firing line."

In short, learn to communicate early on. But from day one, avoid the label one headhunter put on an executive applicant: "He was a dese, dem, and dose guy," the consultant said.

The Growing Role of Public Spokesman

Sharpen your speaking and communicating skills before you sit in the big corner office. Once you get there, the demands (public and corporate) are so consuming, there's little time to develop speech skills.

The Tylenol poison scare spotlighted the skills of Johnson & Johnson chairman James Burke. I attended his closed-circuit TV press conference networked to major cities. Burke's calm, masterful handling of questions was widely hailed. (During the telecast, one executive whispered to a colleague, "They didn't teach him anything *this* valuable at Harvard Business School!") Without Burke's strong public presence, Tylenol's comeback would not have been anywhere near as rapid.

"Tylenol was the most successful OTC [over-the-counter] product ever marketed," Burke said later. "Before the murders, it had 46 percent of the market. Right afterward, that dropped to 6.5 percent. As of now, we're back up to 18 percent. There's ample evidence that American consumers want Tylenol."

If the CEO does the other parts of the job well and is also an effective public spokesman, this is a plus. If you're bad in your public pose, people will judge *all* aspects of your performance by your speech, just as they do for political candidates. The technique is often called people-skills, but it boils down to power speech. Irving Shapiro, former DuPont CEO, said in *Dun's Business Month:* "Above all, the CEO must have the ability to relate to people, both within the organization and outside. He is no longer just running plants and selling goods. Today, he is a quasi-public official, who needs as much skill in dealing with people as any Senator."

Speech: Key to Group Communications

Why take the time and trouble to become effective speaking to groups? Because:

1. Speaking to groups is the quickest and most effective way to develop courage, poise, and self-confidence.
2. You gain recognition from people who count, and others will follow your leadership.
3. Speaking will do wonders for your self-image and self-esteem and will propel you forward in business, civic, and community activities.
4. Because an effective group leader is noticed by employers, he or she will get promoted faster.
5. The higher up the ladder you go, the greater your need for this kind of leadership.
6. You'll be an inspiration to others. You'll teach them to be more self-confident and courageous.

Good speech doesn't attract attention to itself. Use the standard speech of the leaders in your community. And when you're making a formal speech, heed syndicated columnist Jenkin Lloyd Jones: "A speech is a solemn responsibility. The man who makes a bad 30-minute speech to 200 people wastes only a half hour of his own time. But he wastes 100 hours of the audience's time—more than four days—which should be a hanging offense."

Often the stakes in formal speaking are quite high.

A midwestern university invited a man to come halfway across the nation to speak at a convocation. But the real purpose was to size him up for the presidency. His speech was a test of his mental stature and ability. He got the job.

H. L. Mencken, on the other hand, found one-on-one boredom the problem. "The capacity of human beings to bore one another seems to be vastly greater than that of any other animal. Some of our most esteemed inventions have no other apparent purpose, for example, the dinner party of more than two, the epic poem, and the science of metaphysics."

There's no mystery to good speech. You can learn and apply the principles as well as anyone else. None of the techniques in this book is illegal, unethical, or patented. Ignore them and you turn your back on the accumulated knowledge and experience of speakers who achieve, night after night, week after week, the very results you seek.

WRAPPING IT UP

Why power speech? The great entertainers have it. Top executives have it. Super salesfolk have it. Virtually every successful person utilizes power speech. You can have it, too. Power speech can be *your* key to success—at work and in your personal relationships.

Effective speech is a means to a happy and influential life. When you master power speech, people listen. You rivet and hold attention. You sell your opinions, ideas, products, and *yourself*.

Power speech is synonymous with winning, whatever your field or profession, whatever your purpose or goals. It gives you what you want. It helps rocket you to the top.

As you acquire effective speech, barriers start to crumble. Disappointments give way to success. Goals you thought impossible become reachable. You feel positive, confident, secure—guiding the conversation at social gatherings or speaking to groups, large or small. Your speaking prowess brings about a presence others can sense, a presence that says you're strong, determined, persuasive—that you mean to get what you want, that you're a winner.

Conversation is more enjoyable. Others pay attention. Interruptions are reduced. People care about your opinions and views.

Promotions come faster. Employers are always on the lookout for leadership. Power speech tells your boss: This person is born to command!

You'll be in demand to chair committees, lead groups, speak publicly. Others will look to you for instruction.

When you begin speaking, people who once patronized you will count you as a friend. Effective speech can upgrade your professional status. Shabby speech can tear it down.

Your listeners, conditioned by word-portraits on screen, stage, and in novels, judge your background and your probable future by what you say and how you say it. This instant impression can be good or bad. It's your choice.

Sterling speech moves its possessor to the apex of corporate pyramids, to the forefront of non-profit associations, yea, even to the White House.

2

Speech: Your Inescapable Calling Card

I was half asleep one Saturday when a headhunter called. "We want to explore a job with you," the telephone voice said. "A friend tells us you are blocked in advancement in your present post and just can't get nowheres."

Nowheres? This discordant note quashed my interest. Yes, I was in the market for a new job. But I felt no confidence in Mr. Nowheres. A man who spoke that incorrectly must be a moron. Place my future in his hands? Forget it.

The man lost a candidate. We'll never know if he figured out why or not. Gross speech works that way. The higher up the ladder you are, the more it's assumed you will speak correctly. In fact, you probably won't get credit for good speech—you don't want or need it. But you accumulate demerits for poor speech.

The Society Election

In covering an annual professional women's convention for *Marketing Times,* I ran into a conflict that was resolved by speech—although I don't think either contestant realized it at the time. Both Josie McGillicuddy and Sandra Brown were campaigning for the presidency of the women's group for the coming year. I recall the meeting vividly—it was in Tulsa and the temperature was 90 degrees.

Both women were highly qualified. However, in speech, Josie had the edge. Originally from Texas, Josie had taken time and trouble to drop her regional sound in favor of fairly standard American speech. Sandra had never lost her original country-store sound.

Both made outstanding speeches at the convention. But when the votes were counted, Josie won the gavel of office. One member, who didn't know either candidate personally, explained her vote: "I just felt we should have a *national* president—not a regional one."

Actually, of the two, Josie was more regional in her policies and practices, but Sandra sounded regional. Score another victory for power speech.

The Old Southern Colonel

I had a similar experience with regionalism when the old southern colonel met me at the airport in Vicksburg, Mississippi. I was on assignment to evaluate plant sites around historic Vicksburg. I knew a realtor was meeting me, but I wasn't prepared for the colonel—or his comment: "Should we stop and have a mint julep first?" he asked. "Or should we go DI-rec-ly to the whoh-house?"

His speech was perfect for Colonel Sanders. But I wanted to evaluate land. Was he really the leading realtor in town?

His speech was fine for an antebellum play. Or a fast-food symbol. He could have been a good realtor—until he spoke. (Like the old Ipana toothpaste ad. Everything's fine—until the beautiful girl smiles. Then you find—horrors!—she's neglected her teeth!)

I quickly found another realtor.

When you open your mouth, do people find you've neglected your speech? No! Instead, they find—as I did with the headhunter—that they don't trust you. Or they cannot see you in the right role, interacting with the right people.

People use speech as a litmus test for assessing class. Gauche speech can belie your true abilities. Effective speech, on the other hand, will give you points you don't deserve.

Eliza Doolittle, as the whole world now knows, was passed off successfully as a duchess just because she talked like a duchess. Her upper-class speech, plus a fine gown, was the only change Henry

Higgins had wrought in the cockney flower girl. Yet she got instant acceptance.

If you, on the other hand, talk about *biddness* when you're saying *business,* or use *innarested* when you're trying to say *interested,* you may as well go to a formal party in a bikini. (That's a distraction, all right, but not the kind that pushes you forward. Remember, the freak show is never held in the main tent.)

Four Kinds of American Sound

You may look, think, and perform like a winner, but if you don't sound like one, forget it. That's the thesis of Communispond, a New York–based advisory service to executives. Communispond's Joseph McIntyre says poor speech is often the major factor that holds back careers.

McIntyre isolates four levels of American speech (the higher the level, the more power):

1. *Aristocratic speech.* Less than 5 percent of the population speak this way. The grammar is polished; the syntax sophisticated. "William F. Buckley, Jr. has a special sound. You know he'd have no trouble meeting the chairman of the board."

2. *Standard (unaccented) American speech.* (Used by 25 to 30 percent of the population.) Standard speech is "what's needed for executive success and advancement in the professions," McIntyre notes. "Banking recruiters have historically looked only at Ones and Twos."

3. *Regionally accented speech.* Colloquial, perhaps ungrammatical. "A number of Threes find themselves not moving up and don't know why," McIntyre observes. "By changing their speech, they can avoid a lot of frustration. People want leaders who speak newscaster English, who sound convincing to them."

4. *Sub-standard speech.* Limited vocabulary, incorrect usage, difficulties in self-expression.

"Imperfect speech may be a roadblock," McIntyre says. "But it's not a dead end. With patience, a good ear, and mimicry, speech can be upgraded."

But don't think your chi-chi right-school background guarantees effective speech. In the movie *Reds,* George Plimpton was typecast as a snob because he comes across that way. His speech is a cross between the country-club honk and the Yale sniff.

Jacqueline Kennedy's White House tour on TV was a perfect example of speech belying true ability. Jackie tore down the public's impressions of fabled Camelot because her speech said vapid, frivolous, silly—in contrast to her true abilities, which are considerable. Vaughan Meader in his *First Family* album parodied Jackie's speech.

(Today hear *The First Family Rides Again* with Rich Little on the Reagan White House. It's worthwhile for the student of speech and the appreciator of fine humor.)

So being snotty isn't the answer. It takes good speech plus the common touch—Ronald Reagan, John F. Kennedy, and Franklin Delano Roosevelt—to get highest appeal.

Speech: Your Calling Card

Ken Mantel, a New York investment adviser with Oakwood Counselors, manages millions in trust funds. Mantel is a Renaissance man with a multiplicity of interests and talents. He admits to judging people by speech, although he fights against it. Says Mantel: "When I meet a college president with a rustic accent, I hear my subconscious saying: 'The man's dumb.' Then I reply to my internal self: 'He's *not* dumb. He's a college president. It's just the *way* he talks.' "

Yet in more hurried or less analytical moments, Mantel judges by speech. To vast numbers of other movers and shakers, your speech *is* what you *are*. They don't even think about it.

Commodore Cornelius Vanderbilt, the ferryboat and railroad tycoon, was skittish about sitting down with British nobility. "I know I'm smarter than they are," he said. "But they *sound* smarter than I do."

As John Malloy and other savants of power dress have pointed out, you cannot call on the board chairman in overalls and expect to be persuasive. You're simply not on his wavelength. But fine clothes alone won't do it. Dress a pig in a tuxedo and it still *sounds* like a pig. Artificially impose power speech on a sanitation man and the falseness still shows through.

Fine speech, like fine clothes, is basically a matter of good taste. This taste cannot be injected into the vein. But power speech can be yours—if you work at it. No labor pays greater dividends. Effective speech, like appropriate dress, places you on a *par* with the people you seek to influence. That's not only important, it's *vital* in climbing the ladder.

In England, until 1800, a number of dialects prevailed without one dominating—until the so-called Oxford accent began to gain influence. At that time, the sons of upper-class families started attending the great "public" schools (Eton and Harrow) and then went on to Oxford and Cambridge. They became the power elite in the military, church, business, and society. The Oxford accent was their entrée. Without it, as the English say, "You simply don't belong."

In America, distinctions are made along different lines.

High Brow vs. Low Brow

In the United States, right after World War II, Russell Lynes of *Harper's* coined the expressions *high brow, middle brow,* and *low brow.* Taste, Lynes said, separates the classes in America.

In 1983, social commentator John Brooks asked Lynes to update the rankings for *American Heritage.* Some aspects remained constant. In the 1980s, the high-brow person looks for the "surprisingly good jug wine" (reverse snobbism) or obscure imported beer. The upper middle brow tries to order French wines. The lower middle brow still drinks martinis, and the low brow domestic beer.

Today, however, it's speech, not taste, that sets the classes apart, with standard speech winning out over even high-brow speech. Hugh Downs is a perfect user of standard speech on TV's *20/20* show. Do you ever stop to analyze the way Hugh Downs says something? No. Your subconscious tells you: "He speaks the way I do. Now I'm going to concentrate on what he's saying." That's power speech in action.

Look at examples of high-brow, standard, and low-brow speech shown in Table 1. You'll see that neither high brow nor low brow is power speech, because it calls attention to itself, not its meaning.

Table 1. Sample words from each of three classes of speech.

Word	*High-Brow Speech*	*Standard Speech*	*Low-Brow Speech*
Can't	CAHn't	cant	caint
Cemetery	sim-etry	sim-uh-teri	sim-uh-teri
Leisure	LEH-zur	LEE-zur	time off
Potato	po-TAH-to	po-TAY-to	taters
Secretary	sec-uh-tri	sec-re-tari	my girl
Tomato	to-MAH-to	to-MAY-to	ter-MAY-ter

Aping high-brow speech will merely mark you as pretentious and detract from what you say. The examples of low-brow speech shown in Table 2 can creep into the speech of otherwise educated persons. Roust them out.

Table 2. Power speech vs. low brow.

Word	Power Speech	Low-Brow Speech
Amateur	am-uh-ter	ama-chur
Clique	kleek	click
Company	COM-pan-i	com-pny
Exquisite	EX-quisite	ex-QUIS-it
Furniture	fur-ni-chur	furni-ture
Government	guv-vern-ment	gub-mint
League	leeg	lig
Mischievous	MIS-chi-vuhs	mis-CHEE-vi-uhs
Umbrella	um-brel-uh	UM-bu-rel-ah
Valet	va-LAY	va-let

Regionalisms you've heard all your life may sound right to you—but they are not considered standard American English. Table 3 presents some examples of regional pronunciations that may be considered low-brow. Note the power speech variants to their left.

Table 3. Regional pronunciations.

Word	Power Speech	Low-Brow Speech
Couldn't	KOOD-nt	KOONT
Creek	creek	crick
Finance	fuh-NANCE	FIGH-nance
Fire	fi-er	far (rural) fi-yah (urban East)
Get	get	git
Guarantee	gair-un-tee	gar-un-tee
Insurance	in-SHUR-ants	IN-sur-ants
Italian	it-TAL-y'n	EYE-tal-yin
Long Island	Long I-lund	Long Guyland
Singer	sing-er	sing-gah
Theater	THE-a-ter	the-AYE-ter
Tremendous	tree-MEN-dos	tree-MEN-dis
Vehicle	VE-hi-kl	vi-HIC-l
Wouldn't	WOOD-unt	WUNT

36   *Power Speech: Why It's Vital to You*

Land Mines in Pronunciation

American Presidents have held on to favored pronunciations:
George Washington pronounced *pumpkin* "PUMP-i-uhn." Andrew Jackson, they tell us, insisted on saying, "di-FIK-'l-ti" because he liked his old schoolmaster who pronounced *difficulty* that way. Teddy Roosevelt made "DEE-light-ed" famous.

You can use these pronunciations—or others—once you've attained celebrity status. But the smart-money speaker learns the rules before cutting new trails. Keep an eye out for the land mines listed in Table 4.

Table 4. Low-brow land mines.

Word	Power Speech	Low-Brow Speech
Antipodes	an-TIP-u-deez	anti-POHDS
Arctic	ARK-tic	AR-tic
Bade	bad	bayd
Chiropodist	kee-RAHP-uh-dist	chee-RAHP-uh-dist
Dour	dour	dower
Drowned	dround	drownd-ded
Eleven	i-LEV-n	LEV-n
Err	ur	ehr
Grevious	gree-vuhs	gree-vi-us
Heinous	hay-nus	hee-nus
Quay	kee	kway
Sacrilegious	sac-ri-LEE-jus	sac-ri-LIGE-us
Sine qua non	SIGH-nee kway NAHN	sin que non
Soto voce	so-to vo-chay	soto vohs
Vaudeville	VOD-vil	VAWD-i-vil

Turn *See* Words into *Say* Words

Unusual words, encountered more in reading than speaking, must be converted from *see* words to *say* words. Table 5, opposite, is your conversion chart.

Table 5. Words to incorporate in power speech.

See It	*Say It*
Dramatis personae	DRAM-uh-tis per-SOH-ne
Enervate	EN-er-vayt
Ennui	AHN-wee
Ensign (banner)	EN-sighn
Ensign (officer)	EN-sin
Entrée	AHN-tray
Epistle	i-PIS-l
Epitome	i-PIT-uh-mi
Esoteric	ES-uh-TEHR-ik
Espousal	es-POUZ-l
Ethereal	i-THEIR-i-l
Fete	fayt
Finesse	fi-NES
Forbade	fer-BAD
Gondola	GAHN-duh-luh
Grimace	gri-MAYS
Gunwale	GUHN-l
Hospitable	HAHS-pi-tuh-bl
Hussar	hoo-ZAHR
Hyperbole	high-PER-buh-li
Incognito	in-KAHG-ni-toh
Jocose	joh-KOHS
Logy	LOH-gi
Mayoralty	MAY-er-l-ti
Meerschaum	MIER-shm
Mellifluous	muh-LIF-loo-uhs
Morass	muh-RAS
Opined	oh-PIGHND
Orion	oh-RIGH-un
Patois	PAT-wah
Perpetuity	PER-pi-TYOO-i-ti
Placard (n.)	PLAK-ahrd
Plethora	PLETH-uh-ruh
Portend	por-TEND
Protestation	praht-es-TAY-shun

See It	Say It
Pumice	PUHM-is
Scimitar	SIM-i-ter
Scintillate	SIN-ti-layt
Scion	SIGH-un
Scourge	skerj
Sepulcher	SEP-ul-ker
Stipend	STIGH-pend
Tempestuous	tem-PES-choo-uhs
Zealous	ZEL-uhs
Zoology	zoh-AHL-uh-ji

The list could go on—but that gives you a sample. I'd be greatly surprised if you didn't find something in it that needs changing in your speech.

When to Preserve Your Accent

Standard American speech has a purpose: It enables you to speak to powerful persons in their own language. Sometimes keeping an accent has a purpose, too.

On CBS-TV's *Cagney & Lacey,* Marybeth—one of the two policewomen—turns to her partner, Chris, and says: "Do me a favah, willyuh? Go see a doctah or sompin." Her pure New Yorkese is a perfect way of establishing character, background, and station in a few seconds.

Albert Kner, former director of package design at Container Corporation of America, started out with a Hungarian accent. When he saw it worked well for him in business, his accent got heavier and heavier. "If Albert keeps this up for another five years, we won't be able to understand him at all," a colleague said. "But we'll still think it's wonderful."

Dr. Ruth Westheimer, the sex doctor for a popular call-in show, uses her European accent to the fullest, saying things that would sound too forward (even in today's permissive society) in standard American.

"With her accent, she's scientific," one viewer said. "Without it, she'd be a nosy busybody."

I do not believe that all the psychiatrists who sound German or Austrian *are.* Yet many talk the way they do because that's what the public wants. British lecturers get more British on the platform. James

Stewart played characters on the screen that conjured up visions of democracy in the raw: small-townspeople going to meetings to debate the school tax.

At one time, ethnic accents were part of the entertainer's arsenal. Fanny Brice started out doing heavy Yiddish routines. Bert Lahr did a Dutch accent, which, in early vaudeville days, meant low German. The appeal of Amos and Andy was based on black patois. (Today such accents are considered demeaning. In the forties, I worked with a black butcher, Raleigh Randolph Holley, certainly no Uncle Tom. But he listened religiously to Amos and Andy—along with the rest of the nation.)

In time, this great melting-pot nation must view accents with a healthy perspective. Already trends are emerging. In 1982, *Marketing Times* reported that Robert Podesta, an unabashed Italian-American in northern California, established that accents are beautiful (and profitable). He published *The Italian No-Joke Success System,* a series of "teach cards" that advise career-climbers via Italian vernacular.

"I make you beeg success," Podesta tells audiences from the lecture platform. "I provide teach cards. I tell you good what smart guys teach me. You want to be a rich guy? You want to be real happy guy? Whatever you want, write it down on a card. Everybody likes a winner—only bums like bums—so be a winner!"

Podesta uses Italianese from the podium to make a point. But he speaks differently with program chairmen about appearing as a Waldorf-Astoria dinner speaker (which he did). Podesta uses accent for a purpose. But again, if you're not making a point, people wonder where you're from rather than what you're saying.

When to Preserve and When to Discard
Nonstandard Usage

One evening, at the Orkney Springs Hotel in the Shenandoah Valley of Virginia, we waiters were invited to hear Harry and Morton—the two bellmen—sing and play guitar. By way of introduction, Harry said proudly:

"I sing tenor."

That left a logical question for Morton:

"What do *you* sing?"

"Just straight voice," he said.

I was struck then—as I am now—by the perfection of that phrase: *straight voice.* Much better than *the lead* or *the melody.* Here is local language well worth preserving. The power speaker draws on local patois to enrich and enliven speech.

In the novel *Addie Pray* (on the screen: *Paper Moon* with Ryan and Tatum O'Neal), Addie says: "Some people don't know *B* from bull's foot." This traces back to early schoolbooks: *A* is for apple pie (drawing of pie). *B* is for bull's foot (drawing).

Today we're left with a colorful expression. Not to know *B* from bull's foot is to be lacking, indeed.

The Frontier Inheritance

Other American comparisons also show a closeness to the frontier:

- She's so ignorant she couldn't drive nails in the snow.
- The water is so muddy the trout had to swim backwards to keep from getting dirt in their eyes.
- He's grinning like a jackass eating briars.
- He's so bucktoothed he could eat corn on the cob through a picket fence.
- He'd climb a tree to tell a lie before he'd stay on the ground and tell the truth.
- I'm as happy as a dead pig in the sunshine.
- He'd fight a snake and give it 10 bites head start.

In the mountains and remote rural areas, we still hear authentic comparisons so valuable that if they were tangible artifacts they'd be shipped off to the Smithsonian as national treasures:

- Hogs so thin that it takes six of them to cast a shadow.
- So stingy he sat in the shade of the hackberry tree to save the shade of the porch.
- So ugly that he had to sneak up on the mirror to shave.
- That dog could track a grasshopper over running water.
- He'd stretch the truth so far it died of thinness.

The Urban Tradition

In the city of New York, you encounter speech traditions from another kind of frontier—the urban neighborhood. Many ethnic expressions have endured because of their vigor and aptness. To *schlepp* (to carry) connotes a lot of packages and an onerous trip. Nothing says what *schlepp* means as well as *schelpp* itself.

A person who bumbles and splutters in speech is *fumfering*. In no other way is it possible to so accurately describe a verbal botch or false start.

Ask a New Yorker what kind of a day it's been. She shrugs and says, "Don't ask." The message: It's so bad I cannot consider discussing it. If the day's been good, the woman says: "Not so terrible," meaning rather good, in fact.

Kids playing stickball on the street describe hits as *one-sewers* or *two-sewers*—graded by how many manhole covers the ball passes over. Folk creativity favors distinctive *sewer* over drab *manhole cover* (and gives tyro sportscasters practice in language-crunching: "Schwartz two-sewered in the first inning").

The Many Sounds of Americans

In the United States, many accents have emerged. We developed southern speech in several forms, New England speech (with variations including Down East), urban eastern (New York–New Jersey), and general American, also called standard American.

You may think you don't have an accent. But you do.

Merv Griffin, normally Mr. Standard American as a talk-show host, dips back to rustic for his pronunciation of syrups—it comes out *surps*.

If you started out in New England, you probably (as even John F. Kennedy proved) say *Cuber* for *Cuba* and *sofer* for *sofa*. David Lebedoff, social commentator who divided people into the "New Elite" and the "Left Behinds," said JFK's remarkable charisma came from his ability to appeal to *both* groups at the same time:

> Many Left Behinds supported him because they could identify with his roots—his religion, the closeness of his family, his immigrant grandparents.
>
> The New Elite admired his style. They heard the accents of Harvard, not Boston. They liked his clothes and wit, the quotes from Aeschylus, the cello concert in the East Room.

Such two-tier appeal is rare. Most of us need to adapt a standard speech that makes many segments of listeners think: "He's one of us."

Regional Usage: When and How to Blend In

The real value of power speech, when you get down to it, is your ability to adjust your conversation to regional circumstance.

I found this out visiting a coal mine in West Virginia to gather article material and supervise photography for the Oak Leaf Coal Company.

Coal miners distrust strangers. The best way to get cooperation during the day is to socialize at night. Socialize to coal men is spelled p-o-k-e-r. The first night, they still felt I was a stranger. Normally, I *bet* a dollar at the poker table. In West Virginia, they *check* a dollar. Soon I was hollering "check a dollar" right along with them. Before long, I blended into the group. But the next day, back in New York, I had to leave West Virginia talk behind—along with $36 they'd *checked* out of me.

In New York, *regular* coffee is served with cream. In Chicago, *regular* is black. *Soda* can be generic for soft drinks, but it's *pop* to the midwesterner, *tonic* to the Bostonian, and *dope* to the southerner. *Soda* can also be *club soda, clear soda, white soda,* depending where you are. In New York it's *seltzer,* after sparkling water from the Niederselters district of Germany—or better yet, *2¢ plain.*

Ask New Yorkers the name of that hard-crusted monster sandwich filled with lettuce, cold cuts, and cheese. They'll say, "A hero." In New Orleans where it may have originated, it's a *po'boy;* in New England, a *grinder;* in Philadelphia, a *hoagy;* and in other places, it's a *submarine* (after its shape).

Speech of the Sidewalks

The native New Yorker usually has the hardest time changing speech because he or she is so seldom aware of an accent. In their parochialism, New Yorkers assume the whole world speaks and thinks the way they do. Yet this accent is extremely grating to the non-New Yorker.

My friend Madeline Finch, who speaks very well, is still enough of a native New Yorker to call her daughter *Dianar* instead of *Diana.* Yet she never says *gent-ul-men* and *bot-ul* for *gentlemen* and *bottle* as do many New Yorkers. Other Gothamites add extra syllables to *ath-uh-lete* and *cock-a-roach.* They leave the *r* off *bettuh* and *summuh*—and quickly add it back on to *Chinar* and *La Guardiar airport.*

For a real treat, catch Tony Curtis on late-night TV in *The Prince Who Was a Thief,* an Arabian Nights movie. The horses come galloping over the sand.

Curtis (in Arab dress):   I vant to retoin to da land of my fadders.

Enough to make Hollywood speech coaches take up a new calling.

Nor does radio catch them all. On Orson Welles' famous "War of the

Worlds" (the show that panicked the nation into thinking Earth was being invaded), the announcer described dance music coming from the *Plazar* Hotel. There's nothing otherworldly about *Plazar*.

WRAPPING IT UP

Gauche speech can make you a permanent outsider. Power speech assures you of blending into society's elite—at each level.

Snotty speech isn't the answer. Neither high brow or low brow wins points. Develop standard American. At times, you can deliberately use an accent—but make sure you know the rules first.

An exhilarating benefit of a deep knowledge of American speech: You draw on it to be effective in a particular time and place. Say precisely what you want to say; select the proper emotional overtones and grace and force and beauty to accomplish your objectives.

Make a conscious effort to increase your professional and personal power through better use of your mother tongue. Fine speech, like fine clothes, is basically a matter of good taste.

America is rich in local usage. Revel in this distinctive heritage. Use local language to blend in. Discard it when you want to mesh with standard speech. Pick it back up when you seek color and distinction.

Hew to the line on *meanings,* however. Say what you mean to say. Wrong meanings label you as a dolt—or run you off a cliff by miscommunication.

Be careful: False elegance can tempt you to follow rules out the window. Common sense is often your best guide.

Make deliberate decisions about speech—be it on-track or offbeat. Don't leave your speech behavior to chance. Warning: Learn the rules before you decide to break them.

Power speech is the most potent weapon available in modern society. Acquire it and you accrue many other abilities. Ignore it and non-power speech can kick you in the slats. It's just that simple.

PART II

The Awesome Power of Content

3

What You Say Makes All the Difference

When I worked in a butcher shop, I found that cuts of meat rarely fall evenly into pound or half-pound measures. Yet the customer always asked for a specific weight: "Two pounds of pork chops." I'd read the scale and say: "That's 2¼ pounds. Is that all right?" "No," the shopper would say. "Give me what I asked for."

Then I'd do a juggling act, trying to get chops to weigh out exactly. But I soon got tired of this. With one customer, I put the meat on the scale and said: "That comes to $2.47. Will that be enough?" "Oh, quite enough," the woman said.

I never mentioned weight from then on. Just the amount and the magic phrase, "Will that be enough?"

Hundreds of shoppers reacted positively to the phrase—my first use of word power to persuade. It was a real eye-opener.

Whenever you're trying to get people to do something, there's a good, a so-so, and a bad choice of words to use. Find the right words, and the riches of King Solomon's mines are yours for the asking.

In the classic movie *The Grapes of Wrath*, Henry Fonda as Tom Joad is driving the Joad family into an orchard to get a fruit-picking job. The truck goes through a series of checkpoints—with harrassment by fascist guards. Finally, a guard repeats for the third time:

"Name?"

"It's still Joad," says Fonda, getting riled.

"I was just asking," says the patronizing guard.

"Well, *ask right*," says Fonda.

Ask right! A wealth of power speech counsel in two simple words.

My friend Hugh Edwards, president of The Research Guild, Atlanta, knows that asking right leads to better marketing research work. When he found respondents resisting the question "What was your last year of schooling?"—he designed a new question: "How many years of schooling did you have the opportunity to acquire?"

The question's response rate rose 55 percent. "After all," respondents figured, "they want to know about the *opportunities* I've had." A small difference? Yes, but a vital one. Remember Napoleon's assertion: "We rule men with words."

How Presidents Deploy Words

John F. Kennedy's use of *quarantine* instead of *blockade* defused the Cuban missile crisis. It allowed Russia to back down and save face—a formidable achievement in international head-knocking. This one word—*quarantined*—may have prevented nuclear holocaust.

Kennedy went about his wordsmithing quite deliberately. Said his speech writer, Theodore Sorensen:

> Our criterion was always audience comprehension and comfort. This meant: (1) short speeches, short clauses, and short words, wherever possible; (2) a series of points or propositions in numbered or logical sequence, wherever appropriate; and (3) the construction of sentences, phrases, and paragraphs to simplify, clarify, and emphasize.
>
> The test: not how it appeared to the eye, but how it sounded to the ear. His best paragraphs, when read aloud, often had a cadence not unlike blank verse—indeed at times key words would rhyme. He was fond of alliterative sentences, not solely for reasons of rhetoric but to reinforce the audience's recollection of his reasoning . . .[2]

Kennedy regarded words as tools of precision, to be chosen and applied with a craftsman's care. He liked to be exact. But if the situation required a vagueness, he'd deliberately choose a word of varying interpretations—rather than bury his imprecision in ponderous prose.

He wanted both his message and his language to be plain and unpretentious, but never patronizing. He avoided *suggest, perhaps,* and *possible alternatives for consideration.*

Kennedy used little or no slang, dialect, legalisms, contractions, clichés, elaborate metaphors, or ornate speech. He refused to be folksy or corny, tasteless or trite. He rarely used words he considered hackneyed: *humble, dynamic, glorious.* No speech fillers ("And I say to you that you've asked a legitimate question and here is my answer").

He departed from strict English when proper usage ("Our agenda are long") sounded pretentious to the listener. He believed that using topical, tasteful humor when opening his speech was a major route to audience rapport. He worked diligently for the right kick-off witticism.

Other presidents placed great value on words as weapons. Lincoln's political eminence was based squarely on his skillful and persuasive use of *lingua Americana.*

After the Cooper Union Address in 1860, Lincoln left New York in company with an acquaintance who said, "I want very much to know how you got this unusual power of 'putting things.' No man has it by nature alone. What has your education been?"

Lincoln answered:

> Well, as to education, the newspapers are correct. I never went to school more than six months of my life. But, as you say, this must be a product of culture in some form. I have been putting the question you ask me to myself while you've been talking.
>
> I say this: that among my earliest recollections, I remember how when a mere child, I used to get irritated when anybody talked to me in a way I couldn't understand. I don't think I ever got angrier at anything else in my life.
>
> I can remember going to my little bedroom after hearing the neighbors talk of an evening, with my father, and spending no small part of the night walking up and down and trying to make out the exact meaning of some of their, to me, dark sayings. I could not sleep, though I often tried to, when I got in such a hunt after an idea, until I caught it; and when I thought I had got it, I was still not satisfied until I had repeated it over and over, until I put it in language plain enough, as I thought, for any boy I knew to comprehend.
>
> This was a kind of passion with me, and it has stuck, for I am never easy now, when I am handling a thought, till I have bounded it north and bounded it south, and bounded it east and bounded it west. Perhaps that accounts for the characteristics you observe in my speeches, though I never put the two things together before.[3]

In modern times, word-oriented persuaders use the same stock-in-trade.

In the 1950s, Eisenhower delegates to the national Republican convention were challenging the seating of Taft delegates. Herb Brownell, Ike's astute manager, introduced an amendment to the rules that set Ike's people well ahead. He labeled it the Fair Play Amendment. This reduced Taft supporters to speaking against "the so-called Fair Play Amendment." You do not have to be a political buff to know they were licked before they started. Taft never made it to the White House. Brownell, of course, went on to become Ike's attorney general. This brilliant lawyer understood and used power speech.

James Webb Young, a word master who retired to New Mexico, set about selling apples grown on his own ranch—Uncle Jim's Apples. One fall, disaster struck. Just before picking time, a hailstorm hit Jim's orchards, putting small pockmarks in otherwise perfect fruit. At first Jim thought of returning money to his customers. Then inspiration hit. With each bushel, he said:

> You might see some small pockmarks on my apples this year. They're hail marks. They won't hurt the flavor or texture. They're your proof that these delicious apples were grown up here in the high mountain country of New Mexico where the air and soil are just about as perfect as you can find for apple growing.[4]

Not one customer asked for a refund. In fact, for the next couple of years, customers asked if Jim could sell them genuine hail-marked apples!

The difference between the right word and the almost right word, as Mark Twain reminded us, is the difference between the lightning and the lightning bug.

Words to Put Money in Your Pocket

Carefully chosen words are worth their weight in gold—literally—in terms of the money they can spoon into your pocket. Certain words ring a bell with your customer; they appeal to his or her viewpoint.

When you use *you,* you bring the buyer into the conversation. Instead of resisting, he can actually help you make the sale.

Design your questions at order-asking time to include *profit. Profit* has power. It's the reason your business customer is in business.

Value has a strong appeal. The buyer always wants to make sure she's getting her money's worth.

Opinion is good. When you ask the buyer his opinion, you're adding air to his ego balloon.

Rock Lubin, ace real estate salesman, likes take-charge words. "Take charge of the sales interview from the start," Lubin says. "Stay in charge through getting the name on the dotted line." In demonstrating a house, Lubin says to the prospect: "Follow me." Then he turns and walks away—never looking back.

Patter phrases work wonders when the customer is making a decision.

Lubin: What color checks do you have?
Prospect: Green.
Lubin: Good. That's the kind we're taking today.

Another effective patter phrase while customer stands pen-poised over contract: "Press hard. This pen must print through three copies."

By shifting the prospect's attention to the mechanics of writing, you take the spotlight off the decision and give him or her an easier matter to consider.

In Lubin's lexicon, the living room is always the *great room.* The entrance is the *foyer.* A kitchen is never small, it's a *step-saver kitchen.*

Effective salesfolk never say, "Sign here." They say: "I'll place my O.K. here, and just above my name is a place for your approval—then the problem of keeping your rugs free from dog hair will be solved!" (She signs.)

"Tremendous trifles make or break a sale," Lubin says. "Offer a win–win choice: 'Would you like the shorter term or the greater savings?' "

In a movie theater snack stand, one group of clerks asked, "Large or small" when the movie-goer ordered a soda. Clerks in the other group were instructed to simply ask, "Large?" Seventy percent of the second group's buyers nodded *yes.* One word increased the second group's sales volume 35 percent over the first group's.

Texaco wanted service stations to push a new motor oil. Many motorists, when asked, "Check your oil?" responded: "No, I just need gasoline, thanks."

Texaco's wordsmith changed the query to: "Is your oil at the proper driving level?" The response was magic. Service station operators looked under a million hoods in one week! Words are dynamite. The motorist thinks: "Suppose my oil *isn't* at the right driving level? What could happen?"

Skilled persuaders don't ask *if,* they ask *which.*

The Hoover vacuum cleaner salesperson closes with: "If the Hoover goes, dirt stays; if the Hoover stays, dirt goes. Which do you prefer?" This question is hard to answer other than: "I want the Hoover to stay."

Hoover salespeople are also experts in providing flattering product descriptions. The salesman doesn't talk about his product's gray color. Instead he says: "It's stratosphere gray." *Stratosphere* evokes images of speed and lightness.

Bloomingdale's doubled its sales of furniture polish by having the clerk hold up a bottle of polish and say: "It cleans and polishes in one easy operation." The salespeople stressed operation, not polish.

I can hear you saying: "Sounds like a lot of painstaking trouble over words." I refer you to Ernest Hemingway. On why he rewrote the ending to *A Farewell to Arms* 39 times, an interviewer asked Hemingway: "What was it that stumped you?" "Getting the words right," Hemingway said—in true Hemingway style.

De-Personalize to De-Sting

Certain advisers (in this book and elsewhere) exhort you to speak in the active voice. In most cases, heed them. But not when you want to take the sting out of personal words.

You're talking to an erring employee about consistent lateness. You could say: "You've been late three times this week and I won't stand for it." Clear enough—but rankling. Here's a better approach: "The job calls for the employee to be here on time—9 A.M. sharp. There's no way the job can be done without that." The *job* says. An employee can't get mad at the job.

You're interested in setting an appointment with a prospect. You want to insist without making it personal. You say: "The calendar says that 3 P.M. Tuesday would be a good time for us to meet." How can your prospect get mad at a pushy calendar?

Lee Stanley, president of Solar Additions, Greenwich, New York, does get personal at times, especially when an employee asks him a busywork question. "That sounds like a personal problem," Stanley says. "Be creative." The employee goes away—sometimes with a puzzled look on his face, but he does go away.

What Not to Say: Double Meanings and Other Gaffes

Newspaper headline writers are constantly alert to two-faced headlines, those that carry the original meaning plus something else. Nevertheless, purient heads do slip through the net, such as the *Boston Globe*'s eye-catcher about a university dean's opposition to new construction in Harvard Square: DEAN FIGHTS ERECTION IN SQUARE. Or the sports-page headline about the Cincinnati Reds' defeat of an opposing baseball pitcher: REDS HAMMER PETERS.

Nor are songwriters immune, particularly since they like telling us about heartfelt separations. Witness the line from "Red River Valley": "Would you leave her behind unprotected?" Or the song made popular by the Clancy Brothers and Tommy Makem about the sadness "In leaving Miss Nancy Sears behind."

Don't think it doesn't happen with spoken words too. In modern times, a woman with a bad cold decided to avoid dinner-party embarrassment by hiding an extra handkerchief in her décolletage (her sheath evening gown had no pockets). Later in the evening, when hanky number one became sodden, she reached inside for her reserve. Alas, it had slipped down just out of reach. With her nose running, she frantically searched in her bosom—creating exactly the kind of attention she'd hoped to avoid. Feeling all eyes on her, she said: "I *thought* I had *two* when I came." That brought the house down.

A fellow at an airline counter was flustered by the well-endowed female ticket clerk. "Two pickets to Tittsburg," he said in reflex.

It can happen to anyone. My friend Connie Jason, surprised to meet Jack Lemmon in a bistro, blurted out: "Oh, Mr. Lemmon, you've been a fan of mine for years." She's never forgotten the incident.

Professionals also succumb to hoof-in-mouth disease, much to their eternal shame. Harry Von Zell, in introducing Herbert Hoover on network radio, said: "Ladies and gentlemen, Hoobert Heever."

And no listener will ever forget the announcer who introduced banjoist Eddy Peabody with: "Eddy Playbody will now pee."

Nor is Ronald Reagan, an overwhelmingly popular president and trained performer, immune. At a dinner welcoming him to Brazil, President Reagan said: "And now won't you join me in a toast to the people of Bolivia?"

At a meeting of big-city mayors, Reagan failed to recognize his own housing secretary, Samuel Pierce. To Pierce he said: "How are you, Mr. Mayor? I'm glad to meet you! How are things in your city?"

How to avoid gaffes? The more you speak, and the more varied the situations in which you speak, the more you'll be in control. Tension brings out the gaucheries; relaxation tends to reduce them.

When it does happen, make it funny—if you can. Humorist H. Allen Smith told us how:

You (looking at picture):   Who is that frowsy old harridan?
Host: That's my mother!
You: Is there a revolver in the house?

Finally, harken to the counsel of the March Hare and the Mad Hatter in *Alice's Adventures in Wonderland:*

"You should say what you mean," the March Hare said.
"I do," Alice hastily replied. "At least I mean what I say—that's the same thing, you know."
"Not the same thing a bit!" said the Hatter. "Why, you might as well say that 'I see what I eat' is the same as "I eat what I see!' "

The Astounding Power of Words

"Worship words, you fellows," said the sales manager to salesfolk. "You don't eat without them."

True. Whatever your product or service or mission, your main inventory is words. To be a power speaker, you must collect, savor, caress, feed, and groom words. File them away carefully in your active retrieval system. Categorize your inventory these ways:

Think of Words in Full Color

Blackball	Greenhorn
Black Hole	Green Thumb
Black Magic	Red Alert
Blackmail	Rednecks
Blue Blood	Red Tape
Blue Chip	Red Undancy (paying attention?)
Blue Laws	Silver Lining
Blue Moon	White Elephant
Blue Notes	White Noise
Golden Rule	White Papers
Gray Matter	Whitewash
Greenbacks	Yellow Fever
Greenbelts	Yellow Streak

Collect Words that Motivate

Use beautiful words: *dawn, hush, lullaby, murmuring, tranquil, mist, luminous, chimes, melody*. Such words, because of musical sounds and rich meanings, are easy to pronounce attractively. Say them sincerely, thinking what they really mean, to make an impression.

Treat words with reverence. Richard Price did in his review of Peter Dexter's book *God's Pocket:* "*God's Pocket* sings, snarls, mugs, wisecracks, buys you a drink, steals your wallet, and takes you home to meet the folks."

Read the King James version of the Bible to collect a trove of simple, powerful words. After all, as Solomon said in Proverbs: "Pleasant words are as a honeycomb, sweet to the soul, and health to the bones." Simple words winged with imagination are like Wordsworth's Lucy, "Fair as a star when only one is shining in the sky."

John Gielgud has been a lifelong conversationalist. When sitting over lunch at the Ivy, an old theatrical restaurant in London's West End,

Gielgud, according to friends, is an irrepressible Mr. Chat—full of observations, anecdotes, and gossip.

"You needn't say a word when you're with him," said the late Ralph Richardson, a close friend for 53 years. "Sometimes all I will say is *yes* or *no* or *really?* Afterward he will tell someone, 'I had a wonderful talk with Ralph.' And I didn't say anything! He's a continual firework of words."

Yet Gielgud has no secret cache of conversational grist. The words he employs are all available free—in the Bible, in Shakespeare, in your dictionary. And some, we hope, in your own word inventory!

Wilfred J. Funk tells us that the man or woman who's a master of words is likewise a master of people.

WRAPPING IT UP

Once you make word collecting automatic, you will be well on your way to mastering a significant component of effective speech—the awesome power of content.

At work, try out power phrases that persuade customers, colleagues, employees, bosses. De-personalize to de-sting. When words work, add them to your arsenal. Discard the bummers and keep building.

In persuading people to pay money, be particularly alert to phrases that reassure. Give them small choices to make that take the pressure off the decision to buy. Avoid frightening words.

At leisure, carefully build your speech inventory based on its effectiveness in entertaining and motivating.

In both work and leisure hours, avoid the trite, hackneyed phrases that irritate and establish you as part of the thundering herd. Be precise. Say what you mean. Choose words that speak for themselves. Collect and use winners. Isolate and expunge sinners.

4

Suiting Your Message to Your Audience

During the heyday of American folk music, Huddy Ledbetter—more often called Leadbelly—was a performing legend. He got himself out of a prison by composing and singing "Good Night, Irene" for the Louisiana governor. He then became a popular recording artist and concert folksinger.

In the 1940s, producers of a Lincoln's Birthday benefit asked Leadbelly to perform at historic Cooper Union in Manhattan, where Lincoln had spoken in 1860.

"Can you tailor your performance to Lincoln's birthday?" the producer asked. "Sho' can," Leadbelly said.

On performance night Leadbelly delighted the audience with "Midnight Special," "Good Night, Irene," and "Ella Speed." During the first half, nothing about Lincoln. At the break, the worried producer asked: "When's the Lincoln part?" "Coming up next," Leadbelly said.

Back on stage, he strummed through several songs, getting big sounds from his 12-string guitar. Then, in the midst of one song, he stopped and said loud and clear, "Happy birthday, Mr. Linkum," and then finished the concert.

Portrait of a man tailoring performance to an audience.

Of course, Leadbelly had a loyal following. He could (and did) do as he pleased. The rest of us who perform—and that's exactly what a speaker does before large groups or small—must be much more diligent about suiting the message to specific ears.

You *must* suit the message to the audience. Basic? Absolutely. Often ignored? All the time.

Back in the Middle Ages, learned savants debated the following for hours: "If a tree falls in the center of the forest and nobody is there to hear the crash, does it make any noise?" The yeas and nays have been evenly divided to this day. Now it can be resolved in terms of human speech.

If you're talking, and your message isn't geared to your audience, you're *not* making any noise—or, for that matter, any progress. You're wasting everyone's time.

Churchill on Suiting Words to the Audience

Winston Churchill drew his power from adroit choice of simple work-horse words—the more classic, the better. Churchill loved words.

Lloyd George, a Churchill critic, said to call Mussolini's conduct in Ethiopia "at once obsolete and reprehensible," as Winston had, was meaningless. Unchastened, Churchill replied, "Ah, the *b*'s in those words: 'obsolete, reprehensible.' You must pay attention to euphony."

When short words hit hard, he used them. ("I like short words and vulgar fractions.") Needing military equipment after Dunkirk, he told the United States: "Give us the tools and we will finish the job."

He did not declare that the Allies had "consented to a coalition" or "agreed to cooperate." Instead, they "joined hands."

On other occasions, he didn't hesitate to dip into his enormous vocabulary. Once he dictated a note to the Admiralty: "Must we have this lugubrious ingemination of the news of our shipping losses?" At first the sea lords thought his secretary had mistyped *insemination.* Then they consulted the Oxford English Dictionary and found that the word means *redundancy.*

Like most power speakers, Churchill had his favorite words: *unflinching, austere, somber, squalid.* He said *aircraft,* not *aeroplane,* and *airfield,* never *aerodrome.* He did not use *adumbrated* and *coordination.*

He also liked to gather adjectives in squads of four. Bernard Montgomery was "austere, severe, accomplished, tireless." Joe Chamberlain was "lively, sparkling, insurgent, compulsive."

Said Churchill biographer William Manchester: "He would open a speech with a sluggish large tempo, apparently unsure of himself. Then he'd pull out his vocal organ's Grand Swell and the Vox Humana, and deliver a bold, ponderous, rolling, pealing, easy rhythm, broken by vivid stabbing strokes."[5]

He hated euphemisms. He scoffed at bureaucrats who called the poor "a low-income group," or trucks "commercial vehicles," or homes "accommodation units." Once Churchill astonished the House of Commons by bursting into song: "Accommodation unit, sweet accommodation unit, There's no place like accommodation unit." In 1940, when he took over as prime minister, he changed "Local Defense Volunteers" to the "Home Guard."

No wonder Churchill said: "The short words are the best, the old words best of all."

Adapting Speech to One-on-One Situations

James A. Newman, vice chairman of Booz Allen Hamilton management consultants and my co-author on *Climbing the Corporate Matterhorn*, is a past master at adapting one-on-one techniques to his audience. When he was in charge of executive recruiting for Booz Allen, Newman was seeking a general manager for a new paper mill in Canada. He contacted many pulp and paper executives, heads of companies, and members of associations and consulted industry directories.

Out of his search came four names—men with the right background, the right training, the reputed personal characteristics—including a man in lower Quebec named Brian McBrae. Jim Newman called McBrae and said: "We have a problem in the pulp and paper industry, a peculiar kind of problem. We think you can help us solve it—if you're willing to give us your time." McBrae agreed.

In person, Newman told McBrae his problem: locating the ablest person in Canada to head up a huge new paper mill. As they got into the discussion, Newman asked McBrae what his three greatest objectives were. McBrae replied: "My first objective is to my family. I feel responsible for its growth and upbringing. I intend to do everything I can to see that they get every opportunity and are as happy as possible."

He really meant this. He didn't care about a better job. He was already president and general manager at a paper company. But he was very much concerned about his family. (Later he took Newman home and proudly lined up his eight children—as sharp as a Green Beret squad. He introduced each and spoke about achievements.)

"My second objective is to discharge a debt I owe to my employer, the Smith-Howard Paper Company. This Scottish company advanced me from the lower levels of a paper mill, selected me to come overseas, gave me a chance in this current mill, helped me rise to general manager. For that opportunity, I'm grateful.

"On the other hand, I've pretty well discharged that debt. We've made this company quadruple in size. Profitability has more than doubled. I have a great cadre of young managers. Any one of them could take my place. So I do think that my employer has been well rewarded."

Newman already knew about McBrae's success—one reason he emerged as a top candidate.

"My third and perhaps my greatest objective is to try to break down the strife between the Anglican Church and the United Church of Canada—two excellent well-meaning organizations. I just can't understand the backbiting and bitterness that exist between them. Here in this Quebec town, I've made a lot of progress through the country club where I'm president and the community house where I'm on the board. But I travel a great deal across Canada. I know this bitterness exists in many other towns."

Newman decided he had uncovered the candidate's hot button. We jumped on it instantly. "In the town where we want you to move as president," Newman stated, "some of the toughest religious strife in Canada exists. The United Church launched meetings trying to dramatize faults of the Anglicans. The Anglicans are reacting in the same way."[6]

Boy, did Brian McBrae react! Not because of the modest increase in money, not because he was moving up the slope (he was already at the top), but because the new post offered him the chance to achieve an unsatisfied personal objective. He took the new job and was abundantly successful in reducing the religious strife. He also made an outstanding CEO.

Several lessons from the Brian McBrae story: (1) A power speaker must tailor his or her personal persuasion to the prospect's needs, and (2) you probably won't know the prime needs until you uncover them on the spot in direct conversation. Once you identify needs, move quickly.

Adapting Selling Words

The same principle works with small groups, too. John Henderson, a computer hardware salesman, was presenting his products to three owners of a medium-size commercial art studio. Henderson arrived in his three-piece suit—with detailed proposals in his attaché case.

To his surprise, the three owners were late, and all wore jeans and running shoes. Quickly sensing these men were not likely to sit still long, Henderson made a brief opening statement on his company, took off his coat and unbuttoned his vest, and indicated that he preferred to have his customers design their own system. He asked the owners to go to the blackboard in their office and, using their imagination, diagram a system to handle their needs. "Don't worry about hardware names," he said. "Just indicate what you want it to do."

When the owners finished, Henderson went to the design, and using a red marker, put the names of hardware components over each appropriate place in the design. He then stepped back, looked at the design, and said: "Gentlemen, that's a helluva system." After Henderson quickly demonstrated his components, the owners placed an order. They never saw Henderson's detailed proposals.

Less-flexible speakers insist on following a pre-arranged plan: If they've worked hard to put together a presentation, then by God they're going to show it. They follow their plan right out the side door and onto the street. The best speech in the world is worthless if the audience isn't receptive.

Dr. Paul Mok, a Dallas sales trainer who teaches the style-flex system, says: "Discern the customer's style. Then match your style to his during this encounter. It closes sales." In short, suit the message to the listener.

In selling (where the effect of power speech is easiest to measure— rising sales mean it's working), suiting the message to the prospect often means listening carefully and then analyzing what the person really means.

George Higpen, an outdoor advertising salesman in Nebraska, called on Samuel Geist, a department store owner. Several times Geist told Higpen: "Listen, I don't want any personal publicity. So just forget about that." Actually, Higpen hadn't planned a campaign based on personality. But after Geist repeated several times "no personal publicity," Higpen got a glimmer of the real need. He came back with a campaign built on Geist's speaking out for his store on vital local issues. He closed the sale.

"Most people hate to admit they're seeking personal recognition," Higpen said. "They think it makes them look ego-involved. So they articulate the opposite of what they actually want. This is particularly true if the prospect repeats the same phrase several times—that's a dead giveaway."

Discover your persuadee's *real* needs. Convert them to your objective.

That's particularly true when you're dealing with a "Contrary," says Phil Taggart, who sells a financial relations service to top management in Houston. Taggart's Uncle Harry is a prime example of the Contrary in action:

> If Harry's wife wants to get him out to dinner, she must call and say she'd like to fix dinner at home. "Oh, no," Harry always says. "I want to eat out."
>
> If she wants to visit relatives on the East Coast, she suggests to Harry they go west. "Oh, no," he replies, "it's high time we went East." The only way possible to get him to take a specific action is to suggest the opposite course.

The corollary in power speech: Suggest to the Contrary that he cannot afford to buy at this time. Or that perhaps the proposition under discussion isn't really for him.

Don Fields is a highly successful office furniture dealer. When he's talking to a chair manufacturer, he makes sure he knows about chairs. "Did you know that each person on the average sits in 13 chairs per day?" Fields will say. They listen. Here's a man who took time and trouble to find out something about their business they didn't know.

The person you're persuading is hardly ever impressed by *your* jargon. He's impressed when you use his jargon. An encyclopedia salesman told a chef: "This first volume is yours free. It's just an hors d'oeuvre. Then you start getting one volume per month. That's your entrée." The chef signed. Here was a man who understood the important factors in life—food. A message tailored to its audience.

Barnes & Noble, the giant book retailer, is sharp about its New York audience and understands how it speaks. The retailer once listed itself in two places in the Manhattan yellow pages. There was the expected listing under Barnes & Noble. But knowing that native New Yorkers don't pronounce the *r*, canny B & N ran a second listing as *Bonds* & Noble. "That way, if they *say* it like they *see* it, we're in. If they *see* it like they *say* it, we're in," a Barnes & Noble marketer said.

Insightful response to audience. Too bad B & N doesn't still do this!

If you go overseas with your product, you have another kind of audience-tailoring job on your hands. Words do not mean the same thing everywhere. Even gestures are not universal. The American O.K. sign (thumb and forefinger joined in a circle) is an insult in Latin America. Never stop analyzing your audience to ensure appropriate language. (The American importer of a Japanese appliance called FACOM had to change the name to suit U.S. ears.)

Never forget timing. Be inspired by a Washington, D.C., theater's action during the frenzied four-day Reagan inaugural bash in 1985. Unperturbed, the proprietor had the theater marquee announce its newest Shakespeare play: *Much Ado About Nothing.*

Getting into Your Audience's Shoes

The only way to really tailor your message is to put yourself in your listener's shoes. Think the way she thinks. A psychiatrist gave a woman a thematic apperception test (the patient looks at a series of pictures and relates what is happening in each). The woman watched carefully and discussed a sexual happening in each frame. In conclusion, the doctor said, "You really are obsessed with sex." "Well, look who's talking," the woman said. "What about you, Doc, showing all those dirty pictures!"

But it's not always that simple. You've mastered your presentation. You deliver it impressively without a hitch. *You* know all about your product or service. But your prospect may be unable to assimilate the facts, especially about high-tech. Maybe you aren't getting through at all!

He may be like my Japanese prospect. His English was poor. I wasn't smart enough to fit my presentation to his capacities. At the end of five minutes, he said to me: "I no get. I no buy. Good-bye."

Remember the graffiti:

> I know you believe you understand
> what you think I said.
> But I am not sure you realize that
> what you heard is not what I meant.

Think about that when you analyze your audience.

One thing is guaranteed: You can't phony up an understanding of your audience. It must be genuine, based on honest interest in your target (be it customer, client, friend, or other person you need to influence).

Hubert Bermont, a Washington, D.C., consultant, found this out when he broke into retail selling. It wasn't working until he found a simple, classic principle: The customer's needs come first. Says Bermont:

> When I was a young salesman, a top-notch colleague always went home with the biggest commission check. He had 30 years' experience. Having armed myself with product information as the old-timer had, I went into combat with customers: wheedling, cajoling, charming, telling jokes, and even threatening them with consequences of not buying.

I was the good guy trying to make sales to support my new young family. They were the bad guys trying to prevent me from making sales. After each infrequent sale, I was emotionally exhausted.

Mr. Experience had no such days. He was easygoing, calm, and lost very few sales. One day, he took me aside and said:

"Kid, I like you. I'm going to explain why you have the wrong approach and the wrong attitude. These customers aren't your enemies. They don't wander in by accident or to come out of the rain. They come here because they want something.

"You act as if they're here to give you a rough time. As if it's your duty to remind them they came in to buy something. They have a genuine need for what we sell, but they're frightened. These are tough times. They work hard for their money. They are terribly concerned about buying something they don't need nor want.

"Your job is to calm them and help them part with money. Your job is not to fight them and try to grab their money because of your own needs. Their needs come first."[7]

Make sure you're not misunderstood. Remember the motto: "Whatever can be misunderstood, will be misunderstood."

How can you make persuasive speech absolutely understandable? J. E. Kennedy, a pioneer in mass selling, said every presentation should be in language of primers used by five- and six-year-olds—everything simple, everything in one-syllable words when possible.

"Clear language is the language which carries the most conviction—the only language the average person understands," he said. "How foolish to believe a person merely hearing your talk, which bristles perhaps with technical and trade terms, will understand it as well as you, who have been over it 1,000 times."

Try your presentation out on uninformed persons. Kennedy used young people between ages 14 and 20. He'd present his talk to them, noting their expressions and asking whether they understood every word. If he found a puzzled look, he'd stop right there: He knew he wasn't getting through. Only when his talk sailed along and every kid understood it did Kennedy know his prospects would.

Does such rehearsal seem like a lot of trouble? It is. But it makes for effective speech, and what else matters?

Another Kennedy rule: During your talk, before you close, summarize what you have already told the customer. You've said it. He's heard it. Repeat it. Bring your entire talk into focus so there's no misunderstanding anywhere.

All successful communicators, from prophets to trial lawyers, go to great lengths to get complete understanding. They agree with the Apostle Paul in his epistle to the Corinthians: "I had rather speak five words with understanding than 10,000 words in an unknown tongue."

Suiting message to audience is even more important when your job is motivating an employee, a child, or a peer who needs encouragement.

In audience analysis, heed the counsel of Douglas F. Starr in his book *How to Handle Speechwriting Assignments:*

- Each audience member will interpret the same information differently.
- Women are easier to persuade than men.
- Younger people are more easily persuaded than older people.
- People generally seek out information that supports beliefs they already hold and tend to disregard information that contradicts those beliefs.
- People are often not rational about their attitudes and beliefs.
- People tend to accept the ideas expressed by charismatic and well-known individuals, but they don't necessarily retain those ideas.
- People are changing: The old orientation toward family, home, and work is fading. The precepts of duty before pleasure and sacrifice on behalf of the children no longer dominate. Values have shifted to favor rights and pleasures, work that is meaningful to the individual, rights for women and minority groups, a simpler and less-structured existence, and less government control.

"The most effective method of analyzing the audience for your speech: telephone the program director and take notes while getting information on the speaking engagement," says Starr. The simplest route is often the best.

My longtime friend Jack Wright, when he operated Wright Advertising in Newport News, Virginia, once managed a campaign to legalize sales of liquor by the drink.

At a political rally, one candidate was asked how he stood on the liquor amendment. Wright reports that the candidate decided to give both his pro and his con speech at the same time. Said the candidate:

> I had not intended to discuss this controversial subject at this particular time. However, I want you to know that I do not shun a controversy. On the contrary, I will take a stand on any issue at any time regardless of how fraught with controversy it may be.
>
> You have asked me how I feel about whiskey.
>
> If when you say whiskey, you mean the devil's brew, the poison scourge, the bloody monster that defies innocence, dethrones reason, destroys the home, creates misery and poverty, yea literally takes the bread from the mouths of little children; if you mean the evil drink that topples the Christian man and woman from the pinnacles of righteous, gracious living into the bottomless pit of degradation and despair, shame,

helplessness and hopelessness, then certainly I'm against it with all my power.

But if, when you say whiskey, you mean the oil of conversation, that philosophic wine, the ale that is consumed when good fellows get together, that puts a song in their hearts and laughter on their lips and the warm glow of contentment in their eyes; if you mean Christmas cheer; if you mean the stimulating drink that puts the spring in the old gentleman's step on a frosty morning; if you mean the drink that enables a man to magnify his joy and his happiness and to forget, if only for a little while, life's great tragedies and heartbreaks and sorrows; if you mean that drink the sale of which pours into our treasuries untold millions of dollars, which are used to provide tender care for little crippled children, our blind, our deaf, our dumb, our pitiful aged and infirm, to build highways and hospitals, and schools, then certainly I am in favor of it.

This is my stand and I will not compromise.

The audience loved it. After all, each side felt he spoke their language.

Sometimes you plan deliberately *not* to speak the audience's language—to achieve a certain effect. Jimmy Carter did this in the New Hampshire primary. Carter forces loaded two buses full of southern ladies drawn from Atlanta, Savannah, Macon, and other such citadels of gentility and transported them to the frozen sidewalks of Manchester, Exeter, and Keene.

There they accosted prospective voters: "Pahdun, me, suh, but may ah talk to you jus' one li'l ol' minnit about Jimmy Carter of Jawjuh?"

The Yankees could understand barely one word from these crinoline beauties. But they fell under their spell. Carter romped home a length ahead of Mo Udall and two lengths ahead of Birch Bayh.

The group was suited to its audience because it was *different* enough to get attention.

Some of the world's biggest failures occur when an unknowing person ham-handedly tries to suit the message to the audience. My friend Alayne Ambrogio, a Bronxville real estate saleswoman, found this out while visiting a sales/marketing association in Appleton, Wisconsin. The local group dispatched a man to meet her at the airport with instructions that, "Nothing's too good for our guest."

When Alayne got off the plane, the host said: "We've never had a real EYE-talian visit us before. We've made arrangements to take you to a real EYE-talian restaurant."

Alayne said fine. When they got there, she found it was the local Pizza Hut! An audience adaptation that failed miserably.

The classic case of speaking the audience's language came when John F. Kennedy went to Berlin. He spoke to a large crowd (and the world) on pride in being a Berliner. Most of his words were in English. But at a critical dramatic point he said the now-famous German phrase: "Ich bin ein Berliner!"

The effect was seismic—one of history's great moments in crowd-swaying. Audience tailoring *par excellence!*

WRAPPING IT UP

The world's best conversation or speech is the world's worst if it's unsuited to the audience. Tailoring to specific ears sometimes means using short, classic words or using longer, unusual words and all gradations in between. Find out who specifically you're talking to, then keep in mind that group's interests and attitudes.

In vital one-on-one conversation, be prepared to zoom in once you uncover the listener's hot button. Strike quickly when opportunity arises. Your listener's needs—not yours—dictate the content and style of what you say.

Get in your listener's shoes. Or else move so far from the norm you attract attention by contrast. But develop a plan for suiting your speech to your listener.

5

Harnessing the Power of Names

In newspapers, local names make news—as I found out when sending hometown press releases for the Army. In show business, names make news because they have already *been* widely publicized. (TV talk shows pride themselves on "top-name guests.")

In one memorable experience, I turned a non-name into a name—just because they *thought* it was a name. When I was living in Chicago, Bill Sheehy, my friend from Army days, asked me to get him on the *Welcome Traveler Show.* I said I would and then realized I didn't have a notion as to how. *Welcome Traveler* was a much-sought-after network show originating in Chicago. Bill Sheehy did have a good story to tell (hitchhiking camel caravans in North Africa), but, of course, the name *Bill Sheehy* meant nothing to the producer.

Then I had the idea: Why not encourage them to assume Bill Sheehy *is* widely known? That way, I could harness name power and put it to work. Two weeks before Bill arrived, I mailed *Welcome Traveler*'s producer a series of teaser memos, each with a stark message: *Bill Sheehy's coming to town.* Nothing more. Then the day before his arrival, I sent a telegram:

BILL SHEEHY ARRIVES TOMORROW. GREAT STORY.
ROY ALEXANDER.

On the day of the show, the warm-up men circulated through the studio audience to pick guests. One selector held a stack of memos and the telegram. (This was back when Western Union actually delivered telegrams.) Bill Sheehy arrived and got an aisle seat, as per plan. When the selector came near, Bill said to him—quietly, "I'm Bill Sheehy."

He got on the show, related his camel caravan story, and won hundreds of dollars worth of prizes. Afterward, the producer said: "I'm delighted. But I have only one question. Who's Roy Alexander?" Bill's answer was quick: "He's my camel driver."

I later heard the producer had decided to go into other work.

This example of harnessing name power carries several morals. In certain industries (broadcasting for one), the really smart money prides itself on knowing Big Names. Hit them with a name they think everyone *else* knows (but somehow *they don't*), and they'll act like they *do* know it. You can play on that.

Further, people are looking for an excuse to single you out of a crowd. Give it to them.

Finally, even though this was a case of short-term name building, the same principles apply for long-range goals. Always work at building recognition value for your name.

The Unforgettable Name

I played poker each Thursday with Ed Fellerman, a New Jersey restaurant equipment salesman and designer. But at trade shows, much to my surprise, I found he introduced himself to prospects as George Kockenlocker. Why?

"You don't think they'd forget a name like George Kockenlocker, do you?" Fellerman said.

No, I don't. It reminds me of the slogan: "With a name like Smucker's, it's *got* to be good." (If the name is bad enough, play on that.)

Now I'm not really sure that giving a phony name pays off. Sooner or later, you must tell them your real name. But Fellerman, a professional character, makes it work. And it does point out the value of a memorable name.

Always Use the Correct Name

Shortly after I started work for Mid-States Corporation, our Kalamazoo mobile-home plant hired a Dutch engineer named Peter Visser. I met Visser when he came to Chicago as one of CEO Bill MacDonald's guests at the season's first White Sox game.

En route to Comiskey Park, Visser kept calling a regional sales rep, Al Warren, by the name Bob. Every time Visser said "Bob," Warren pleasantly said, "It's Al." Visser, tired of being corrected, finally said: "Vat's da difference!" Warren said nothing. But he avoided Visser at the ballpark.

Later when I suggested doing a press release about Visser joining the company, my boss said: "Hold up. They're not too happy with Visser in Kalamazoo. I don't know why." I knew why. Anyone openly contemptuous of people's names is a disaster looking for a place to happen. Visser left the company a few weeks later. A qualified engineer, a flop in human relations.

In evaluating yourself as a persuader, ask this key question: "Do I capitalize on the full benefit of using people's names favorably and flatteringly?" Many otherwise accomplished speakers do not, and lose power in the process. The formula is simple: Find out names immediately and use them constantly. Successful politicians do this. Louisiana Governor Edwin Edwards' advance man stands near him on tour to provide a wife's name or a daughter's name in each receiving line.

Another way to satisfy this want-to-believe hunger: reading name tags. "You call them by their name and they think you're great for remembering," Governor Edwards says. "They forget they're wearing the tag."

"They *want* to believe they're remembered," said Bruce Shine, former advance man for Hubert Humphrey. "Let them believe."

The truly persuasive person knows that no sound is prettier to a listener's ears than the person's own name—his or her symbolic extension. The persuasive person remembers names. Suppose that you meet five or ten new people a day. Write each name down. Review the name and its association a few times, and then put the paper away. Go back to the paper when you need it. Soon you'll have the name.

Finally, never make a joke about Mr. Bright or Miss Short—believe me, they've already heard it *ad nauseam.* Maybe they should have changed their names, but they didn't. Don't win the quip and lose the quarry.

Adjustable Names

In your arsenal of speech, *your* name stands out as a force for power or impotence. You may say: "This is my name and I'm stuck with it." Think again. Names are adjustable.

As a journalist, I once interviewed Raymond Hollis, a newly arrived immigrant from West Germany. He told me he'd changed his name when he arrived in the United States. "What was it before?" I asked. "I fear you will laugh at me," he said. "Why would I laugh?" I said. "So it's a German-sounding name, why not?" "All right. I'll tell you," he said. "It was Raymond Horshitz," he said.

I kept a straight face. But it wasn't easy.

It was even harder when I got into medical publicity and worked with a Dr. Passwater. To make it completely beyond belief, I found out his first name was Dick.

Truth is indeed stranger than fiction. Now I expect the unusual. (When I met Miles Long and a stockbroker called Lota Kahn, I didn't even blink.)

I haven't met the people listed below—all real, John Train tells us in *Remarkable Names of Real People*—but I do think changes might be easier than fending off double takes and titters:

Ave Maria Klinkenberg	Joy Bang
Buncha Love	Katz Meow
Carlos Restrepo Restrepo	Memory Lane
Restrepo de Restrepo	Miss Pinkey Dickey Dukes
Reverend Christian Church	Shine Soon Sun
Hugh Pugh	T. Hee
John Senior, Jr.	

If you're saddled with a name that gets the wrong kind of laughs or projects the wrong image for you, change it. The precedents are many and varied.

> Norma Jean Baker, as the world knows, moved on to become Marilyn Monroe. Emanuel Goldenbogen became better known as Edward G. Robinson. You know Allen Konigsberg as Woody Allen. Avram Goldbogen is famous as Mike Todd. James Baumgarner didn't change too much to become James Garner. Joseph Levitsh, as do many changers, kept the same initials as Jerry Lewis. Lucille Leseur became Joan Crawford.

> Bernie Kaplan decided to become Bart Lytton and emerged as a California savings and loan tycoon. Arthur Flegenheimer became Dutch Schultz. Lester Gillis told police his name was George (Baby Face) Nelson. Helen Leonard became Lillian Russell. (Tip: The *l* and *m* and *n* add beauty to a name. The *r* adds power. Ronald Reagan, for example, is a name that shouldn't be tampered with, and wasn't. Nor was Elizabeth Taylor.)

Tamara Ruth Alexander (not bad to start with) became Scotia Carvelle. Leonard Slye became Roy Rogers. Sadye Marks was known to the public as Mary Livingstone. Eunice Quedens you know as Eve Arden. Archie Leach became Cary Grant. Bernie Schwartz is now Tony Curtis. Jerome Silberberg is known today as Gene Wilder.

You *can* change your name to enhance your speech power. It's done every day. Keep in mind the following:

- Is the name too hard to pronounce? Simplify it. Jozef Korzeniowski became Joseph Conrad.
- Avoid a name that's too simple. George Scott became George C. Scott.
- Is the meaning too well entrenched in another area? The character Pansy O'Hara became Scarlett O'Hara just before *Gone with the Wind* came out. It's hard to imagine Pansy as a household word that doesn't make people snicker. Scarlett, both colorful and distinctive, is immortal.
- James Stewart changed his name to Stewart Granger because Jimmy Stewart had a lock on Granger's actual name in the public mind.
- You aren't limited to one change. Edna Rae Gilooly became Edna McRae on stage and then Ellen Burstyn.

If your name is Victor Frankenstein, a change is in order just to put a stop to the "Are you related to . . . ?" comments.

In many cases, new names are American versions of the original. Barry Goldwater would have been Barry Goldwasser had not an earlier generation changed the family name. Not that an international shift in nomenclature is always indicated. Anglicize Guiseppe Verdi and you get Joe Green. Doesn't sound exactly operatic, does it?

If you're starting with a clean slate, remember the most pleasant-sounding name is described in poetic terms as a dactyl and a spondee (an emphasized syllable followed by two unemphasized syllables in the first name followed by two equally emphatic syllables in the last name). Example of such a name: Jer-e-my Spar-row.

In creating names, remember the fashions of the times. In the 1930s and 1940s, performers sought non-ethnic names. In the 1980s, people are ethnic-aware—as the names George Segal, Kevin Kline, Tony Lo Bianco, and Bob Prosky indicate.

The point: In changing or altering a name, decide what gives you the greatest power of speech. After all, as Othello said: "Good name in man and woman . . . is the immediate jewel of their souls . . . he that filches from me my good name . . . makes me poor indeed."

Enhancing Mob Monikers

Even working yeggs need colorful names to enhance their unstable (and often short) existences: Charley (Lucky) Luciano, Frank (The Enforcer) Nitti, Paul (The Waiter) Ricca, Cherry Nose Gioe, Joe Bananas, Tough Tony Arcardo, Vincent (Mad Dog) Coll, Sam (Golf Bag) Hunt (Sam Hunt alone sounds almost respectable).

Actually, though, mobsters have problems with name confusion, too. When I was a kid, we used to play FBI. Impersonating the most wanted criminals was always the envied slot—with John Dillinger and Baby Face Nelson the clear favorites.

My mother, woefully uninformed by our standards, came out one day and announced: "That's enough. You've been playing *Bad* Face Nelson all day." (We weren't too surprised in later years when she reported seeing *Fiddler on a Hot Tin Roof* on TV.)

Good Names vs. Bad

In choosing a name, remember there are good and bad names—or so the public thinks. Jack Trout and Al Ries tell us about two psychology professors, Dr. Herbert Harari and Dr. John W. McDavid, who checked out why elementary-school students made fun of classmates with unusual names.

They placed two popular names (David and Michael) and two unpopular names (Hubert and Elmer) on student compositions. Each composition was given to elementary-school teachers to grade as ordinary school papers. Compositions bearing the names of David and Michael averaged a grade higher than the same compositions attributed to Elmer and Hubert. "Teachers know from past experience," the professors reported, "that Hubert or Elmer is generally a loser."

What about Hubert Humphrey and Adlai Stevenson? Both eventually lost to men with the popular names of Richard and Dwight. Ron, Jimmy, Jerry, Richard, Lyndon, John, Dwight, Harry, Franklin. Not since Herbert have we had a loser name in the White House. And who did Herbert Hoover beat in 1928? Another loser name: Alfred. In 1932, when Herbert ran against Franklin, he lost big.

Edsel was a loser name before Ford introduced the Edsel car. And the name contributed to the marketing disaster. People expect a Cyril to be sneaky and a John to be trustworthy.

An experimenter found two women who were rated as equal in beauty by a group of people. Then, for a second group, he named the two women Jennifer and Gertrude. What do you think happened when the second group voted on which woman was prettier? The results were 158 votes for Jennifer, 39 for Gertrude. Evidently Gertrude is a word that distorts people's view of things. But Trudy, its short form, works— and often turns up as the ingenue name in frothy movie musicals.

So when you name yourself, keep these associations in mind. And think twice before passing on a thoughtless label to a child. Five minutes of whimsy on your part could result in a lifelong millstone for him or her.

William Swanson (who won't reveal his own middle name for just those reasons) says people with funny names have more problems (getting good grades, getting dates, getting raises) and may therefore grow up maladjusted, cankered, maybe even dangerous. In a magazine article he wrote:

> Those who argue that Percy (a) was good enough for Granddad and is good enough for the kid, (b) will be back in fashion, like plus fours, given sufficient time, or (c) is only a name, so why get all excited, are missing the point. We do not live in a rational world, nor one that is always kind to oddballs, and, whatever else he may be, a kid named Percy is, in the eyes of his contemporaries, an oddball.

Names are distinguishing labels that define, describe, detract, diminish, limit, enlighten, enrich, enable, expand, or endanger us. In the realm of names and naming, good intentions mean nothing. It is of fleeting comfort to a kid to know his namesake wrote enduring poetry or invented the iron lung. His tormentors care little about poets, less about saints.

So the same diligence employed in naming the latest high-tech widget must also be marshaled to prevent an Algernon, a Hugo, Yerta, Phedra, or Gaspar in your family.

As James Russell Lowell said: "There's more force in names than men dream of."

Names that Discourage Competition

On the greenswards of Manhattan's Central Park, where I pitch softball during the sweaty months, teams are formed ad hoc day to day. This requires instant group naming. One team captain said: "We're the 69th Street team. What's your team?" Replied the savvy second captain: "Our team is called the Winners."

How can you compete? Certainly not with the Losers! A name that puts down competition is extremely valuable. No-Nonsense panty hose, for example.

In this competitive era, the single most important marketing decision you can make is what to name the product. The name is injected into speech dozens of times each hour.

Make sure your name travels well if you're going to sell in another country. The word *Nova* sounds new and even related to the solar system, right? You'd think it would be a good name for an automobile. In English, it is; but translate it into Spanish, as one automaker did, and you get *no va* ("it doesn't go"). Disaster.

While we're talking about cars, consider Mercury—possessor of a large *M* as a product symbol. Fine in English or Spanish. But it's murder in French, given that graffiti artists scrawl *M* throughout all of Gaul— meaning *merde*. Better watch it, buddy.

And speaking of successful product names, if you can convince shapely posteriors all over America to wear your name on constant quivering display, you've *really* arrived. The idea of people voluntarily becoming human billboards defies understanding. But as the jeans manufacturers say: "Don't knock it while it lasts."

William Swanson, writing in the *TWA Ambassador,* sees it as a part of a surging sociological movement: "Today labels and designations cover the body like hair. For many of us, our own names, discreetly tucked away in pocket or purse, are no longer sufficient: we pay to wear the names of others on our shirts and slacks and shorts. We care as passionately about these purchased names as we do about our own."

Strange times. Strange society.

Organizing Organization Names

Now that you realize the importance of individual names, take it one step further and examine names of organizations.

Since you do have a say about your club chapter name, your part-time business, or your professional group, you should capitalize on name power.

In popular paraphrase, Shakespeare said: "A rose by any other name would smell as sweet." But does it? Hog Island was going nowhere until it became Paradise Island. Now it attracts tourists. After all, who would turn down a trip to Paradise? (Heaven, Pennsylvania, might have worked out too, except for its proximity to Intercourse and Blue Ball, two nearby Pennsylvania towns that have titillated generations of undergraduates.)

The point is that power speech is composed of two parts: delivery and content. If the content is preposterous, people tend to think about that, instead of the communication.

When it comes to naming organizations, Dr. Joseph R. Mancuso, director of the Center for Entrepreneurial Management, New York, says selection of a name is vital "because it's so visible." (Amen! *Audible,* too, which is our concern here.) Continues Dr. Mancuso:

> Most of the "good" names have already been picked. Many bad names have been picked too.
> Ego-tripping founders often christen fledgling companies in their own image. Bob Jones University. The Karen Smith Organization.[8]

Many entrepreneurial ventures fail, and when the business contains your surname, your name has failed too—so you can use it but once. (Nevertheless, your own name may often be the best choice.) The Harley Simpson Company is easy to remember, human (you're not dealing with computers, just good old Harley), and distinctive.

Advertising, accounting, public relations, and law firms often use people's names, often to good effect—except attorneys, who never know when to stop adding names. Brown and Brown is enough—why make it Brown, Brown, Brown, and Brown? Why not $Brown_4$ if you must give each Brownie a point?

Bob Newhart's joke about Helen Ferguson's Airline and Aluminum Storm Door Company makes the point. When the name tells what you do, you're ahead, provided the name isn't a real jawbreaker or confusing. A financial institution in the New Jersey town of Red Bank bought out a rival in neighboring Long Branch. People in Long Branch now deposit their checks in the Long Branch branch of the Red Bank bank.

The name Weight Watchers not only helps customers understand what the group does but also has a positive connotation. Fat Losers or Nonfat People would be offensive as well as negative.

Names to Depict Disgust

Of course, if your mission *is* to disgust and sicken your audience, the right name will do wonders. Harken to joyously nauseating names of punk rock performers:

Johnny Rotten
Sid Vicious
Sharon Tate's Baby
The Dead Kennedy Brothers (known as The Dead Kennedys for
    short)

We could go on but won't. Instead, let's use the moment to pray for
a temporarily (we hope) deranged youth that responds to such a sick
lexicon.

Make Names Memorable

Your organization's name should be easily identified, distinctive, and
easily remembered. All three criteria must be met, not just two out of
three. When Missouri Beef Packers merged with Kansas Beef Industries, the combination was christened MBPXL—from Missouri Beef
Packers and the Excel brand of Kansas Beef. The name looks more like a
printer's error.

George Eastman named his camera company with an abrupt word
that begins as it ends: Kodak. The same holds with Xerox. Both are
distinctive, identifiable, descriptive, and easily remembered. MBPXL is
not.

Columbia Broadcasting System and National Cash Register ex-
panded beyond the original businesses, and the names became misrep-
resentations. Now they use only initials—poor substitutes for descriptive
titles.

You should examine prospective names, slogans, and themes early
on for their power speech qualities. First National City Corporation
changed its name to Citicorp and maintained an association with its
previous name. But, more important, the new name also allows expan-
sion into Citicard, Citicash, Citicredit. The company made a significant
net gain without the loss of a historic tie.

The computer, all-pervasive in modern society, has also entered
name-finding—probably not to anyone's surprise. Name-it computers,
of course, must be fed and goosed. One champion caretaker is San
Francisco-based NameLab (its own name a product of its system).

To position a Nissan automobile, NameLab came up with *Sentra*. For
NYNEX, a splinter that emerged from the AT&T breakup, NameLab
suggested *Datago* for the company's chain of retail computer stores.

Movie titles are also product names. NameLab changed the *The
Making of Emma* to *Foxtails* for ABC Motion Pictures.

An article on "name calling" in *Inc.* magazine (July 1984) reported the way NameLab founder Ira N. Bachrach sees it: "A successful brand or corporate name can put a new company on the marketing map, set a product head and shoulders above competitors, and even make its way indelibly into the language."

On the other hand, left to chance or collective company wit, a misnamed entity either gets accepted into the Edsel Hall of Fame or risks becoming just another whatsis.

WRAPPING IT UP

The savvy power speaker looks on names as effective or weak content for presentation. Whenever you get a chance to improve your speech content, do so.

In this name-oriented society, if you can make people think a non-name is a name, it soon will be. If you don't like your own name, or that of your product or organization, change it. Create a name that enhances power speech. Names are handles for speakers and reassurance to customers all day every day. Names are invaluable tools of power speech.

6

Words: Choosing, Creating, Updating— For Better Speech

Abraham Lincoln is far and away the most quoted American president. Yet if Old Abe came back to visit the rapidly fleeing twentieth century, you'd probably be disappointed. After all, you're accustomed to the orotund on-screen tones of Raymond Massey or the winning professional style of Henry Fonda as *Young Mr. Lincoln.* (Hal Holbrook in his made-for-TV movie *did* add some roughness and nasality natural to the Great Emancipator.)

But if these celebrated performers had actually pronounced words the way Lincoln did, you'd be elbowing your seatmate, saying "Did you hear that?" or "How's that again?"

Lincoln said *howdy* to visitors. He *sot* down and *stayed a spell.* He came *outen* a cabin and *yearned* his wages and *made a heap.* He came from *whar* he had been. He was *hornswoggled* into doing something against his better judgment. He *keered* for his friends and *heered* the latest news. He pointed to *yonder* stream and addressed *Mr. Cheermun.* And he got an *eddication* and *larned* about adversity.

The way Lincoln talked certainly wasn't acceptable to scions of the eastern establishment (like his treasury secretary, Salmon P. Chase). But much of his language was perfectly understandable to ordinary folks—most of whom talked the same way. What sounds quaint or just plain silly today was standard then.

Language change is constant. The power speaker must keep an eye on and an ear alert for changing words. You must know what's in and what's out, what's a passing fad, what's old-fashioned, what's trendy, and what's been overdone and thus must be avoided. From this knowledge, you then cut your verbal cloth to fit or defy the fashion, to gain this or that end.

As late as 1949, speech mavens were exhorting the diligent to pronounce *bone fide* as bona fy-day. By the mid-1980s, *Reader's Digest* (that great arbiter of commonality) said: "Say bona fide [to rhyme with clyde]. Join the common people on this one."

In the early 1950s authorities advised saying *syndrome* as sin-dro-mi. Today with the rise of social science, you'd sound silly sounding the final *e*. And no one does.

Experts once said we should say VY-uh for *via*, but today the power speaker says VEE-uh. And not that it'll last long (teen speech never does), but ba-a-ad from a youthful mouth currently means *wonderful*.

Of course, if you're making a movie showing life in the 1920s, you're equally concerned about change—in reverse. When *Chief*, starring Charlton Heston, was being filmed in Georgia for 1985 release, a creative press agent arranged for Heston to telephone *New York Times* language pundit William Safire to check out the script for 1920s authenticity. (Clever promotion: Safire reported on the call in his Sunday column. You and I are talking about it right now. And the cycle goes on.)

Heston asked Safire about the phrases *so I lied* and *wear it in good health*. Safire doubted if either was used in Georgia in the 1920s: "Yiddishisms both," he added. "Harry Golden, who did not move South and become editor of *The Carolina Israelite* until the 1940s, used the expressions, but it is unlikely that many Southerners in the 1920s would have spoken that way. Today, sure: 'Y'all weah it in good health, heah?' Not three generations ago, before television."

Other word contrasts, then and now: *Uptown* meant *ritzy*, before *ritzy* became *upscale*. Words that were *risqué* in the 1920s and *off-color* in the 1940s are *dirty* today. Back then, she'd warn a fella not to *get fresh*, rather than telling him not to *come on*. People packed *valises*, not *carry-ons*. They came down with *grippe* rather than the *flu*. *Fooling around* was relatively innocent. Now it means *sexually active*. *Affairs* have become *relationships*.

Is Your Word Choice In or Out?

Today your use of "in" words indicates status. Phyllis Martin formalized this list for Safire to make sure you know who's on first:

Out	In
Tuxedo	Black tie
Washrag	Washcloth
Bathing suit	Swimsuit
Cake of soap	Bar of soap
Clap	Applaud
Honeymoon	Wedding trip

"Only fuddy-duddies go to the *gym* or to the *drugstore*," pundit Safire says.

The upscale (formerly hoity-toity) crowd goes to the *spa* or to the *pharmacy*. The truly avant-garde know that nobody who is avant-garde uses *avant-garde* anymore: They are the *trendies*, or on the *cutting edge*.

People who used to say *phonograph* were tittered at by people who said *record player;* now they in turn are looked down upon by those who say *turntable*. When was the last time you heard a young, rich-affluent-wealthy type use *railroad station?* Upper-class use is now *train station*.

Forbidden Words

Probably nothing changes as dramatically as the list of forbidden words. At one time, certain words used freely on the Broadway stage were verboten in movies. Today you hear words on the screen that no self-respecting producer will allow on stage.

Before James Jones wrote *From Here to Eternity,* in 1950, certain words were not printed by reputable publishers. Jones told about detailed paring sessions held with his publisher's lawyer in which they reviewed a scoresheet of four-letter words.

Today nothing is barred in books—but newspapers are still chary of repeating what books print and performers say. ("No part of Richard Pryor's comments," *Variety* said, "could be reproduced in a family newspaper—or any other newspaper for that matter.")

Such is the changing world of forbidden words. Naturally, you can use words in conversation that won't wash on the platform or in a media interview. If you're in doubt about a word, don't use it. Never risk offending your listener; it's not worth it. The power speaker always has many word choices.

Creating Your Own Words

The vendor stands outside Madison Square Garden yelling in a hoarse, gravelly voice: "Red hots! Getcher red hots heah! Red hots!"

What's he selling? Frankfurters in rolls, of course. Why doesn't he say so? Because *franks* or *frankfurters* or *rolls* don't play well to crowds— they're words with no audience-stopping power. The idea of something red and hot gets attention—even if it's untrue. The frank is barely pink (and that thanks to dye) and lukewarm at best (it's never hot).

The vendor created a phrase to do a job where the true description failed. Power speakers often create, adapt, adopt, and just plain change words to make them work better.

Lewis Carroll created *chortle* (or was it *snortle*?) by combining *chuckle* and *snort,* and we're richer for it. (Why not *snotle* for a runny nose? See how it starts?)

Stripper Georgia Sothern asked H. L. Mencken to suggest a tony word for her occupation. The sage of Baltimore obliged with *ecdysiast,* from the Greek word for *shedding an outer layer,* the way a snake or an insect does—or, for that matter, the way a bird molts (Miss S. had a feather act). Today public molters are called exotic dancers, forever restricting the use of *exotic* in any other way.

Mencken also created *Bible Belt.* Today we have *BB*'s descendants— *sun* and *frost. Bad-mouthing,* meaning *to publicly and verbally flay another,* has been with us since the 1960s. Now we have the fallout: *big-mouthing (to promote loudly).*

Résumé may well be pushed aside in favor of the more sensible *biodata,* which sounds much better.

If the words you create are good enough, you'll soon hear your creations echoing back. Several of comedy writer Rich Hall's word-children appear to have real staying power. For example:

> *Brattled.* The unsettling feeling you get at a stop light when you think that the busload of kids that just pulled up beside you is making fun of you.
> *Snorfing.* The game waitresses love to play of waiting until your mouth is full before sneaking up and asking: "Is everybody O.K.?"
> *Chwads.* The small disgusting wads of chewed gum commonly found beneath table and counter tops.

Cinemuck. The combination of popcorn, soda, and melted chocolate that covers the floors of movie theaters.

Furbling. Wandering through a maze of ropes at an airport or bank even when you are the only person in line.

Petribar. Sun-bleached prehistoric candy that's been sitting in the window of a vending machine too long.

Jim Wayne Miller, professor at Western Kentucky University, in Bowling Green, points out that Appalachians have been creating their own words for centuries—as I can confirm from personal experience. Miller cites these mountain-talk examples:

The children played in the spring drain and *benastied* themselves.

A creek *turkey-tails* out into little forks.

Children drive mothers to distraction, giving mothers the *all-overs.*

A person in declining health is on the *down-go.* It's better to be *survigrous.*

People who combine piety with an extraordinary power to annoy are *harrassmatic.*

Maintenance awarded a spouse for prolonged toleration of unorginal views and insipid opinions and attitudes is *banalimony.*

Saying "you know," "really," or "O.K." repeatedly is *illiteration.*

Word creations or adoptions can become as famous as the power speaker behind them. Theodore Roosevelt was a big contributor to the American lexicon. He described the White House as "a bully pulpit," a valiant platform for speaking out. Words either minted or popularized by Roosevelt include: hat in the ring, big stick, pussyfooting, malefactors of great wealth, weasel words, mollycoddle, muckraker, parlor pink, and lunatic fringe.

He also inspired the Teddy Bear and the popular song that went with it: "Teddy, You're a Bear."

Teddy's daughter, Alice, followed tradition by inspiring "Alice Blue Gown." In later years, as a noted Washington hostess, she personified the D.C. gossipvine by saying to a guest: "If you don't have anything good to say about someone [stage pause], sit right down here beside me."

Creating Both Meaning and Sounds

Remember what Lewis Carroll's Humpty Dumpty said to Alice: "When I use a word, it means just what I choose it to mean—neither more nor less."

For that matter, words mean whatever your listener thinks they mean—as Dan Rowan and Dick Martin proved on TV's *Laugh-In* with "you bet your bippy." What's a bippy? Your guess is as good as—nay, better than—mine. When you give the imagination room to work, it's almost always stronger than a literal statement.

When I was with the Valley Players in Holyoke, Massachusetts, visiting actor Al Paschall (also production manager of Ralph Edwards' *Truth or Consequences* show) created *cransel* and *plootch* and applied them everywhere. On meeting a friend: "How's your cransel?" In singing "The Old Gray Mare": ". . . hitch Old Dobbin to the plootch."

"One's an un-word and the other's a non-word," another actor said.

The lurid field of sports commentary lends itself to created phrases. The precedents are classic. Dizzy Dean, after leaving the diamond for the microphone, described a ballplayer who *"slud* into third base." He also said: "What this team needs is *spart.*" A colleague didn't understand. "You know, *spart,*" O'l Diz said. "Like the *Spart* of St. Louis where Lindberg *flowed* to France."

Creative wordsmith at the anvil.

Sportswriter Art Plotnik believes such magnificent fractures in the *lingua cuerpo* should be labeled for our guidance. He calls it *base-babel.*

When infielders dispute over who made an error, that's *infield accusative.* If a commentator says "if we'd a-gotten a man to third, that fly ball drives him in easily"—that's *past-second-base subjunctive.* And back in Leo the Lip's day, we had *umpirative imperative*—a suggestion from manager to umpire, usually directional.

Don't hang back. Create words and phrases in your own field—to the enrichment of your speech. It's gratifying.

As editor of *Marketing Times,* I coined *salesfolk* to apply to both men and women. I'm delighted to see it's taking hold.

Such are the growth sources of the vigorous and dynamic American language. Today's creation, with cultivation and luck, becomes tomorrow's dictionary item.

Because: Workhorse Word

When Rick DuBrow and I (and six other students) lived in a quonset-style hut at Northwestern University, I rather efficiently (I thought) kept a supply of postage stamps in a cigar box. When I had outgoing mail, the stamps were ready—no hustling out to Hoos Drug Store to get stamps at the last minute.

DuBrow didn't plan that far ahead. When he needed stamps, he took mine—and put money for them in my cigar box. Of course, this inconvenienced me. When I needed stamps, I had coins instead. But as

DuBrow explained it: "I took the stamps because I had some letters that had to go out."

I felt I was being had at the time. Now I know I was being flummoxed by *because*.

Use *because* at the right time and you usually get your way easily and without grief. Social psychologist Ellen J. Langer of Harvard University proved it. Langer went up to people waiting to use a copying machine and explained: "Excuse me, I have five pages. May I use the machine because I'm in a rush?" Ninety-five percent of those asked let her move ahead in line.

When she made the request without *because* ("Excuse me, I have five pages. May I use the machine?"), only 60 percent stepped aside. The crucial difference between the two requests: *because*.

Just as the cheep-cheep of turkey chicks triggers an automatic mothering response from a polecat, the word *because* triggers an automatic compliance from people.

People exist in an extraordinarily complicated environment. To deal with it, they need shortcuts. They can't recognize and analyze everything—they haven't the time, energy, or capacity. Instead, they classify things according to a few key features and then respond automatically to these triggers.

Use *because*. This trigger-word will put you out front.

The Surprising Power of *What If?*

Suppose you're in the *middle*—trying to get A and B to agree on a price so you can make a commission (a position common in real estate). The phrase *what if?* is worth its weight in uranium. Says Robert E. Baxter, a Los Angeles real-estate ace:

> I had a three-story office building listed for sale. The owner wanted $155,000—$60,000 in cash. The property had a $40,000 mortgage on it. The owner offered to carry a second mortgage of $55,000. A lot of repairs were needed. I figured if the owner wanted to sell *as is*, the property was overpriced by about $20,000.
>
> For three months, I got no offers. The owner was softening.
>
> Then, one day I got an offer of $140,000 instead of the $155,000 asked. Of this he'd pay $45,000 cash, not the $60,000. Further, he wanted the air conditioning and plumbing repaired. Air-conditioning repairs alone would cost nearly $8,000.
>
> I presented the offer and just about fell over when the owner said he'd accept, provided the buyer'd split air-conditioning repair costs.
>
> I ran back to the buyer—sure the sale was in the bag. It wasn't.

The quick reply caused the prospect to think: "Boy! this owner really wants to sell. I'll just hold out for the whole package." The prospect didn't sign. So I took a counteroffer to the buyer. And a counteroffer to the counteroffer. I never got them together.

I should have remembered to use *What If!*

When I went back to the prospect with the owner's agreement I should have said: "I am having a tough time trying to get the owner even to consider your offer. He knows he has a good piece of property. He might lower that price a little but he balks at paying for repairs.

"But Mr. Prospect, *What If* I got the price down to $140,000. *What If* I get the owner to pay for the plumbing and parking surface repairs, and split the cost of the air conditioning? I don't know if I can do it, but *What If?*"

This makes the buyer want to deal. So he'd probably say: "Yes, I'd accept that kind of agreement. See what you can do." I'd wait a day or two before I brought back the owner's agreement (which I had in my pocket all along).

When the buyer signed, he'd feel like a clever fellow who'd driven a hard bargain.[9]

Use *what if* the next time you get caught between A and B in any field. You and power speech will win the day.

Choosing Competitive Words

When you're negotiating with an adversary, check your word inventory for effective ways to answer objections and make polite put-downs.

One day Harry Truman told his aide to get a one-armed economist. Naturally, the aide asked why. "So he won't be able to say 'on the other hand' all the time," said feisty Harry.

Sometimes it's best to voice the unthinkable. Ad agency pioneer Claude Hopkins did it when a prospective advertiser said: "I don't know if I'm wasting my ad money."

"I do know," said Hopkins. "Your advertising is utterly unprofitable. I could prove it to you in one week. End an ad with an offer to pay five dollars to anyone who writes you that he read the ad through. The scarcity of replies will amaze you."

A week later he got the account.

When you're battling an adversary, don't give your opponent *any* free points—as Caspar (Cap the Knife) Weinberger did in indoctrinating media people right after the Reagan administration invaded Grenada. The reporters were furious because Weinberger had denied on-the-scene coverage.

"While it may not seem credible to you, the government did not allow reporters because we want to provide for the security of newspeople," Weinberger said.

No, it did not seem credible. He gave away *game* and *match* to his adversary.

John Brinton, who sells in Camden, New Jersey, doesn't give his adversary—a woman considering purchase of an encyclopedia—anything. Even when she says she's decided *not* to buy. John does nothing for a moment. He just stands there as if dazed. Then he says:

> Madam, you have just told me you're *not* going to buy these books for your children. Do you know what you're really saying? You actually said you're willing to let your children struggle on without every help you can give them. Who knows, you may be needlessly handicapping them in getting along in the world. You're telling me you're willing to let those children struggle against odds! When just 10 cents a day would give them a better chance!
>
> But I don't think you meant that, Mrs. Johnson. It's a dime a day against the handicap of inadequate preparation. You ought to be willing to invest that to give those children a start in life.

Strong language? High pressure? Yes to both.

"But they don't seem to resent it, and it saves at least one sale out of five," John declared.

Using Stories to Counter

Stone Wheaton, who calls on retailers in the South, uses stories to counter objections. Listen as he works retailer John P. Atter:

"Do you know Conner and Tedmon of Nashville?"

"Very well," Atter says.

"What do you think of them?"

"They've built a tremendous business in the face of great competition."

That's Wheaton's go-signal. He launches into his story.

When he first called upon Conner and Tedmon, Wheaton relates, he found such and such a condition prevailed. (It "happens" to be almost exactly the same business condition John Atter faces.) Mr. Conner wasn't exactly sure whether Wheaton's products would correct the condition and give him what he needed in profit. (Neither is Atter sure at this particular moment.)

As an experiment—but only as an experiment—Mr. Conner decided to put in Wheaton's line. (That gives John Atter courage: Maybe he also could try it. Here's a respected precedent to follow.)

"But now Conner and Tedmon are thanking their lucky stars they experimented," Wheaton says. "Sales increased 30 percent in a year's time. Their inventory turnover has speeded up. Profit is better than ever. They have attracted a new type of customer."

Thus does Stone Wheaton talk, confirming his statements, of course, with evidence.

In effect, he's saying: "Don't take my word for it. Follow someone else who's already done the experimenting for you."

Meanwhile, John Atter is telling himself that if Conner and Tedmon can make such a record with the line, he can do as well, maybe better. Further, Conner and Tedmon's acceptance is a recommendation for him to accept it—evidence to overcome his own wavering.

Wheaton tells stories that use the third-party endorsement. His prospect unconsciously (if not consciously) compares his business with the character in the narrative. Success of the central figure in the story is *his* success. The prospect thus sells himself.[10]

Stone Wheaton reacts to objections by telling a story. His finesse also illustrates another principle of power speech: It's your responsibility to communicate your feelings and persuade your audience. But don't bully them. They'll resent it. Show them the light—don't blind them with it.

Effective speakers present arguments so that listeners are convinced *they've* discovered the truth. Read Marc Antony's funeral oration in Shakespeare's *Julius Caesar*—a masterful example of manipulating a crowd into accepting a viewpoint without beating them over the head.

When you react, don't get defensive. During the Bush-Ferraro head-butting in 1984, George tried to upstage Gerry by calling on locker room language: He referred to *kicking ass*. In a *USA Today* interview, Ohio Governor Richard Celeste saw this as a reaction to anxiety: "That sort of defensive thing happens whenever women get close to power. Men just don't know how to handle it."

When your defensive bare-bones show to another professional in the field, you're not winning points. As historian Barbara Tuchman said: "Words are seductive and dangerous—material to be used with caution."

Use Flattering Words Adroitly

Many are the commercial uses for flattering words—to make a rose by any other name a lot more impressive. Rock Lubin, real-estate maven, says sales soar or droop on the way you describe the house to the buyer.

Lubin exhorts real-estate salesfolk to use *power* words: *year-round-comfort control, husband's retreat, slumber area, countrylike atmosphere, extra touch of quality, indoor/outdoor living, country-style kitchen, programmed family comfort.*

"Semantics can turn an ordinary floor plan and community into a highly attractive place to live," Lubin says. "The consumer must be romanced."

I've seen flattering words influence public opinion in marked ways. When we represented *American coal,* we talked about *foreign oil* as a competitor. We said *surface mining,* never *strip mining.*

In working for Renault, we stressed *imported* cars against the drab *domestics.* But when we promoted *California wine,* we scoffed at *foreign* wine. (Our adversaries took the opposite tack: They pushed *imported* wine vs. *domestic* wine.)

In assisting the National Pest Control Association, we extolled the local *pest control professional* (never, God save us, the *exterminator*).

In the housing field, we discussed *mobile homes* (never *house trailers*) and *log homes,* not *log cabins.*

Take a hard look at the way you describe your products, services, company, or industry. Are you giving your enemies free points? Don't.

Walter A. Lowen, a pioneering headhunter, once saw an astonishing sight in a candy store. One salesgirl was waiting on shoppers who were standing on line for her. Other salesgirls were idle. Customers appeared quite willing to wait for the already busy salesgirl.

When the crowd thinned, Lowen asked the successful girl: "Why do they come to you in preference to the others?" She lifted her scoop and said, "It's easy. The other girls scoop up more than a pound of candy and then take some away to make exact weight. I scoop up less than a pound and add to it."

Each girl allocated customers one pound. But the ace salesgirl gave *more.* Think about it. There are ways to tap into power, if you describe it right.

A word can be a hero in one context and a bum in another. *Old-fashioned* is wonderful if you're selling lace, ice cream, hotel service, craftsmanship. (When cars get old, they're *antiques.*) But if you're selling jet airplanes, computers, or copying machines, *old-fashioned* is the last phrase you want to be using.

Remember, too, that a prophet is often without honor in his own country. That's why you buy Kansas City steaks in New York and New York strip sirloin in Kansas City, and why an expert is a person with a briefcase 50 miles from home.

We is a power word with potential for both good and bad. When an accountant sees a client and talks about *our* problems (meaning the client's), that's good. He's showing concern as a part of the corporate family. When a doctor or nurse asks a patient, "How are we feeling today?" it's childish and patronizing.

The double face of *we* occurred when the Lone Ranger and Tonto were attacked by a force of 500 Amerinds. Said the masked man:

"My God, what are we going to do?"

Said Tonto: "What's this *we* shit, white man?"

Give the same reply to your doctor or nurse. Help stamp out patronizing pother.

And while we're snuffing pointless diddle, help kill off the habit of saleswomen in ladies' clothing shops. A perfect stranger walks in and it's:

"Come in, *sweetie.*"

"Yes, *honey,* what can I show you?"

"Yes, *dear,* did you have something in mind?"

I've polled 50 women, and I've yet to find one who likes this mawkish twaddle. Since no one wants it, why do it? This is power speech in reverse. Overfamiliarity in public to a stranger is a sure way to win the booby prize—even if you do sell lingerie.

WRAPPING IT UP

Fashions in speech change. The power speaker changes with the times— indeed, as you grow in influence, you'll help mold the cutting edge of what's "in." Once you learn the rules, you can cut new trails.

Change words to meet new needs; create phrases to fill gaps. Such action is constantly at work in the ebb and flow of the mighty American language.

Yes, you can artfully use outdated or vanguard words to create a planned effect. But using such words in ignorance or thoughtlessness distracts your listener and places you outside the mainstream—without benefit.

In confrontations, don't give your adversary any free points. Tell stories to counter objections.

In using forbidden words, err (if you must err) on the conservative side. When in doubt about a word or phrase, don't use it. The power speaker always has a variety of options in word choice.

Collect workhorse words that motivate and make your work and leisure tasks easier. The right words rule the world.

7

Avoiding Staletown or Jargon City— Lest You End Up in Dullsville

The speaker, dog-tired, had been busy as a beaver all day. So he hit the hay hoping to fall immediately into the arms of Morpheus and sleep like a log. But his mind was full as a tick, and he didn't get a wink of sleep.

"Oh God," he said, "this is a pretty kettle of fish. I'm going to shuffle off this mortal coil unless I can hit the sack and greet old Sol for another day/another dollar. Stop this nightmare and I promise *never to use clichés on the platform again!*"

"Can we depend on your permanent reform?" the voice asked. "Better take a look at this chapter first. See if you can get the monkey off your back."

Clichés Sap Your Power

A cliché is a term of speech that once had a dash of cleverness about it. Through overuse, it has become stale and tiresome.

"Whoever first thought of a cucumber as the type of a particular kind of coolness or conceived that the hinges were likely to be the hottest part of hell or suspected that one part of a brass monkey was more susceptible to cold than the rest had a droll imagination and deserved applause," says Dr. Bergen Evans, author of *A Dictionary of Contemporary American Usage*. "But those who repeat such expressions, now that all life has left them, are doubly damned.

"Your use of clichés shows you'd like to be thought witty yet are actually a parroter of failing echoes. Your very attempt to be clever shows you to be dull."

The New Yorker's classic attack on clichés in 1934 provided us with Mr. Arbuthnot, the certified public cliché expert, an enduring character:

Q. How do you cliché experts reveal yourselves, Mr. Arbuthnot?
A. In our true colors, of course.

Q. And you expect to live to . . .
A. A ripe old age.

Q. When you are naked, you are . . .
A. Stark naked.

Q. In what kind of daylight?
A. Broad daylight.

Q. What kind of outsider are you?
A. I'm a rank outsider.

Q. How right are you?
A. I am dead right.

Q. And your horizon?
A. I broaden my horizon.

Q. And when you are drunk?
A. Lots of leeway there. I can be as drunk as a coot or a lord or an owl or a fool or a skunk . . .

Q. What kind of precision are you cliché users partial to?
A. Clocklike precision.

Q. And you shroud things . . .
A. In the mists of antiquity.

Q. And you are destined . . .
A. To go far.

Q. How do you point?
A. I point with pride, I view with alarm, and I yield to no man.

Q. What do you throw?
A. I throw caution to the winds.

Q. Everyone who has listened to you here today will be a better cliché user for having heard you.
A. It's been a pleasure, I assure you, and I was only too glad to oblige.[11]

Go Back to Originals

Do you feel the irrepressible need to use "gild the lily"? At least go back to the original from Shakespeare's *King John*, where Salisbury complains about the "wasteful and ridiculous excess" of John's second coronation. To crown him a second time, says Salisbury, is:

> To gild refined gold, to paint the lily,
> To throw a perfume on the violet,
> To smooth the ice, or add another hue
> Unto the rainbow . . .

Returning to the original is often refreshing:

- Oft-heard phrase: "Trip the light fantastic."
  Original (John Milton):
  "Come and trip it as you go
  on the light fantastic toe."

- Oft-heard: "A rose by any other name."
  Original (Shakespeare):
  "What's in a name? That which we call a rose
  By any other name would smell as sweet."

- Oft-heard: "He does not suffer fools gladly."
  Original (The Bible):
  Paul the Apostle says: "For ye suffer fools
  gladly, seeing ye yourselves are wise."

Not only does the original refresh your audience, it establishes you as learned—which makes listeners more receptive to what you say.

Don't refer to the "old adage." An adage isn't an adage unless it's old. So an *old adage* is redundant. Worse is "as the old adage says." Even worse is "as the old adage hath it."

If you want to use an adage, don't telegraph your punch. Just go ahead and use it. Don't apologize for using it with an announcement.

When someone says "Alas," you can bet even he's going to add "poor Yorick, I knew him well."

If you insist on using a well-worn phrase, go back to the original and get it right. As he took the skull of Yorick, the king's jester, from the clown in the churchyard, Hamlet said: "Alas, poor Yorick! I knew him, Horatio."

Speakers often salivate to quote Shakespeare because their knee-jerk reaction is: "Quoth the Bard" (yuck!).

A bard was a professional singer who composed and sang songs for his tribe's heroes. To apply bard to any poet is, as Bergen Evans warns us, "to indulge in a low grade of frigid jocularity" with "a lamentable piece of stilted nonsense."

Thoughtless speakers love to use "in one fell swoop." When Macduff learns his wife and children have been "savagely slaughter'd" by. Macbeth, he cries:

> All my pretty ones?
> Did you say all? O hell-kite! All?
> What, all my pretty chickens and their dam
> At one fell swoop?

The hell-kite is Macbeth, who had swooped on his victims (Macduff's little chickens) like a hawk. *At one fell swoop* has since plummeted into clichéland. *Fell* has nothing to do here with fall but means inhumanly cruel, savage (from Latin *fello*, a wicked person). Remember the meaning of *fell* by calling to mind the old Mother Goose rhyme:

> I do not like thee, Dr. Fell
> The reason why I cannot tell.
> But this I know and know full well
> I do not like thee, Dr. Fell.

Kneejerk Filler-Words

So much for the classics. Today's passion for filler-words is an even bigger scandal. Topping the list is *you know*. This fad has reached gigantic proportions. I recently heard one teenager telling another: "You know, I don't know, you know."

Injecting *you know* between every word is deadly.

One clubwoman recently used the phrase *to be honest with you* four times in a presentation to new members. One prospect aptly said:

"Anybody who keeps saying 'to be honest with you' scares me. What else is she supposed to be but honest?"

No one these days, it seems, attends high school or college. They study at the high-school level or at the college level. When tempted to use *level*, ask yourself whether it helps meaning, clarity, style. *Level* is almost always filler-word clutter. Expunge it.

In its current fad use, *hopefully* is substituted (grossly and ungramatically) for *it is hoped*. An effective fund raiser would never say, "It is hoped you'll consider donating to our fund."

Remember this: *Even when correctly employed, the passive voice isn't the persuasive voice.* Further, when you use *hopefully* as an introductory word, it marks you as a filler-mongering clod. And your listeners will not be persuaded.

"*Hopefully* is a knee-jerk word, like *yunno*," John Bremner wrote in *Marketing Times.* "And most of the time it doesn't make sense. It makes sense when you say, 'Hopefully, he awaited the jury's verdict,' because he was full of hope. It doesn't make sense when you say, 'Hopefully, the plane will be on time,' because the plane is not arriving full of hope."

The power speaker, of course, merely says: "We hope you will join us," or "We'd be delighted if you can join us," or "We certainly do hope this will work out to your liking."

Frankly inserted in front of each sentence is just as bad. It makes the listener wonder if the speaker is candid. Other variations: *To be truthful, Honestly speaking, To tell the truth.* Does a spoken assurance of honesty ever ring true? Remember Shakespeare's admonition: "Methinks she doth protest too much!"

Then there is the statement: "I only want a minute or two of your time." If you have anything of value to offer, how can you possibly present it in a minute or two? And, "I doubt this will interest you," probably won't interest anyone.

Avoid using *basically* at the beginning of sentences ("Basically, I liked the move"). It is fast joining *hopefully* and *you know* as a gaucherie.

By and large, originally a sailing term, is now a knee-jerk filler used while the speaker tries to decide what to say next. It's an excellent phrase to avoid.

Conspicuous by his absence sticks out like a sore thumb, as does *pregnant pause.*

When you tell someone, "Every effort is being made to look into the matter," your listener knows that (1) nothing has yet been done, (2) nothing will ever be done, or (3) nothing can possibly be done.

When a stock phrase like "That's incredible!" becomes the title of a

TV show, you know we're in deep trouble. Over-use by "out" people has made *incredible* indigestible.

Don't say, "It is interesting to note," or, "I heard an interesting story." Let the listener decide whether it was interesting. (Frequently, it isn't.)

For some time, the word *outstanding* was overworked. "Outstanding," said H. L. Mencken, "began its career among the pedagogues, and they still overwork it cruelly, but it is now also used by politicians, the rev. clergy, newspaper editorial writers, and other such virtuosi."

Revitalizing the Overworked Cliché

Don't tell your listeners to "Have a nice day!" Why be the fourteenth person to say this before 10:30 A.M.? It brands you as unimaginative. To show you how old the phrase really is: In the 1890s, a friend told Mark Twain, "It's a nice day." "Yes," said Twain, "I've heard it spoken of very highly."

Twain believed in retreading clichés. When done inventively, this revitalization makes your speech bright and memorable. That's what Dorothy Parker did when she said: "You can lead a whore to culture but you can't make her think." She did it again at the Yale prom: "If all these sweet young things were laid end to end" [here you expect an analogy about reaching halfway around the earth], "I wouldn't be the slightest bit surprised."

She did not simply retread the trite, she added a surprise—that vital element of genuine humor.

You can also improve the over-familiar by adding an out-of-context second line. William R. Espy suggests these starters:

Marlowe	Was this the face that launched a thousand ships? *No wonder there're keel marks on her hips.*
Shakespeare	Full fathom five thy father lies. *I pushed him. I apologize.*
Congreve	Music has charms to soothe a savage breast. *So I keep a flute tucked inside my vest.*
Milton	When I consider how my light is spent, *I'm glad utilities come with the rent.*
Poe	Once upon a midnight dreary, *Late-late show starred Wallace Beery.*[12]

With a little work, you can be a sparkling source of shocking second lines. You can also give clichés a second life without being poetic. Just change the script: "Something's gone ascrew," or, "He threw a wrench in the monkey works." Or, as the unintentionally creative woman said to her restaurant tablemate while looking in her compact mirror, "I look like the raft of God hit me."

If you feel the undeniable urge to commit a cliché, use shorthand. Let your listener figure it out: "I don't have a red" (cent), or, "I haven't the foggiest" (notion).

The most pathetic of all is the speaker diligently trying to use clichés—and botching them in the process. Mark Twain clobbered James Fenimore Cooper for not getting his clichés right. When Russian propagandists work in English, they attempt breezy journalese familiar to Americans and don't always bring it off. A news statement released by the Soviet Embassy stated: "The people strove to break away from the medieval dark." (You don't break *away* from the dark, you break *out* of it.)

If you're hell-bent on using a cliché, jump right in without *proverbial* to soften the blow ("He hit the proverbial hay"). Don't add a patronizing phrase such as, "if you'll pardon the expression," "to coin a phrase," or "as the old saying goes." You might as well say: "Look, I'm using a cliché. My speech is so poverty-stricken I can't do any better."

John Bremner suggests you create *new* clichés. Since "American as apple pie" is overdone, why not as American as "baseball, divorce, pizza, and french fries," or, "McDonald's"?

Of course, your created clichés can come back to haunt you— witness Nixon's "I want to make one thing perfectly clear." Rich Little made it immortal.

Answers to the Unasked Questions

You can also breathe fire into the well-worn by merely providing answers to overworked questions (in the manner made popular by Johnny Carson). Here are answers-only from Bruce Feirstein's compilation in an article that appeared in *The New York Times Magazine:*

> By definition, still waters don't run at all.
> Not always last; sometimes those guys finish next to last.
> They won't spoil the broth—but too many will, in fact, absolutely mangle a chicken.
> It honestly doesn't matter whether you starve it or feed it. Just do everyone a favor and stay home.

Let's settle this once and for all: It doesn't matter whether it's half full or half empty; the important point is it's evaporating while we discuss it. Come on. Everybody knows it's the egg.

Occupational Argot: The Army

When Ronald Reagan pronounced the word *liaison* LEE-a-zone, speech experts all over the republic took notice.

"Surely it should be li-A-zon," the correctors said, delighted about catching the President in error. When he was governor of California, Reagan explained his sin in a letter to a constituent, who later forwarded it to William Safire:

> You are absolutely correct about mispronunciation of the word liaison. I can only plead old military habit. For some reason, in the old Army where I served, liaison was always pronounced LEE-a-zone. In fact, my first assignment was as liaison officer. I have one other word from my cavalry days. I've managed to break the habit better on it but still not completely: oblique. It comes out Army-style o-BLIKE.

He's right. When I was at Fort Dix, Platoon Sergeant Jim Collins explained o-BLIKE this way: "Now I know there're some of you men here who've been to school and you're gonna correct me on o-BLIKE— say it should be o-BLEEK. Not in the Army. A group of men marching can hear o-BLIKE better. There's the right way, the wrong way, and the Army way."

True. O-BLIKE travels better outdoors when you're commanding a platoon to march half right or half left. PRO-ceed is so pronounced for the same reason.

The Army has other peculiar argot. VEE-hick-l become vee-HICK-l. In-SUR-ance becomes IN-sur-ance. (Some say these pronunciations merely reflect the high southern percentage among career noncoms. Could be.)

Put *longevity* in olive drab and it becomes long-DIV-ity. And in the old cavalry, if you remember the movie *Fort Apache,* Henry Fonda refers to a new second lieutenant (John Agar) as a KAY-det—meaning a ca-DET fresh from West Point.

Army speech isn't always standard, by any means, but it's often creatively vulgar. The anonymous GI who coined the phrase for pay-day—"when the eagle shits"—deserves veneration. Squeezing money out of the national bird is gloriously graphic.

But when Army speech rises to the general's quarters, the patois is usually designed to obscure failure. Union General George B. McClellan spent much time working out language to suit his nature. (Said Lincoln: "He has a terrible case of The Slows.")

When McClellan decided against assaulting the Confederate defenses at Richmond in 1862, he conducted what he called a *change of base.* This official description of movement away from the enemy capital got a skeptical reception in the northern press.

The star-collar term for moving rearward is *withdrawal.* When that became transparent, generals announced *redeployment. Pull out* has been in colloquial use for a century. It became *bug out* during the Korean War. In Vietnam, the ordinary grunt said it much more simply: *haul ass.*

Understanding olive-drab jargon is valuable in talking to military folk or understanding what they say to you. Army words also add vigor to the great American language.

Occupational Speech

Much occupational jargon adds tedium to the language.

▪ *Airlines.* The stewardess comes on the intercom: "Please extinguish all smoking materials." When you first get on she announces: "If there's anything we can do to make your flight more comfortable, please don't hesitate to call on us." The captain will explain that, "Due to the clouds and haze, your visual reference to the ground will be considerably restricted." Noxious twaddle. And it never changes.

If your work calls for regular conversations with the public, please make sure you're not committing similar outrages.

▪ *Data-processing* language needs reform, Peter McWilliams tells us in *USA Today.* McWilliams distributes this product literature along with his McWilliams II word processor:

> Prints characters from every known language, uses no energy, does not lose its memory during power failures, is user friendly and comes with a five-year unconditional warranty. To create a file: Place a sheet of paper under point of McWilliams II. To delete a file: Crumple the paper and toss in wastebasket.

Now the truth: The McWilliams II word processor is a pencil.

▪ *The newspaper field* is awash with jargon. As Roy Peter Clark notes in *Folio,* it contains consistent images of death and violence:

First a reporter writes in a style called the *pyramid* (which is a tomb), often starting with a news *hook* and ending with a *kicker.* At the end, he writes *30,* a telegraphic end-it symbol and metaphor for death.

The story fills a *news hole,* a shallow grave left by advertising. Editors *cut, kill,* and *bury* stories. They spike *dead* stories. Editors on the *graveyard* shift earn nicknames like *Hacksaw, Butcher,* or *Knife.*

Editors also write *drop heads* and *jump heads.* They eliminate *widows.* Even punctuation is violent. Exclamation points are *bangers.* Stories are riddled by *bullets.* In layout, sometimes editors are guilty of *tombstone* makeup.

In the hot-metal days, pressmen threw lead scraps into a bin called a *hell box.* Today stories are written on a *terminal* with buttons for *cut, kill, search and destroy, purge, execute.* Hit the wrong button and *Fatal Mistake* flashes on the screen.

Finally, the newspaper goes to bed and an editor yells: "We're *dead* for tonight." The following day, all today's stories go to the *morgue* (library).

Argot in Adland

Down the street at the advertising agency, men and women wrestle with different concerns. Roger Myers, a New York advertising agency executive, tells how in *Ad Digest:*

> Here's *pitch patter* used by agency people presenting for new business—followed by plain English translations.
>
> *Pitch:* "Rather than take up your time with our speculations and guesses about your particular advertising needs, we've decided to provide you with a general overview that will help you appreciate our experience, resources, and capabilities."
> *Translation:* We're going to show you a canned presentation.
>
> *Pitch:* "Rather than subject you to a one-sided recitation of our experience, resources, and capabilities, we've decided to use this time to talk with you informally so we can get to know each other."
> *Translation:* We don't have a canned presentation to show you.
>
> *Pitch:* "We're prepared to add to our staff to provide for your account. And, of course, we will consult with you in the selection and hiring."
> *Translation:* We're willing to hire your nephew.

Buck Fanshaw's Revenge

Obviously, when your occupational jargon needs translation, you're in deep trouble. Don't be like Scotty and the preacher in Mark Twain's

"Buck Fanshaw's Funeral." In the story, Scotty, river-wise but rough, is trying to arrange a funeral with a sheltered, un-worldly preacher:

> "Are you the duck that runs the gospel mill next door?"
> "Am I the—pardon me, I believe I do not understand."
> With another sigh and a half sob, Scotty rejoined:
> "Why, you see we are in a bit of trouble, and the boys thought maybe you would give us a lift, if we'd tackle you—that is, if I've got the rights of it and you are the head clerk of the doxology works next door."
> "I am the shepherd in charge of the flock whose fold is next door."
> "The which?"
> "The spiritual adviser of the little company of believers whose sanctuary adjoins these premises."
> Scotty scratched his head, reflected a moment, and then said:
> "You ruther hold over me, pard. I reckon I can't call that hand. Ante and pass the buck."
> "How? I beg pardon. What did I understand you to say?"
> "Well, you've ruther got the bulge on me. Or maybe we've both got the bulge, somehow. You don't smoke me and I don't smoke you. You see, one of the boys has passed in his checks and we want to give him a good send-off, and so the thing I'm on now is to roust out somebody to jerk a litte chin music for us and waltz him through handsome."
> "My friend, I seem to grow more and more bewildered. Your observations are wholly incomprehensible to me. Cannot you simplify them in some way? At first I thought perhaps I understood you, but I grope now. Would it not expedite matters if you restricted yourself to categorical statements of fact unencumbered with obstructing accumulations of metaphor and allegory?"

When each party insists on his own jargon, communication cannot take place. The two viewpoints are vastly different. Always check carefully to see if you're communicating. The chances that you are? Only fair!

Misfires and Mislicks

Adults often delude themselves into thinking children understand. Alas! The truth is otherwise—particularly in formal religious ceremonies, as these celebrated misunderstandings indicate:

Actual	*Understood*
Round yon Virgin (in *Silent Night*)	Round John virgin
Give us this day Our daily bread	Give us this day Our jelly bread

Actual	*Understood*
Lead us not into temptation	Lead us not into Penn Station
Gladly, the cross I'd bear (line in a hymn)	A cross-eyed bear named Gladly
Hallowed be Thy name	Harold be thy name

There's an enduring lesson here for power speakers: It's not what you say that counts—it's what listeners *think* you say.

Nice-Nelly Language

Use of euphemisms ("speaking fair") may be motivated by reverence, kindness, decency, and fear. But under such circumstances folly and bad taste often emerge. When you employ euphemisms, you're obscuring what you *do* mean to spare the listener's (assumed) delicate ears.

A hundred years ago the genteel referred to legs as *limbs,* trousers as *unmentionables,* and pregnancy as *being in the family way.*

Billy Graham has amended the seventh commandment to "Thou shalt not commit immorality."

Today death is *passing away,* false teeth are *dentures,* and a stroke is a *cerebral accident.* But death and taxes remain unsweet by other names, as do most other human ills.

Though nice-nelly words are meant to be soothing, there is something nastily condescending in such expressions. We resent the speaker's superiority to life's unpleasantnesses and his attempt to hoodwink us and lead us past them.

In most cases, you are well advised to expunge euphemisms. You and your listeners will be happier and healthier.

Fad Words

During the 1984 presidential campaign, a Mondale spokesman praised the improved *atmospherics* in the Ferraro camp. In computerland, machines develop *glitches.* In Washington, politicians accuse others of dealing *only in rhetoric.* On PBS's *Washington Week in Review,* panelists tell us what *the rap* is on a certain official.

All are fad words, and there are many more. They streak across the verbal firmament like Halley's Comet, strut and fret their hour on the stage, then are heard no more.

Rather than a bad back, Oswald has a *bad-back situation.* A company is in a *hiring mode.* Children, we hope, are having a *learning experience.* A *surprise condition.* A *landing pattern.*

In a newspaper article, Bill Rabe, professor at Lake Superior State College, Sault Sainte Marie, Michigan, calls fads "non-meaningful expressions," and his annual Unicorn Hunters Award alerts us to the worst examples. He honored these winners: *State of the art,* which Rabe says is applied to everything from garbage cans to contraceptives. *Signals,* which are often sent by foreign powers in news stories. Asks Rabe: "Don't diplomats talk anymore?" *Caboose words,* like *conceptualize,* "where people add *ize* at the end to a perfectly good word." And the classic bummers *meaningful* and *at this point in time.*

Rabe's witchhunt illustrates the problem with fad words: They overstay their welcome. Fresh-coined fads can add trendy verve to your speech when less than 10 percent of speakers use these words. But the moment fads become popular with the Great Unwashed, bail out, old boy and old girl. Use the most Out Person you know as your weather vane. When he or she starts mouthing a fad, get yourself gone. (Several doughty Outs serve me well as an early warning system.)

Doubletalk and Triplespeak

With regret, we now turn to that loathsome scourge that shows every sign of growing geometrically: doubletalk or gobbledygook or over-talk. Arrest it. It's wanted for murder.

"The following inputs," said the account executive fresh out of business school, "should be sufficient for you to generate a sales presentation." What he meant: "Here's the information you need to write the presentation."

Peter Hockstein of Ogilvy & Mather advises you on ways to get so gobbledygooked you'll be sure to be *mis*-understood:

> 1. *Use buzzwords* from the mathematical and computer sciences, misapplied to business. Instead of saying: "Let's make up a prospect list," say, "Let's input a probability sequence within firmly limited parameters."
> 2. *Use nouns as verbs.* Example: "The cancer scare will impact our market."
> 3. *Use gobbledygook.* These well-known quotes, rendered in gobbledygook, are translated back to the American language.

> Hopefully, if they input their caloric requirements with pre-sweetened high-yeast-content baked goods products, they will have an

affirmative nutritional experience of adequate dimensions. *(Let them eat cake.)*

I am faced with the options of continuing to function as an entity or aborting the process and terminating all operations. *(To be or not to be, that is the question.)*[13]

Phrases like these move people to actions, to meet objectives, to do the bidding of motivators. Which versions are best for power speech? You know the answer.

George Orwell, in his essay "Politics and the English Language," translated the clear prose of Ecclesiastes into gobbledygook (even before it was called that):

Original: "I returned and saw under the sun, that the race is not to the swift nor the battle to the strong, neither yet bread to the wise, nor yet riches to men of understanding, nor yet favour to men of skill; but time and chance happeneth to them all."

Over-talk: "Objective consideration of contemporary phenomena compels the conclusion that success or failure in competitive activities exhibits no tendency to be commensurate with innate capacity, but that a considerable element of the unpredictable must invariably be taken into account."

Any doubt about which is the most effective? Not to the power speaker.

Every so often, even a judge cries "Hold, enough." Said New York federal judge Jack B. Weinstein, in ordering the government to explain itself more clearly on Medicare forms: "The language used is bureaucratic gobbledygook, jargon, double talk, a form of officialese, federalese, and insurancese, and doublespeak. It does not qualify as English."

In 1984, the National Council of Teachers of English got exercised and issued Doublespeak Awards to:

- The Pentagon, for referring to combat as *violence processing* and peace as *permanent pre-hostility.*
- The National Transportation Safety Board, for calling an airplane crash a *controlled flight into terrain.*
- The White House, for calling the Grenada invasion a *pre-dawn vertical incursion.*
- A Chicago discount store, for advertising *a hydro blast force cup*—a toilet plunger.
- New Jersey, for having no more death row. Now it's a *capital sentences unit.*
- A large oil company, for calling planned layoffs *eliminating redundancies in the human resources area.*

Log Jam on the Potomac

When you go to Washington to influence legislators, it's vital to understand and use their jargon of artful ambiguity. In an atmosphere of mutual back-scratching, congressmen and congresswomen try, in their own phrase, "to keep options open as long as possible."

Representative Morris K. Udall, an Arizona Democrat who's been around long enough to know evasive strategy when he hears it, says a common response to the sticky question, "How do you stand on Bill X?" is this seemingly straightforward assurance: "I'm all right on that one."

Another response, "You can count on me," indicates support but does not specify precisely what the politician can be counted upon to do.

One congresswoman responds to vote solicitation by saying: "Don't get me started on that one," accompanied by a roll of eyes and shrug of shoulders. The implication: The answer is so obvious, the position so clear, there's absolutely no point in further discussion.

Another Potomac-fever response: "A lot of people have been asking me about that." The desired impression: The position has been carefully honed in response to repeated questions and is not in doubt. (What that position *is* remains unsaid.) Or as one senator said: "Some of my friends are for that bill and some are against it, and I'm going to stick with my friends." Then there's the smoke screen: You bore listeners with a wealth of irrelevant detail, or you address an entirely unrelated issue. If all else fails, you can always say: "I'll stand behind the president on that one."

Washington, sometimes described as 71 square miles surrounded on all sides by reality, excels in excesses. Should gobbledygook be exempt? No. Potomac palaver confuses even dedicated doubletalkers.

Only in Washington do you find an *assistant administrator to the administrator.* Or any of these job titles:

Self-explanatory

- National Supervisor for Shell Eggs, Agriculture Department.
- Senior Liquidator at Large, Federal Deposit Insurance Corporation.
- Chief Sculptor and Engraver, U.S. Mint.
- Staff Officer for Red Meat Slaughter, Food Safety and Inspection Service.
- Solar Eclipse Coordinator, National Science Foundation.

Non-explanatory

- USSR Input-Output Bureau Chief, Census Bureau.

- Internal Operations and Screwworm Eradication Staff Senior Staff Veterinarian, Agriculture Department.
- Journey-to-Work and Migration Statistics Bureau Chief, Census Bureau.
- Welfare Whereabouts of Americans Abroad Bureau Chief, State Department.
- Umpire, Government Printing Office.

Obscure

- Special Assistant to the Assistant to the Secretary and Director in the Office of the Secretary, Treasury Department.
- Special Assistant to the Special Assistant to the Secretary for Civil Rights, Department of Health and Human Services.
- Principal Research Silviculturist, National Forest System.

In fact, Washington speech-mangling is so organized that word-torturers formed their own association in the 1980s. (Why not? Everyone else has one.) The group, based in Washington (naturally), is the National Association of Professional Bureaucrats (NATAPROBU). The founder is Jim Boren, most suitably a former State Department aide. NATAPROBU's motto: "When in doubt, ponder. When in trouble, delegate. When confused, mumble."

To raise standards in its field, Boren regularly awards The Bird—an ugly unfeathered talisman—to the most professional bureaucrat in America. Boren is currently forming two other groups: Department of Adjusted Procedures and Orchestrated Clearances (DAPOC) and Office of Orderly-Overruns, Permutations, and Statistics (OOOPS).

At times, Boren talks of taking his philosophy of orchestrated harmonics on the sawdust trail. A sample of his campaign speech: "The economy must be regulated in order to meet the proliferation standards of wage-price harmonics and monetary proficiency within the special contingencies of the corporate linkage with the anticipatory disparity of domestic portfolios."

Boren has tested his theories in testifying before Congress on—you guessed it—ways to cut red tape. Said Boren: "To deny a dedicated finger-tapper an adequate supply of paper on which to record the results of his prodigious pondering is to deny him the tools of creative nonresponsiveness."

Only one thing worries Boren: NATAPROBU is dangerously close to actually accomplishing something. That, as the anarchist said when he resigned from the anarchist society because it was too well organized, would be murder.

WRAPPING IT UP

What have you learned about power speech vis-à-vis jargon, clichés, doubletalk, euphemisms, overspeaking, and gobbledygook? These simple and valuable principles:

- This is the heaven-forbid minefield of speech. Use this knowledge to know what *not* to do.
- Recognize those traits in your competitors as lethal and play up your own straight talk as a real plus, which it is.
- If you insist on dipping into the well-worn barrel, at least be creative and adapt!
- Fads are all right in their extreme youth. Once the "out" people get them, bail out.
- Jargon is sometimes colorful, but make sure you're getting your meaning across.
- Learn to laugh at our national tragedy of confusion—it's better than crying (the only other sensible alternative).

8

What Not *to Say and When* Not *to Say It*

Speech advisers recommend positive thinking and positive speaking. That's sound counsel, in most cases. But at times you're better off knowing when to speak *negatively,* when *not* to speak at all, and what *not* to say.

First take nay-saying. At the right moment, it wins the Kewpie doll.

Nay-Saying in Action

Bruce Alexander, a Tennessee real-estate expert, believes that assertive nay-saying often wins the day. Says he:

> In real estate, always take house-viewers to see property in your car. Don't be chintzy and think you're going to save gas by going in their car. You have no control in their car. *They* can decide when they've seen enough. Keep control.
>
> En route to the property, don't drive by vacant lots and eyesores. Choose the most scenic route. Don't spend valuable drive-out time in idle chatter. Spend that time talking negatively: "It's an excellent value but needs painting inside and outside."
>
> If you *don't* mention that en route, the viewers are going to mention it to *you* when they get there. Take that ammunition away from them.

If the property's a mess, make it a bigger mess. Say: "The walls have got this and the carpet needs this and the lawn is this high. Oh wow, it really needs an awful lot of work. It's in terrible condition. But I'll tell you this. It's about $6,000 under the normal market price.

When they get there, they're all excited about the terrific price. When they see the property, they'll say:

"You know, it's not *that* bad."

If you don't tell them in advance, they're going to spend the next 15 minutes bending your ear about the fortune it's going to cost to fix it up.

When you're showing property, get the viewers to tell you *then* and *there* anything they don't like. Sense what turns them on the most—that fabulous den, the lovely kitchen, the patio. After they see it all, wander back to that high-appeal spot. Make their last memory the best memory.

You know there's a built-in dishwasher, but you *don't* point that out. Say:

"Gee, Tom and Mary, this property has all the features you wanted— lovely den, complete modern kitchen, just about everything. Wait a minute. I don't remember if it has a built-in dishwasher. Did you notice that, Mary?"

If she didn't notice, let her go back into the kitchen and say to you: "Hey, it *does* have a built-in dishwasher. It even has that!"[14]

And you reached the desired destination by assertive nay-saying—at times, a valuable ingredient of power speech. As David warned, in the book of Samuel: "Tell it not in Gath. Publish it not in the streets of Askelon."

When to Clam Up

In speech, the silence *is* golden. On the stage, often the most dramatic occurrence is a strategically placed pause. Sometimes the white space in an ad is more eloquent than the large headlines. In negotiation, the pause, the block of silence, often closes the deal.

A pause enables you to control the interview like nothing else can. It helps you unpoise your adversary and recover your own poise. Silence is a powerful tool in controlling others.

You've been trying to convince a colleague about an increase in budget. She's turned you down. Her objection is specious and you know how to answer it. Instead, you pause. You look at her, smile, and remain silent. The pause gives you an advantage. She'll be unbalanced, wondering what you're going to say. Your silence also compliments her; you're taking time to think *before* answering her objection.

The pause does require courage. Silence, as Nick Dikum, a wise California philosopher, once said, is a tremendous weapon—if you have the willpower to use it. Practice until you can employ the pause without difficulty, until it becomes second nature.

You've directed the conversation. Your adversary is under psychological pressure to commit himself. You've made it easier for him to say yes than no. Close mouth firmly. Wait for him to speak.

At times, the first person to speak loses. You're eyeball to eyeball. Refuse to break the silence. It's his move. If you don't like his first remark following the silence, *continue* to remain mum. Force him to alter his position. Silence is powerful.

Don't Be a Tattlebasket

The Scots say it with color: "Don't be a tattlebasket." My colleague Ed Blanchard brought it up to date: "There's no law in the state of New York that requires you to tell everything you know."

Seldom, if ever, does gossip advance your case as a power speaker. When in doubt, shut your mouth. Never get suckered into character assassination. James A. Newman learned this while working for Ingersoll Steel. Says Newman:

> Working for Ingersoll wasn't easy. I learned a lot there—like don't talk too much, buddy buddy, with people. I learned this when Roy Ingersoll fired me.
>
> Roy, as head of the Ingersoll division, reported to Howard Blood, the chairman of Borg-Warner. Howard's son, Jack, was in the Norge division in Detroit.
>
> Jack Blood invited me out on his father's yacht, tied up on the river north of Detroit. We had a few drinks.
>
> "Jim," he said, "in Borg-Warner, we're having a terrible internal political battle. Awful fights about what Roy Ingersoll, your boss, is doing. Yet I think each division is trying to achieve its own objectives. Don't you think that's right, Jim?"
>
> "Well, I suppose to a degree that's true," I said. "We see evidence of these kinds of things."
>
> The next morning, I got to the office. *Bzzzzz:* my intercom—direct to the CEO's office (status!).
>
> "Jim, come in here," the voice said. Feeling something amiss, I went in.
>
> "I understand you think we have terrible wars in Borg-Warner and I'm battling with Howard Blood all the time and we have great strife," Ingersoll said. "You're fired. We do not need this kind of stuff around here."
>
> Apparently young Blood had talked to his father and attributed to me what *he* had stated. All I'd said was a grudging, "I suppose so." But obviously I shouldn't have gone that far.

Dazed, I went back to my office. I decided to ask the advice of Ray Sullivan, the manufacturing head.

"Just ignore it," Ray said. "Go right about your work. Do everything you're supposed to do. Don't say anything."

So I went ahead. But I had trouble sleeping at night. After Roy Ingersoll had been out of town for 10 days, *bzzzzz* went the intercom: "Jim, come in here."

When I got to Roy's office, he said, "What the hell's the matter with Kalamazoo Furnances! Look at the cost those bastards are reporting. They're doing a terrible job up there. Jim, you've got to get on top of those guys."

"Mr. Ingersoll, I'm fired."

"Oh, for heaven's sake, get up to Kalamazoo and get them straightened out."

That was the last I ever heard about being fired. But I learned a good lesson. You never gain by tearing somebody else down. Let somebody else assassinate character. Don't you do it.

A telling lesson in power speech. Don't tell A about B. If someone wants to talk about personalities, listen and keep mum. Know when *not* to talk.

An appliance manufacturer said about one of his salesmen:

Dick was a good man. He knew our products and was a great salesman. But he was too nosey. He always had to be the first with the word on everything. He had his own private pipelines all over his territory. People all over the factory fed him information. He was a joyful bearer of bad news. I finally had to let him go. His big mouth kept getting us all into a lot of trouble.

If your mouth spews slime, your own feet will slip in it sooner or later.

Mike Barnett was doing a research study in an Illinois plant for a large steel company. Later, in reporting on findings to headquarters, Mike said to Jen Peterson, the general manager: "Did you know the assistant sales manager is going out nights with the receptionist? I'm amazed at the way they do things out in Illinois."

Peterson wasn't buying any.

"Barnett, God damn it," he said. "We hired you to do a study. Leave all that intrigue stuff alone and find answers to the questions."

The Bible tells us Samson slew 1,000 Philistines with the jawbone of an ass. Each day, thousands of chances to make a good impression are killed by the same weapon. Remember what Tom Sawyer's Aunt Polly used to say: "Never miss a good chance to shut up."

Avoid Hoof-in-Mouth Disease

When you're unsure of your facts, uncertain of the proper tone to employ, or too angry to speak properly—cool it. Say nothing until you're on firm ground.

When Ma Ferguson was governor of Texas, Spanish was proposed as a second language in Lone Star schools. Said Ma Ferguson: "Not while I am governor! If English was good enough for Jesus Christ, it is good enough for Texas children."

She missed a real good chance to keep quiet.

An angry tone is never effective. Present your viewpoint eloquently, but keep a friendly voice and face. In dealing with incompetence, Lou Cerullo, founder of Cerigraf, Inc., Newark, New Jersey, says don't barrel in with: "I asked you to do this twice and it still hasn't been done." Instead, say: "Like every firm, we need good people and I expect you are doing your best. However, in this instance and in several other cases, your best hasn't been good enough. Unless you can do better, I'm afraid we'll have to part company."

In one-on-one situations, when you're unsure about a person's family status, don't ask. Art Harris, a broadcast executive in Schnectady, New York, is savvy about talking family.

"During business or social hours, Mr. S. never mentioned his family," Harris relates. "As we got better acquainted, we went to the Saratoga racetrack together. When he described his forthcoming trip to Japan, I did not ask if his wife was going."

Good thing. Harris later learned Mr. S. had just become a widower. How awkward to come on cornball with, "How's the wife?"

Should You Overstate or Understate?

As a power speaker, your mission is to *under*-promise and *over*-perform. That way, you always exceed expectations. The over-promiser and under-performer is always in hot water.

Understatement impresses. Overstatement invites skepticism. A passenger en route to Southport, Connecticut, told me: "I heard the funniest story yesterday—you won't believe it. You really won't." My first thought was "Oh, yeah?" And after he told the story, I got a distinct that-ain't-so-funny feeling.

Give the listener the facts. And then let *him* tell *you* how impressed he is.

Protesting too much is a form of over-statement. Arrogant people use self-deprecating words to convey fake modesty. In Dickens' *David Copperfield,* Uriah Heep said: "Learning ain't for me. A person like myself had better not aspire. If he is to get on in life, he must get on 'umbly." And his mother, Mrs. Heep, added: " 'Umble we are, 'umble we have been, 'umble we shall be."

Overstatement is dangerous. Understatement is powerful.

The Lethal Effects of Giggle-Water

Generous injections of alcohol cause over-*doing* as well as over-*saying.*

Standing in the midst of his company's Christmas party, the tipsy plant foreman scanned the hotel lobby, fascinated by the enormous, red-bowed wreaths hanging just above his colleagues' heads.

"Whatta ya wanna bet that I can put a chair through the center of that wreath?" Before anyone could stop him, he hurled a lobby chair through the evergreen bull's eye and the massive plate-glass window behind it.

For him, the company party ended with a pink slip.

"As many people ruin their careers at parties as at the office," says John Molloy, the business consultant and author. "Only dummies party at corporate parties."

Don't confuse an office party with fun and games.

"It's not a party, it's a political event," says Marilyn Moats Kennedy, managing partner of Career Strategies, Evanston, Illinois, in a newspaper interview. "The office party is the equivalent of the May Day parade in Russia, where who is standing next to whom, who is seen with whom, is tremendously important.

"You need to circulate, speaking to everyone, even your enemies. Thank the janitorial staff, the switchboard operators. Give everyone a lot of strokes. It will leave your colleagues impressed, and even through a hangover they will remember you as one of the nicest people at this company."

Molloy suggests a more aggressive tack: Arrive a little late, like the executives, and leave a little early. Try to join one of the power groups. "If there is someone you'd like to work for, arrange for an introduction. At the Christmas party, you can get away with saying, 'Hello, Mr. Jones, I'm So-and-so, and if you ever have any openings in your department, I'd love to work for you.' "

There's no obligation, ever, to overstay and do foolish things. I've known many charmers who attend the party and get credit for speaking to the right people; they order a glass of club soda, tour the room, and leave, having done all the right things and none of the wrong.

When I hear someone say, "It's an office thing, I must stay to the end," that sounds like rationalization to me.

Sure, you are often obligated to put in an appearance, but it can be brief if you're courteous and inventive (and if you're not, you're going to have other problems).

What a Tangled Web We Weave

Seldom do scandals trace back to talking too little. Yet too much talk is a classic problem. ("Loose lips sink ships.")

The Crusades (circa 1200) and a cocktail party (circa today) tripped up one man's election to the board of a large corporation.

The candidate, a physician educated in England, boasted idly over cocktails that he had received a particular award presented each year since the Crusades by an English humanitarian group. The remark was overheard by a director of the company the physician hoped to join. He doubted the claim and suggested a reference check. Not only had the doctor never received the award, he'd never even attended the university he'd listed.

Boasting and lying are costly. If you have a good thing going, keep your mouth shut. Or your advantage will evaporate.

If you're privileged to talk confidentially to your boss, that's good. But if you air your feelings too much, you can lose your entrée.

You're on a new job. After three months, you decide you're miscast. You go to your boss and say: "Let's talk about this job. Maybe it's a bad fit. I'd like to see about another assignment."

Your boss might work out a job that suits you better, but not often enough to make the odds good. But some bosses will say: "All right, George, we'll make you a shipping clerk and see if *that's* a better fit."

When and How to Listen

Imagine yourself as a giant set of mammoth ears. (But as former Tennessee Senator Ross Bass once advised a colleague, "Don't keep your ears so close to the ground that grasshoppers get in them.")

The most critical time not to talk: when you can learn (and earn) more by listening. Many promising speakers stumble because they fail to listen.

If you're in personnel, listening is your route to intelligence-gathering. Says Sonny Harris, builder of the growing Window Man franchises based in Durham, North Carolina:

> Before you can listen to a prospective employee, you must flip your attention switch. Set it on full attention. When you find your mind wandering—and it will—pull it back sharply, telling yourself, "Hey, look, if you're going to learn anything about this guy, you'd better pay attention!"
>
> Acknowledge what they say by word, gesture, or facial expression. Focus on *ideas,* not facts alone. When you listen, don't make the mistake of trying to remember a list of facts.
>
> Listen for *keys* to needs, wants, desires.
>
> Listen. Really listen. It's the key to making the right personnel choice.

Be Brief, Be Brief, Be Brief

As columnist Sidney Harris says: "Everyone is a bore on some subjects. The genuine bore is tedious on the subjects he knows best."

Wordiness is a liability that afflicts many. Avoid the heavy use of superlatives and adjectives. Don't talk for 15 minutes to say what could be better said in 3. Don't be a bore.

London publisher John Camden Hotten left us with this epitaph:

Hotten
Rotten
Forgotten

As a result, he's *not* forgotten.

People aren't impressed by pretentious words. Even the educated person appreciates simplicity of speech. Use clear, simple words and statements that anyone can understand. Let terminology fit the slow thinker as well as the fast. A person who doesn't understand cannot be convinced. As you become more aware of speech, you'll tend to associate with people who speak impressively. This will help.

Men and women who cultivate brevity are often memorable. Brevity is rare and refreshing. Brevity is a developed art. When you think you've reduced word power as far as possible to retain sense, think about Victor Hugo. Interested in news of how *Les Misérables* was selling, Hugo penned this letter to his publisher: "?"

The publisher, also something of a card, wrote back: "!"

Let that be your model for brevity in speech.

Mark Twain told about a preacher who began exhorting his congregation to give money.

The preacher made a masterful presentation. Mark Twain, in the back row, was moved. He resolved to give $25. The preacher went on with his talk. After 15 minutes, Twain cut his contribution down to $10.

The preacher didn't close his sale but kept on talking. Twain decided to save half of his $10 and give only $5.

Still the pastor continued to talk. Twain, more bored, resolved to give only $1. At length, after about another half hour, the preacher did pass the collection plate. Instead of giving $25, Twain took $1 out of the plate!

Good product managers realize the fewer words to encapsulate the product, the better.

A look at successful mail-order advertising headlines shows how to state benefits in one sentence:

- The secret of making people like you . . .
- A little mistake that cost a farmer $3,000 a year.
- How a new discovery makes a plain girl beautiful.
- Do you make these mistakes in English?
- Who ever heard of a person losing weight—and enjoying three delicious meals at the same time?
- Another woman is waiting for every man—and she's too smart to have "morning mouth."
- They laughed when I sat down at the piano—but when I started to play . . .
- No more back-breaking garden chores for ME—yet our yard is now the showplace of the neighborhood!
- Imagine me—holding an audience spellbound for 30 minutes!
- It's a shame for you not to make good money—when these men do it so easily.
- A wonderful two years' trip with full pay—but only those with imagination can take it.
- Former barber earns $8,000 in four months as real-estate specialist.

Can you summarize your product or service's benefit in a sentence as dramatic and as compelling? If not, you'd better start working on it.

This poetic statement by Sonny Harris puts it bluntly:

> Tell me quick and tell me true,
> Or else, my friend, "the hell with you."
> Less of how your product came to be,
> And more of what it does for me.

Impressive Precedents for Brevity

Word-parsimony has classic successes. A few years ago, the roadside
Burma Shave signs effectively combined brevity with memorability.

> He Played
> A Sax
> Had No B.O.
> But His Whiskers Scratched
> So She Let Him Go

> It's Not Toasted
> It's Not Dated
> But Look Out
> It's Imitated

> His Face Was Smooth
> And Cool as Ice
> And Oh Louise!
> He Smelled
> So Nice

> With
> A Sleek Cheek
> Pressed to Hers
> Jeepers! Creepers!
> How She Purrs

> Slow Down, Pa
> Sakes Alive
> Ma Missed Signs
> Four
> And Five

Fame and conciseness often go together. Gary Cooper stayed off the
Hollywood gossip circuit by his one-word replies when interviewed
about *High Noon.*

"Is it true, Mr. Cooper, that Grace Kelly will be your co-star?"

"Yup."

"And the plot revolves around certain moral issues?"

"Yup."

Several other questions followed. All got the same answer. Finally
the reporter asked, "Mr. Cooper, is 'Yup' the only word you know?"

"Nope," answered Cooper.

Most power speakers usually need more words than Coop did, but
precedent is all on the side of brevity.

- The Lord's Prayer has 71 words.
- The Ten Commandments have 297.

- The Gettysburg Address has 271.
- The legal marriage vow has two.
- General McAuliffe at the Bulge made his point in one: "Nuts!"

Musical performers often drone on and on about the next song. Not Burl Ives. I recall his concert introduction to "The Ox Driver": "The eye of history seldom focuses on the ox driver—an ordinary man doing a giant's job."

That's it: opening, body, closing. Ordinary words doing a giant's job. Ives is a master of what Francis Bacon described as "the choiceness of the phrase, the round and clean composition of the sentence, and the sweet falling of the clause."

The Value of Brevity in Platform Speech

Donald P. Horton, a popular speaker before business groups, recently advised tyros:

> Here's a simple formula for a successful speech: (1) stand up, (2) speak up, (3) shut up. The first two parts are easy, but the third part most speakers find difficult. When they get to that crucial point when they should sign off and sit down, they can't resist the temptation to keep on talking. Soon they lose their audience. The best speeches are short speeches—where the speaker knows when to shut up and sit down.

The *opening* of a formal address cries for terseness. Said Shakespeare: "Brevity is the soul of wit."

In opening your speech don't write—telegraph! Say it in as few words as possible, then stick to your promise and stay with the points as you've outlined them. Make them quickly, logically, in one, two, or three sentences, and put them in telegraphic speech. In fact, Don Horton advises: "If you don't reach oil in the first two minutes, stop boring!"

Assuming you do strike oil, don't operate the pump all night. In *Speak Up with Confidence,* Jack Valenti, former White House speech writer, offers firm guidelines on turning off the faucet:

1. If you're speaking after dinner at a large gathering of several hundred people who have already endured a long cocktail hour and exhausted all their conversational charm on the person next to them, keep your speech under 15 minutes.
2. If you're one of several after-dinner speakers, or share the platform with entertainers, keep your remarks under 5 minutes.

3. In speaking to a college class, or a seminar convened for the sole purpose of hearing you, 30 minutes is allowed. When the chairman allots you 45, give back part of that time for Q & A.
4. An after-luncheon speaker usually works against a set time for adjournment. When you're introduced, you'll know precisely how much time is left. Even if your chairman says you can linger, don't. Get off on time.

At a convention in Atlantic City, the savvy after-dinner speaker finally got on at 11 P.M.—after several delays and other speakers running overtime. He knew it was a lost cause, so he said: "Ladies and gentlemen, my friend Don Rickles once faced a similar situation. He got up and said: 'Well, folks, the evening just fell on its ass.'

"I won't do that. I'll do this. I'd like to dedicate what is left of this evening to the drunkest man in Atlantic City. He was leaning on the wall, his eyes crossed. But *the second drunkest* man in Atlantic City had him beat. He was pulling the first man's arm—trying to get quarters out of his mouth! With these two men for inspiration, you don't need any more words from me. Good night!"

WRAPPING IT UP

Never miss a good chance to shut up. Pauses are powerful in persuasion. Often the contestant who speaks first, loses.

When you doubt the facts or wonder about the tone or are unsure about a delicate area, cool the brain and close the mouth. Few scandals are traced to talking too little—many to talking too much.

Sometimes nay-saying a persuadee works better than letting the persuadee nay-say you.

Keep off the gossip circuit. You'll advance faster and have less trouble. Don't be a tattlebasket.

Under-promise and *over*-perform. That way, people will always be pleasantly surprised.

Lying and boasting, when put together, are nitro and glycerin. The explosion is just a matter of time.

Listening, really listening, often pays off better than talking.

If you don't strike oil in the first two minutes, stop boring. If you do strike oil, don't keep the pump going all night.

Stand up. Speak up. Shut up.

PART III

The Power of Effective Presentation

9

Whatever You Say, Say It with Style

Back in my show-business days, we presented this vignette to an amused public:

SCENE: A railroad station. The master of the manor, just returned from a trip, is met at the train by George, his faithful family retainer. On the carriage ride home, the following exchange takes place:

The master: Well, George, how's everything been?

George: Just fine, sir.

The master: Come now, George. In three months, nothing happened at all?

George: No, sir. That is to say—nothing much.

The master: What do you mean—nothing much?

George: Well, sir. The old dog *did* die.

The master: Old Tray? My old hunting pardner? How on earth did he die?

George: Well, sir, he died from eating too many burnt chicken feathers.

The master: *(Glaring)* Go on.

George: You see, sir, the chicken house, sorry as I am to say it, *did* burn down.

The master: Burned! How'd that happen?

George: Well, sir, it caught fire from the big house.

The master: The big house? Don't tell me . . .
George: Yes, sir. Sorry to say the big house caught fire.
The master: God save us! Destroyed! Why? Why?
George: Well, sir, you know how we put candles around a person that's laid out for viewing before the funeral? We put candles around the Old Missus, and they set the parlor curtains on fire!

Blackout

Say It Journalistically

The master was experiencing the perils of non-journalistic speech. You'd be surprised at how often this vignette is re-enacted in real life today. The exceptional power speaker knows—and all must learn—to present information in journalistic form. Spit out the most important facts first, then work down. Give them *who, what, when, why, how*—and add the *wow* for listener interest.

In verbal reports, presentations, and speeches: Tell what you're going to tell, then tell it in detail, then summarize what you said. Don't be a modern-day George.

Be a top-down speaker. Speaking journalistically is an important aspect of speaking with style.

Say it with distinction, panache, enthusiasm, courage—qualities most effective when based on knowledge, delivered after practice (with dramatic gestures), and punctuated by strategic pauses.

At times, say it with understatement and a smile. At other times, command presence is your best tool.

Let's see how these style components work.

Say It with Distinction

Walter Winchell, the Broadway columnist who's still heard on the voice-overs of TV re-runs of *The Untouchables,* spoke with a machine-gun stacatto. His clattering telegraph served as pauses between items.

Speed is one key to distinction. Walter Wilkerson, of Kenbridge, Virginia, took top honors at the World Tobacco Auctioneering Championship in Danville, Virginia. Chanting at a lightning 400 to 500 words a minute, Wilkerson can sell a batch of tobacco every four to six seconds, or about 600 piles per hour.

At that rate, the auctioneer could race through the Gettysburg

Address in a mere 40 seconds. He could recite the 796,000 words of the standard King James Bible in slightly more than one day and could breeze through the Declaration of Independence in 3 minutes.

All right. Most of us don't need to speak that fast. But a memorably fast delivery will make you stand out in a crowd.

If you cannot go fast, try whispering. My friend Paul Doebler, a skilled business negotiator, says his most effective adversary whispers at the moment of settlement, as if letting Paul in on a dark secret.

"I leaned forward—not wanting to miss a word," Doebler related. "He continued to whisper. I continued to follow his words. Before I knew it, he asked me to agree. Before I knew it, I whispered I would."

When you don't have much time to make an impression, you must make your speech distinctive. A cameo performer on Broadway knows this. (If you're unknown, it's a bit part. If you're a star, the same role's a cameo.)

The cameo actress isn't the heroine, the best friend, or the young lover. She's the klepto or drunk for comic relief or the last-minute visitor who ties up loose plot strings. When expertly performed, the cameo becomes a miniature portrait—briefly seen but long recalled.

In Colleen Dewhurst's cameo in 1984's *You Can't Take It with You*, Dewhurst plays Olga, the Russian grand duchess who arrives at the last moment to cook blintzes.

Dewhurst enters the cluttered living room of the zany Sycamore family as everyone ineptly tries to pay her proper homage. "I am most happy to be here," she barks like an agitated bulldog. "How soon is dinner?"

That one line, spoken as a command, tells us Olga retains her imperious grandeur but "hasn't had a good meal since before the revolution."

An accent is often memorable—provided it suits the role. Dr. Walter Kempner, the Teutonic Wizard of Fat City (famous founder of The Rice Diet in Durham, North Carolina), has an unforgettable German accent. It's perfectly suited to threats, exhortations, and clucks when he talks to the Ricers (dieters) who flock to him from all over the world.

"Geef us more time," Kempner says when a Ricer announces his length of stay in Durham. ("No matter," one Ricer relates, "if you've agreed to stay *for several years*.")

Dr. Kempner's accent is a component of his total presentation. He has no plan to change it. In fact, his American staff is rapidly picking up German pronunciations. It goes with the territory, or, as they perceive it, with the power.

Cary Grant is an actor of moderate ability who parlayed distinctive style into world acclaim. His own name comes out *Kerry Grent* when processed by his unique vocal apparatus. His distinctive accent stems from an English childhood tempered by touring the United States with a troupe of cockney acrobats.

It was once reported that John F. Kennedy and brother Bobby would often telephone Grant, sometimes interrupting his lunch. "They'd just ask me to talk," Grant said. "They wanted to hear Kerry Grent's voice."

Say It with (Stop) Pauses

Mae West, who invented s-e-x and sold it by the truckload before permissiveness made it commonplace, got her style by exploding *t*'s. (Keep your distance or you'll get sprayed.) "It's not what I say, it's the way that I say it," she drawled, her native Brooklynese still recognizable. "It's not what I do, it's the way that I do it."

When Rick DuBrow, now TV editor of the *Los Angeles Herald Examiner,* visited Mae West in her Malibu home, he noted a well-appointed kitchen.

"Can you cook?" he asked.

"Honey, no one ever asked me that question before," she said—making the most of a triple entendre.

TV's Gomer Pyle speaks and we know right off: Here's a rustic moron. In contrast, his first sergeant's gravel tone says: Here's a street-smart career noncom who doesn't suffer fools gladly.

If you are striving for either of these effects and you achieve them through speech, wonderful. But if you're trying to present yourself as an upwardly mobile yuppie, and you sound like either Gomer Pyle or his first sergeant, you're in deep trouble. So there's distinctive good and distinctive bad.

Your inner personality, whether kind or cruel, thoughtful or greedy, intelligent or stupid, may be largely a function of heredity. But your outer character—manner of speech, appearance, physical carriage—can be learned.

Some power speakers know this instinctively. Some learn it through experience. Some non-power speakers are never aware of it at all.

Effective speech is a uniform that, once donned, tells the audience a great deal about you. General Douglas MacArthur in civilian clothes was a rather colorless man. But in uniform he was a giant, a figure of great authority.

Once you learn how to wear the verbal uniform of the character you're portraying, you've taken a giant step toward living the part.

John Wayne, who started as a stuntman, grew to screen greatness as Rooster Cogburn in *True Grit*. Gravel-voiced Duke explained his style simply: "I cut each sentence in half. I say the first half, stop, then say the second half."

Spencer Tracy was a great stylist. Said movie director Ed Daytrik:

> Spence had developed a trick of naturalistic hemming and hawing, which he used most effectively to cover brief lapses in memory. But sometimes he would go too far. On one such occasion, I called for another take. He feigned hurt surprise.
> "You flubbed just a touch too much on that one," I said.
> "Young fella," he drew himself up. "I've spent a lifetime perfecting that flub."[15]

Let's hear it for *the pause*, that powerful ingredient of distinctive speech. But badly placed pauses result in cluttering. (The Germans call it word-salad.) Your words run together in a mad jumble. Pause at the right time, or you'll give listeners the impression you're a breathless chowderhead.

Say It with Panache

I got on the shuttle bus at LAX, and the driver asked me how I was. Applying a filler response to a filler query, I said, "Fine." He drove two blocks and asked me again: "How are you?"

"Nothing much has changed in the last two minutes," I said.

That driver has a long way to go before he learns to say it with panache. Asking a meaningless question is bad, but asking it twice is insufferable.

Contrast this with a bus driver in Topeka who wished everyone a "Happy Thanksgobble Day" in late November. People are desperate for a fresh approach. They remember the power speaker who gives it to them.

My friend Al White, an army journalist, in impressing his boss with the amount of cooperation he expected from company headquarters, said: "If I call in here for a portable typewriter mounted on the port side of a jackass, I expect it to be provided."

He got attention. He spoke with panache.

Tone of voice can move mountains. A flight to Miami carrying Leo

(The Lip) Durocher, the famed Brooklyn Dodgers manager (certainly the most irrepressible of men—as many an umpire will attest) ran into rough weather. The captain came on the intercom: "Please return to your seats and fasten your seatbelts." Leo, wandering up and down the aisle, paid no attention.

"God bless you," he was telling a baseball fan praising The Bums. He ignored the captain's second request.

Then a 20-year-old stewardess who weighed in at 90 pounds soaking wet came up the aisle and said: "Mr. Durocher, go back to your seat and sit down. I don't want to have to tell you again!"

"Yes, ma'am," Lippy said contritely. He fastened his seat belt and did not say another word. Tone can tame the professional curmudgeon.

The teacher walked into the noisy classroom, slapped her hand on the desk, and ordered sharply: "I demand a little pandemonium!" The class quieted down at once.

"It isn't what you say," she announced later in the teachers' lounge. "It's how you ask for it."

Ben Helms, president of the Maleck Group, Wingate, North Carolina, once lost a key employee, who said, "I got tired of you not saying good morning to me."

"I'd been saying the words," says Helms, "but not really saying it right. People hear what they want to hear. So as far as he was concerned, I hadn't been saying it."

TV emcees, who hear what they want to hear, respond "wunnaful!" to all guest comments. Once during rehearsal, a game-show contestant proved it:

Emcee: And how's everything with this bright-eyed couple?
Contestant: We both just died of cancer.
Emcee: Wunnaful!

Since people hear what they *think* you should say, better make sure your tone is right.

A bright Harvard Law graduate, in the Army briefly during the Vietnam War, barged into his sergeant's cadre room during basic training and sat casually on the bed.

"Get your _____ _____ off the _____ bed and get the _____ out of here, you _____," the sergeant said.

The proper New Englander left. Later his friend, having heard the disturbance, asked what the sergeant had said. "He said it just wasn't *done*," the proper trainee replied calmly.

What the temporary soldier knew—and what a trainee from a less structured society wouldn't have understood as readily—is that each society exists by certain rules. Once you translate unacceptable messages into your own terms, you can explain them to others. The sergeant had powerful speech. The soldier translated it into power speech—in his circle.

Say It with Enthusiasm

You can say nine out of ten things correctly and still fail if you lack *enthusiasm,* says Sonny Harris, president of the Window Man, Durham, North Carolina. He explains why:

> Enthusiasm is highly contagious. If you've got it, everyone around you is sure to get it! It spreads fast. It lights up your face, puts spring in your steps, and a twinkle in your eye.
> Enthusiasm builds power. It pulls you out of the mediocre and commonplace. It makes you sing! It makes friends and builds confidence.
> Enthusiasm makes hard work fun. It tells everyone you like your work, that your company is tops, that your products or services are the best. If you've got it, thank God and give it to everyone! If you haven't got it, get down on your knees and pray for it! Without enthusiasm, you're dead.

Sonny Harris quotes Henry Ford II, who also recognized the power of enthusiasm:

> Enthusiasm is the yeast that makes your hope rise to the stars.
> Enthusiasm is the grip of your hand, the irresistible surge of your will, your energy to execute your ideas.
> Enthusiasts are fighters. They have fortitude, they have staying qualities.
> Enthusiasm stands at the bottom of all progress. With it, there is accomplishment. Without enthusiasm, there are only alibis.

Enthusiasm is knowledge on fire. It's available to you free of charge. So whatever you say, say it with enthusiasm.

Speak with Command Presence

Lee Stanley, president of Solar Additions, Inc., Greenwich, New York, considers command presence vital in person-to-person relations. He's felt that way since he was involved in debating in high school—"trying to accomplish objectives by using the English language."

At first, I was fascinated by using language to put ideas across. I never envisioned it would be useful in making a living. But today speech is a tool I use on an hour-to-hour basis.

When I was in the Army, I learned to call it *command presence.* If you talk, and some people listen, that's command presence. If you talk and nobody listens, you don't have it. The Army considers effective speech absolutely necessary for leadership. An officer must make soldiers listen and carry out orders.

Stanley instructed himself.

I first tried to avoid the constant *ums* and *ahs* so deadly in speech. The Toastmasters Chapters meet regularly to improve one another's speech. Each night they appoint an *ah counter*—a person to make a note every time a person says *ah.* If you log in 37 *ahs* in your address that gives you a clue that you need to expunge yourself.

In hiring people, Stanley grades communications ability (or lack) as a real plus (or minus).

Speech is absolutely essential. In presenting a product (in our case, sunspaces that you add on to homes) you must convey: "We're building a dream." You do this with words and a feeling of imagination. We must establish comfort and rapport with the homeowner—to build confidence. Effective speech goes a long way toward achieving that.

One of Stanley's key people, Ed Reynolds, uses basic power speech. Says Stanley:

He's almost at the "See Spot run" level—like a primer. But people understand him. Even good product knowledge and sincere enthusiasm must be carried forward by effective speech. And if you can develop *command presence,* you're that much further ahead.

Say It with a Smile

In Owen Wister's *The Virginian,* Trampas calls our hero a "son of a bitch." The hero logs eternal fame by replying: "When you call me that, *smile.*"

Say It Briefly

In power speech, less is often more. Many speakers use too many words. We all use too many words sometimes. The fewer words you use to present a thought or image, the greater your impact.

Don't be redundant. The dictionary says *redundant* means "needlessly repetitive," which has led wags to observe that it's redundant to commit suicide in Kansas and that *boring insurance salesman* is a redundant phrase. Other examples: baby puppies, little midget, big giant, long-necked giraffe, 6 A.M. in the morning. *Red in color* is redundant because an object can't be red in size, shape, or age. "Esmeralda picked up a weekly paycheck every Friday." (If it happens every Friday, then we know it's weekly.)

Don't waste words. As William Strunk, Jr. and E. B. White observed in their classic monument to brevity, *Elements of Style:* "A sentence should contain no unnecessary words, a paragraph no unnecessary sentences, for the same reason that a drawing should have no unnecessary lines and a machine no unnecessary parts." Consider the power of this six-word classified ad: "For sale: Baby's crib. Never used."

This doesn't mean the speaker need make all his sentences short or avoid all detail and treat subjects only in outline. It does mean that every word must pull its weight.

Say It with Gestures

Roger Ebert and Gene Siskel, on TV's popular *At the Movies,* talk to one another with animated hand gestures. These gestures add sinew and heart to the show.

"Tie their hands and they'd both be mute," a producer said.

Say It with Boldness and Courage

Poker players say: "Scared money never wins." It's true. No guts, no glory. General George S. Patton, Jr. said it: "Take calculated risks. This is quite different from being rash."

The power speaker must, on many occasions, move out with what Lord Chesterfield called "a decent boldness."

At times, you have nothing to lose and everything to win by taking a chance. Fundraiser George Garmus had been calling on fat cat Walter Hogan for several months. Walter had agreed to donate, but he never would get off the telephone long enough to talk turkey.

George walked in one day, and Walter asked him what he wanted. "Just a few minutes of your time," George said. "Can't do that," Walter replied, reaching for the telephone. "I've got to keep things humming around here."

This is it, George thought. Now or never. He waited until Walter finished the call. Then he grabbed the telephone, dialed the company switchboard, and said: "Please hold Mr. Hogan's calls until further notice." Walter was aghast. George took control. "Walter, three months back, we had a meeting like this—and I never did get a chance to tell you about my charity. That was your day. Today's my day."

Walter, feeling undressed without his telephone, looked at his watch. George then outlined the charity's work in a short, fact-filled presentation.

"O.K., George, you win," Walter said. "We'll give. Now can I have my telephone back?"

George shook his head.

"Not until you make out a check," he said. "I don't dare let you get on that telephone again."

Walter signed the check.

"Little drastic all right," George said later. "But I wasn't getting anywhere the other way. It worked."

When you don't have anything to lose, try a drastic step. Bruce Shine, an active politician in Kingsport, Tennessee, was trying to get a husband and wife to agree to endorse his candidate for office. The woman began writing down what Shine was saying.

"What are you writing?"

"The points you are making."

"Put down your pencil and paper," Shine advised. "These things are all covered in the campaign platform. Why not sign it now?" The endorsers did just that.

Courage implies the willingness to risk failure as a condition of striving for success. Theodore Roosevelt said it this way:

> Far better it is to dare mighty things, to win glorious triumphs, even though checkered by failure, than to take rank with those poor spirits who neither enjoy much nor suffer much, because they live in the gray twilight that knows not victory nor defeat.

Irving P. (Swifty) Lazar, a legendary showbiz agent, is a lawyer by training—and a bold power speaker. In the 1950s, Lazar bet Humphrey Bogart he could close five deals for Bogart before dinner one day.

He did. Bogart paid up and gave Lazar his famous nickname— Swifty.

In negotiating book rights with publishers, Lazar takes a hard line: "Before I go back to the Coast, I want a firm offer."

If the publisher turns him down, which happens even to a legend, Lazar voices the unthinkable: "What's the worst thing that could happen,

Mr. Publisher?" he asks. "The worst is we don't sign an agreement. You'll still be around. So will I."

By appearing offhand—in effect, saying who needs his sale, anyhow?—Lazar whets the buyer's appetite. After all, if he's not eager to sell, does he have a competitive offer just as good? Lazar then bounces right back and starts talking about the value of his property.

"If you keep moving, you won't get hit with a hunk of pie with a brick in it," he says. "If you stop, someone's going to get you. People who stand still are liable to get run over by people who don't."

Folio magazine reported that Charlie Mandel, top-flight magazine ad manager, takes boldness one step further: He asks for more, and in many cases he gets more.

> When an advertiser wants to buy a page, my job is to convince him to buy 12 pages.
>
> Recently, one of my salesmen walked in with a 12-page schedule. I said, "Terrific, let's go back and see him." My salesman thought I'd blow the whole deal. I asked the buyer why he bought 12 pages. He had co-op money he had to spend before Christmas. I said: "Why don't you buy 36 pages?" The order went from 12 pages to 36 pages.

Mandel believes in boldness. The bold speaker eliminates the use of qualifiers.

Non-Bold	*Bold*
Well, I don't think it's a good idea.	I don't think it's a good idea.
That's more or less incorrect.	That's incorrect.
I might like to.	I would like to.
That's somewhat strange.	That's strange.
I wonder if that's a good idea.	Is that a good idea?
Almost no one ever does that.	No one ever does that.
I kind of like it.	I like it.
I'm a little uncertain.	I'm not certain.
I'm pretty sure.	I'm sure.
I'm fairly positive.	I'm positive.
You're probably right.	You're right.

Don't weasel-word.

This also applies to moral courage. Suppose you and your crew have just come back from a convention. Your boss is also back, irate about one of your people. "He was there in the bar talking about intimate company problems to a bunch of dealers," your boss storms. "I never heard anything like it in my life. That man's no good."

Under these conditions, it would be easy to agree with your boss—and condemn the man unheard. Easy but wrong. Better to say: "I don't know what happened, but I'll find out. Let's not judge him too quickly. He's got a fine record, and he's handled a number of things well. Let me find out about this and get back to you. In most ways, I see him as a real asset."

Speak up when good people are under fire. That's when they need it. Speak with boldness and courage.

Say It with Knowledge

When I was a tyro actor with Valley Players in Holyoke, Massachusetts, I played Bill, a high school student, in *What a Life*.

In one scene, I rushed onstage to moan: "On top of that, the cafeteria's closed, and now I'll have to eat the *lunch* my mother made for me."

It was a laugh line—with one problem: The audience didn't laugh. After the first night, Howard Ledig, a veteran actor, took me aside.

"First *you* must understand it before the audience can," he said. "Why do *you* think it's funny?" I didn't know because I hadn't thought about it. Then I realized it wasn't *lunch* that was funny. It was *my mother's lunch*—a horror to contemplate.

The next night I said: "On top of that, now the cafeteria's closed, and I'll have to eat the *lunch* [pause] *MY MOTHER* [groan] made for me."

The audience was convulsed. "My god," they seemed to be saying, "you'd certainly want to avoid *that*."

Engage brain before opening mouth. Power speech must be based on knowledge.

Idle chatter isn't the way to get promoted. Well-thought-out, well-presented contributory comment *is*. Andrew Kershaw, former vice president of Ogilvy & Mather, saw knowledge as the key to power speech. Here's Kershaw's commonsense advice:

> Many people have *talked* themselves out of a promotion. Nobody ever *listened* himself out of a promotion. Don't talk unless you have something to say. Chatter annoys your bosses, who prefer to listen to their own voices.
> It should not take more than a sentence or two to explain things. If it

requires more, the idea is bad or you are making a hash of it. Great ideas are simple. They are easy to communicate.

Good questions can be memorable. Be sure they are good, not ho-hum. A good question elicits this response: "Hm, I haven't thought of that before."

Read everything. Almost indiscriminately. Learn to read fast, and to skip. Digest trade papers and professional journals. The things your bosses read.

Learn to speak properly. Watch for all the little things. Above all: practice. Presenting is theater. Act it out, persuade. Do not try to be dry, impartial, solemn. Rehearsal is the key to learning to be a good presenter.

Half the time, when people present things to me, they do not know all the facts. Don't let this happen to you.

Speak out. You are the most junior person in a meeting. Something worthwhile has occurred to you. Don't hold back. Speak out. Opinions and suggestions do not recognize age, experience, or seniority. Let them discover their level and worth.

Make sure you are noticed. Or heard. The squeaky wheel and all that. But let it be a musical squeak.

A Hungarian proverb says: "Not even a Mother can hear the words of her mute child."

A lot of people, little people, will help to smooth your career, and make you more successful. Be sure to thank them, loudly, and in public, or in writing. This grace will rebound to your credit.

Being good at a job is okay, but it tends to make you deadly dull if that's *all* you know. Most people have *one* hobby or special interest. Outstanding people converse intelligently about dozens of subjects. The more you know, the more valuable and interesting you are. Let your interests be known. Don't hide your light under a bushel.[16]

Walter H. Johnson, Jr., president of Quadrant Counselors, Ltd., New York, sees effective speech as critical but insists that it be based on solid knowledge. Johnson, a popular speaker on business subjects, says:

Knowledge is power. Knowledge of your job. Knowledge of your boss's needs. Knowledge of how to bridge the gap between the two. This power is developed by experience, analysis, and concentration.

Confidence is power. Confidence in yourself. Confidence in product quality and value. Confidence in your ability to meet customers' needs.

Expression is power. Mastery of words is essential in influencing others. When you face a customer, your ability to speak is crucial. Know the emotional power of words. Dress up your ideas with colorful, descriptive words. Develop power of expression by reading, practicing, and collecting powerful words and phrases.

Being affirmative is power. Prospects respond to a positive attitude and a can-do presentation. This is developed when you have pride in your presentation and when personal attitude is positive.

This requires homework as well as office work! Remember what

Mark Twain said about reading: "The man who *won't* read has no advantage over the man who *can't* read."

It works that way with knowledge, too. The power speaker who sees learning as a lifelong challenge and takes positive delight in satisfying insatiable curiosity is a good bet to climb the success ladder.

Say It Actively with Confidence

Be decisive. "Don't sit back and be the smiley one," says a female bank vice president in *The Wall Street Journal.* "Be aggressive but not repulsive. Let them know you're there or they'll never see you." Take a stand.

As Will Rogers said: "Even if you're on the right track, you'll get run over if you just sit there." Society is critical of non-decision-makers.

In *USA Today, Wall Street Week* emcee Louis Rukeyser made this pronouncement about White House fence-sitting:

> Richard Nixon and Jimmy Carter both were guilty of the same crime—terminal vacillation. They were all over the map on all these issues. Nixon's economic program consisted of the most spectacular reversals since Christine Jorgenson. Carter carried on a four-year sequence of non-stop debates with himself—in which, incidentally, both sides lost.

(Carter will go down in history as an indecisive president both for *actions* [as Louis the Leer pointed out] and because of speech style. Even when he was being decisive, it didn't sound that way. And using *Jimmy* in the oval office hardly sounds presidential.)

WRAPPING IT UP

Whatever you say, say it with style.

Speak journalistically. Start with most important facts, work down to lesser facts and details. In a presentation or speech, tell what you're going to cover first. Then live up to your promise.

Say it with distinction. Develop a style that's pure *you.* Sometimes a controlled accent is a plus—if it's appropriate to the role you've assumed.

Say it with panache. Often the way you say it makes it memorable or appropriate. Or acceptable. Or believable.

Say it with enthusiasm—knowledge on fire. But before you start, speak with knowledge. Idle chatter doesn't push your career forward.

At times, draw on *command presence, and eloquence* to make your case.

Use the active voice. Don't waste words. Make each word pull its weight in the beat.

Speak with boldness and courage. Be decisive. Society is run by decision-makers.

Use the familiar word rather than the technical, the concrete word rather than the abstract, the direct word rather than the circumlocution. Choose the vivid word instead of the noncommittal one, the specific over the general, the unusual over the trite.

Say it with confidence. Acquire presentation skills. Speak with precision and clarity in a well-modulated tone.

Effective speech is a self-fulfilling prophecy. Diffidents do not sound authoritative and therefore do not achieve positions of authority.

10

Adding Eloquence to Your Speech

Francis Brown, the rather stuffy former editor of *The New York Times Book Review,* once tried to explain the publication's editorial stance. After several false starts, he finally came out with it: "See here," he said, "we may *be* dull—but we don't *try* to be dull."

Alors! Well, inadvertant dullness does beat drabsville-by-design.

The power speaker, on the other hand, tries *not* to be dull and does actively work at producing stimulating conversation. Distinctive conversationalists (1) are sought after by décolletaged hostess and talk-show host alike, (2) ply their winsome ways with people and make people like it, and (3) appear to breeze through work and leisure hours with the world in thrall.

Note: They *appear* to breeze through. But each scintillating conversationalist diligently inventories words and phrases, creating a storehouse of riches to be tapped when needed.

When Groucho Marx toured the South Pacific for the USO during the Second World War, he reached an army orderly room (company HQ) just in time to hear the telephone ring. Since the company clerk was goofing off, Groucho picked up the receiver and said crisply: "World War *Two!*"

He emphasized *two* to let the caller know precisely *which* war. A match point—doubled.

Back in Hollywood, at a party at Groucho's, a departing guest told The Leering Mustache: "I'd like to say goodbye to your wife."

"So would I," said Groucho.

Ah, yes, you say. If only I could be as clever as Groucho!

Turnipseed! What you mean is: "Too bad I don't work as hard as Groucho at collecting and remembering material."

Julius (Groucho) Marx was a voluminous cataloger and learner of jokes, quips, descriptions, colorful words. His hilarious ad-libs were carefully drawn from his lifetime inventory. If you work just *half* that hard, you can be a power conversationalist.

This does not *mean* asking: "What's new?" "How have you been?" "How's tricks?" "Whaddya say?"

My friend George Hall saw an acquaintance emerging from a medical arts building. He asked immediately: "Is it true they have a quackle of doctors in there? Which duck are you seeing?"

George was making creative conversation—drawing on his stock of Victorian collective nouns. When it comes to colorful plurals, never think you've finished collecting. You know geese on the ground as a *gaggle.* But probably not flying geese as a *skein.* And floating geese as a *plump.*

En masse, ducks are a *flock,* all right. But afloat, they're a *paddling.* And airborne, a *company.* (Is an even larger group a *batallion?* No.) But wait. If the swimming ducks are teal, they're a *coil.*

Now also heed: a *rag* of camels, a *murder* of crows, a *barren* of mules, and a *murmuration* of starlings.

Also a *pod* of seals, a *gam* of whales, a *pride* of lions, a *muster* of peacocks, a *skulk* of foxes, and a *stye* of pigs.

Of course, anyone can play, and you should. To prime the pump, I recommend a *backfence* of housewives, a *garbage* of punkers, an *incomprehensible* of rock musicians, a *maelstrom* of government forms, and a *billing* of home repairmen.

On the business front, I see a *territory* of salesmen, a *delay* of production men, an *agony* of call reports, a *frown* of purchasing agents, a *chart* of researchers, a *gabble* of conventioneers, and a *froth* of inspirational speakers.

Robert Riley, vice president of Baird, Inc., Little Rock, Arkansas, loves collecting plurals (and it helps make him a power conversationalist). Says Riley:

> Three English gentlemen were sitting in their club watching the passing parade. Three ladies of the evening strolled by and the gentlemen sought to discover proper collective nouns.
> The first gentleman suggested a *jam of tarts.* The second suggested a *blare of strumpets.* The third suggested an *anthology of pros.*

Use Distinctive Words

The words you collect need not be commonplace. At times you'll want to trot out highly distinctive words, perhaps to point up your unusual erudition. Try these suggestions from word expert Paul Dickson:

Globaloney.   Cosmic nonsense. Used by Clare Boothe Luce in a speech commenting on the views of then-vice president Henry Wallace.

Oiscallipygia.   Dislike of beautiful women.

Croodle.   Combining crouch and cuddle.

Bathykolpian.   Deep-bosomed.

To Plimp.   To participate à la George Plimpton in a professional sport for participatory journalism.

And don't be content with ordinary words of abuse. Here are verbal punches that *cannot* be returned:

Bezzler.   A sot who steals for liquor money.

Chattermucker.   A blabberer, gossip.

Clinchpoop.   A lout or jerk.

Clodpate.   A stupid fellow; a dolt; a thickskull.

Dandiprat.   A prattling dandy.

Dizzard.   A blockhead, dimwit.

Drumble.   A lazy person or drone.

Dunderwhelp.   A detestable numbskull.

Fadge.   A short, obese lump of a person.

Fopdoodle.   A fool; an insignificant wretch.

Fribble.   A foppish lackwit.

Gongoozler.   An idle person who is always stopping on the street to look at things.

Grouthead.   A dunce or blockhead.

Herkel.   A drip.

Jacksauce.   A rude and saucy person.

Lickpenny.   A greedy, miserly person.

Ninnyhammer.   A simpleton.

Nipcheese.   A cheapskate.

Nup.   A silly person.

Tattlebasket.   A gossip.

Wheech.   Scottish for twerp.[17]

A limerick collector is assured of a responsive audience, as I found out in Egypt while addressing a group of Americans who didn't know one another at the hotel:

> The sexual life of the camel
> It's not what everyone thinks
> One night in an excess of passion
> He tried to deflower the sphinx.
>
> But the sphinx's posterior regions
> Are clogged with the sands of the Nile.
> Which accounts for the hump on the camel
> And the sphinx's *inscrutable* smile.

For Egypt, it was perfect; it wouldn't have been suited to a hotel convention in Kansas City. But this limerick was:

> A lady athletic and handsome
> Got wedged in a sleeping-room transom
> When offered much gold
> For release she was told
> The view is worth more than the ransom.

Collect anecdotes, but do it behind the scenes—not like Red Gardner, a Chicago TV producer. He told amusing stories, but publicly pulling out his list and going over the possibilities at a party reduced their effect considerably.

Finally, you'll need some toasts. Often epitaphs are best:

> When my time is over
> When my race is past
> Be sure to bury me upside down
> So the world can kiss my ast.

Use *ast* rather than *ass*. It rhymes better and it's unexpected (a prime requirement of humor). And if your conversation doesn't sparkle *all* the time, keep trying. Remember what actor Edmund Kean said on his deathbed: "Dying is easy. Comedy is hard."

Word Choice: Making the Critical Decision

Once you've put by a healthy root cellar of words, phrases, and stories, then you must exercise the right choice at the right time.

According to a newspaper account, when Margaret Thatcher, the British prime minister, hosted a diplomatic reception at Holyrood Castle in Edinburgh (where Mary, Queen of Scots once lived), the PM was approached by a counsular official—quite the worse from wine.

"I've always," the man slurred, "had a yen for you, Maggie. Now will you please come across?" (You'll find the Basic Proposition works about the same way even at such rarefied heights and in such a venerable setting.)

The courtly Margaret replied: "You have very good taste, but I really don't think you're up to it right now."

Excellent word choice in a potentially explosive situation, drawing on phrases held in reserve for the diplomatic circuit. Honest, active, specific, and appropriate words give your language power.

A short word that contains the same information as a longer word or a phrase is almost always more powerful. *Rape* is stronger than *sexual assault*. *Mourn* is stronger than *lament*. *Stretch* is stronger than *extend*. *Rich* is stronger than *wealthy*.

"I can see her now in her yellow taffeta dress" is stronger than "I can envision her now in her yellow taffeta dress." Very long words—five syllables or more—are almost always weak.

Now compare these two sentences:

A man entered the room.

A priest entered the room.

Weren't you more interested when I told you the man was a priest? He became more specific. You could see him better. If I'd said a *midget*, a *monk*, or a *thief* entered the room, each would have been more interesting than just a *man*.

When you see writing that appears tailor-made for power speech, read it aloud. If it still works, save it to use in a speech. Imagine grabbing your audience with this glowing paragraph from *The Last Good Kiss* by James Crumley:

> When I finally caught up with Abraham Trahearne, he was drinking beer with an alcoholic bulldog named Fireball Roberts in a ramshackle joint just outside of Sonoma, California—drinking the heart right out of a fine spring afternoon.

That's a wonderful opening to a speech or conversation. Asks Gary Provost in *Writer's Digest:*

> But suppose Trahearne had been drinking with an *alcoholic dog* instead of an *alcoholic bulldog?* Not as fascinating. *Bulldog* helps us focus— not just on the dog, but on the bar, the beer, and the fine spring afternoon. Why? Because by telling what kind of dog it is, you convince your listener you must have been there to see it. How else would you know it was a *bull*dog?[18]

Effective speech is specific and builds mental pictures. Another way to ensure this: Use *activity* words rather than *state-of-being* words. You could say: "A grandfather clock was in one corner, three books were on the table, and the smell of cigar smoke was in the air."

But the power speaker gives each object something to do: "A grandfather clock towered in one corner, three books lay on the table, and the smell of cigar smoke filled the air."

Some words mesmerize, others induce slumber. Choose wisely. Remember the counsel in Proverbs 21:11, "A word fitly spoken is like apples of gold in pictures of silver."

Be a Word Miser

When President Lyndon Johnson was rushed to the hospital for his operation and was minutes away from anesthesia, an aide asked him: "Any last advice for vice president Hubert Humphrey?"

"Yes," said Johnson. "Tell him to keep it short."

Humphrey, a famous extempore speaker, produced many long fire-and-brimstone orations. (As Maxie Schwartz, a New York deli counter-man, said: "A speaker he is, but a short speaker he's not.")

Ergo LBJ's last words to a man then a scalpel's breadth from the presidency: "Keep it short."

Humphrey, effective as he was, could have been greater if he'd been a word-miser. A good lesson for power speech. Even though you put thousands of good words in inventory, be choosy about doling them out. If you were sending a cable to Australia at $2 a word, you'd be careful about word-tonnage. Be just as miserly when speaking. Watch for opportunities to cut four words and put in one. Change "in the event of rain" to "if there's rain." Change "on the occasion of your anniversary" to "on your anniversary."

Make no mistake: Short is harder than long. You must work at using short words and short sentences to build speeches and conversations that hit the mark dead-on. Every word must pull its weight. But the result of this diligence is power speech, effective speech, speech that enhances your professional and personal status. It's the world's best-paying hard work.

Basic Training for Eloquence

"The best way to say something smart," said Sam Levinson, the urban folk philosopher, "is: Think of something stupid, then say just the opposite." Levinson agreed with the classic graffiti: "Do not *operate* mouth without *engaging* brain."

Yes, the reflective speaker says, but who has time to think during the cut and parry of normal conversation?

Good point. A Broadway actress doesn't have time to think up her speeches, either. So she rehearses for weeks before the play opens. Use the same principle by rehearsing your eloquence. Read aloud from the works of great spellbinders. Do this regularly and you'll develop reflex eloquence. It'll dress up your speech.

Traditionally, second-term presidential addresses are not as eloquent as first-term orations. However, Ronald Reagan's 1985 state of the union address may prove an exception—only the marination of history will tell.

But in the meantime, for reading aloud, these Reagan excerpts will build eloquence into your speech:

> Tonight, America is stronger because of the values we hold dear. We believe faith and freedom must be our guiding stars, for they show us truth, they make us brave, give us hope, and leave us wiser than we were. Our progress began not in Washington, D.C., but in the hearts of our families, communities, workplaces, and voluntary groups which, together, are unleashing the invincible spirit of one great nation under God.
>
> This nation is poised for greatness. The time has come to proceed toward a great new challenge—a Second American Revolution of hope and opportunity; a revolution of spirit that taps the soul of America, enabling us to summon greater strength than we've ever known; and, a revolution that carries beyond our shores the golden promise of human freedom in a world of peace.
>
> Let us begin by challenging our conventional wisdom: There are no constraints on the human mind, no walls around the human spirit, no barriers to our progress except those we ourselves erect.
>
> In Europe, they're calling it "the American Miracle." Day by day, we are shattering accepted notions of what is possible.
>
> Our Second American Revolution will push on to new possibilities not only on earth, but in the next frontier of space.
>
> Within the next decade, Americans and our friends around the world will be living and working together in space.
>
> Just as we're positioned as never before to secure justice in our economy, we're poised as never before to create a safer, freer, more peaceful world.
>
> Our alliances are stronger than ever. Our economy is stronger than ever. We have resumed our historic role as a leader of the free world—and all of these together are a great force for peace.
>
> I have spoken of great plans and great dreams. They are dreams we can make come true. Two hundred years of American history should have taught us that nothing is impossible.

This comment by Chicago ad pioneer Leo Burnett isn't widely known. But read it aloud and you'll see how effectively it creates a mood for Chicago-style advertising:

> In the Michigan town where I was raised, you could hear the corn growing on hot nights. I snuck up on Chicago slowly, by way of outlying cities. When I finally got here I was 40 years old and confirmed in my colloquial ways.
>
> People in my home town thought of Chicago as a kind of Rome to which all roads led—beckoning, majestic, maybe a touch or two wicked.
>
> Unlike New York, however, which was a mythical place, Chicago was real. Everyone had an Uncle Charlie or Aunt Mable living here, in Glen Ellyn or somewhere. Whether people approved of Chicago or not, it was *family*, rather like a son who had gone off and made good in an impressive but controversial way. So my little town had a proprietary feeling about Chicago, and when we rubes came flocking in from all quarters of the cornbelt, we recognized each other and knew we were home.
>
> I guess what I'm getting at is that Chicago *is* the Midwest—the heart, soul, brains, and bowel of it. Its ad-making ranks are filled with folks whose heads are stocked with prairie-town views and values.
>
> Now I don't intend to argue that Chicago is in any way a worthier city than, say, New York. But I am suggesting that our sod-busting delivery, our loose-limbed stand, our wide-eyed perspective make it easier for us to create ads that talk turkey to the majority of Americans—that's all.
>
> I like to think that we Chicago ad-makers are all working stiffs. I like to imagine that Chicago copywriters spit on their hands before picking up the big black pencils. I like to think that the language of our ads has been ventilated in the fresh Chicago breezes and rinsed in the clear waters of Lake Michigan.
>
> It seems to me that Chicago advertising draws up a lot of nourishment from the richness of American folklore, restores it, and perpetuates it in a keen and lively sense.[19]

Sometimes the speaker is famous but not the passage. Repeat Winston Churchill's words on Gettysburg:

> The Battle of Gettysburg was at an end. Twenty-three thousand Federals and over twenty thousand Confederates had been smitten by lead or steel. For a week the Confederates stood at bay behind entrenchments with their backs to an unfordable river. Longstreet would have stayed to court attack; but Lee measured the event. Meade did not appear till the 12th, and his attack was planned for the 14th. When that morning came, Lee, after a cruel night march, was safe on the other side of the river. He carried with him his wounded and his prisoners. He had lost only five guns, and the war.[20]

Some prose is really poetry—like Thomas Wolfe's scene-setting for *Look Homeward, Angel:*

A stone, a leaf, an unfound door. . . .
O lost, and by the wind grieved,
ghost, come back again.

Or read this famous John F. Kennedy inaugural address excerpt:

Let the word go forth from this time and place, to friend and foe alike, that the torch has been passed to a new generation of Americans. . . . Let every nation know, whether it wishes us well or ill, that we shall pay any price, bear any burden, meet any hardship, support any friend, oppose any foe to assure the survival and the success of liberty. . . . And so, my fellow Americans, ask not what your country can do for you; ask what you can do for your country.

Eloquent Spellbinders of Yore

No debate in American history is more famous than Robert Hayne vs. Daniel Webster on states' rights, which occurred just before Hayne left the Senate in 1832.

Hayne, who got first licks, was stirring in his argument in favor of states' rights. But even an ally, Senator James Fredell, said in anticipation of Webster: "He has started the lion; but wait till we hear him roar and feel his claws."

In the past, Webster had proved he was no ordinary speaker. Now he'd do it again. Equipped with exhilarating energy and an overpowering demeanor in crisis, Webster was the picture of manhood, tall and foreboding, confident. He stood and addressed the Senate:

Mr. President, when the mariner has been tossed, for many days, in thick weather, and on an unknown sea, he naturally avails himself of the first pause in the storm, the earliest glance of the sun, to take his latitude, and ascertain how far the elements have driven him from his true course. Let us imitate this prudence, and, before we float farther, on the waves of this debate, refer to the point from which we departed, that we may, at least, be able to form some conjecture where we now are. I ask for the reading of the resolution.

The resolution was read, and then Webster continued, holding that vast audience.

I shall enter on no encomiums upon Massachusetts; she needs none. There she is: behold her, and judge her for yourselves. There is her history; the world knows it by heart. . . . There is Boston, and Concord, and Lexington, and Bunker Hill; and there they will remain forever. The bones of her sons, fallen in the great struggle for Independence, now lie mingled with the soil. . . . and there they will lie forever. And, sir, where American liberty raised its infant voice; and where its youth was nurtured and sustained; there it still lives, in the strength of its manhood, and full of its original spirit.

Even Webster's enemies had moist eyes. A group of Massachusetts men wept openly.

When he denounced his opponent, his words clapped like thunder. Webster spoke for three hours before closing with a last great appeal for the Union:

> When my eyes shall be turned to behold, for the last time, the sun in heaven, may I not see him shining on the broken and dishonored fragments of a once glorious Union; on states dissevered, discordant, belligerent; on a land rent with civil feuds, or drenched, it may be, in fraternal blood! Let their last feeble and lingering glance, rather, behold the gorgeous ensign of the republic, now known and honored throughout the earth, still full high advanced, its arms and trophies streaming in their original luster, not a stripe erased or polluted, nor a single star obscured . . . but everywhere, spread all over in characters of living light, blazing on all its ample folds, as they float over the sea and over the land, and in every wind under the whole heavens, that other sentiments, dear to every true American heart—Liberty *and* Union, now and forever, one and inseparable![21]

Webster sat. For several moments no one stirred, so great was the lingering effect. The sectionalism that threatened to divide the nation was, at least for a time, arrested. Soon after, when South Carolina made known her intention of leaving the Union, not one state supported her. Webster's triumph establishes him for all time among history's great orators.

Maybe you don't aspire to be another Webster. But reading his words *aloud* will build eloquence as you move down the road to power speech.

WRAPPING IT UP

Eloquent speakers and scintillating conversationalists don't spring full-grown from the forehead of Zeus. They build eloquence by deliberately working at it. This means you must:

Collect apt words and phrases and keep an inventory, but dole them out the way a miser gives up gold. Choose the single nugget to meet each need.

Add muscle to your speech by using specific, picture-building words—operating words. Choose one telling word or phrase that does the work of four or six in careless usage.

Short speeches, short sentences, short conversations—all are prized. Short is harder than long. Work for short. It pays great dividends.

Read aloud from classic audience-movers to build the reflex of eloquence. Collect your own favorite word magic. Since you're not always able to think out everything in give-and-take speaking, develop reflex eloquence to propel you to power speech—in overdrive.

11

Sloganeering: A Concise Way to Persuade and Motivate

Phillips Exeter Academy, a respected eastern school, surveyed its most successful graduates to isolate the qualities that propel achievers up the ladder. Some of the 20-odd personal qualities that emerged won't surprise you: people-smarts, good time management, directed energy, and a lifelong learning orientation. But the real sleeper was *sloganeering*, the ability to reduce desirable policies to simple values (Thomas J. Watson's "Think" for example). And since a slogan must be communicated to be effective, this means the sloganeering achiever is also a power speaker. He or she coins, adapts, and uses slogans to influence boss, peers, employees, and friends.

Archimedes said: "I could move the world if I had a place to stand." Today we add: "Yes, and the right slogan at the right time gives you a hell of a lot of leverage."

A slogan, especially if it rhymes, has a number of words that begin with the same sound, or has a strong rhythm, will move us to action. "Motorists wise Simoniz" is far more effective than "Simoniz, wise motorists" or "Wise motorists, Simoniz." The witchery of rhythm is a subtle force that influences our minds.

Seduced by "Fifty-four forty or fight," our ancestors almost went to war over Oregon in 1844. And historians trace much of the misery of the modern world to the fascination that Grant's terms of unconditional surrender held for generations of Americans.

Consider that remarkable British phrase, "His Majesty's loyal opposition," which Lord Broughton invented during the reign of George IV (1820-1830). Once uttered, people saw that criticism of an administration could be a part of good government and that a person who disagrees with the party in power isn't necessarily a traitor.

Slogans in Mass Persuasion

Often slogans are simple in appearance but potent in impact. Certainly the question "Where's the beef?" sounds innocuous enough. But when shrieked by Clara Peller, a little old lady who sounds (and looks) like a chicken, it captured the imagination of millions, zoomed the sales of Wendy's hamburgers, and provided Walter Mondale with a spinoff for harrassing Gary Hart in the 1984 primaries.

Nor is the classic slogan always positive. Dr. Samuel Johnson, the coffeehouse sage, coined memorable negative expressions. His comment, "When you're tired of London, you're tired of life," still draws tourists to watch beefeaters at the Bloody Tower.

Fund-raisers are still indebted to Winston Churchill: "We make a living by what we *get*. We make a life by what we *give*."

Phrasemaking that converts the unfathomable into the familiar is good persuasion. Witness Coca-Cola's description of the total amount of Coke consumed so far: "If all the Coca-Cola ever consumed by the human race were poured over Niagara Falls, the falls would flow at their normal rate for eight hours and fifty-seven minutes." Even if you haven't been over the falls in a barrel, this gives you a clear idea.

When you hear successful slogans, they sound natural and simple. Anyone could come up with them, right? Wrong! (As one slogan-creator said: "Where were you yesterday when the paper was blank?") That which appears artless is often so artful you don't see the sweat behind the productivity.

So what good are slogans? When *Advertising Age* announced its selection of the best TV commercials of 1983, 16 of the 75 top commercials had made use of a slogan or jingle. The simpler the idea, the better remembered. Philip B. Dusenberry, executive creative director at

BBD&O, says the key ingredients of slogans are "memorability, believability, longevity."

Honored slogans:

- *The U.S. Army: Be all you can be.* It recast the Army in a believable way.
- *Reach out and touch someone.* AT&T Long Lines' slogan asks you to do something and is warm, almost tender (not bad for a utility).
- *Everything you always wanted in a beer—and less.* This Miller Lite slogan demolished the sissified image of diet beers. It opened the door to the heavy beer drinker.
- *I love New York.* The New York Department of Commerce.
- *Don't leave home without it.* American Express.
- *With the strength of two, it's the one to chew.* Alka Mints.
- *Now you see it, now you don't.* Diet Pepsi's slogan was inspired by magicians, who traditionally say the words over disappearing acts.

Effective small businesses create their own slogans. A recreational-van seller calls his product *Wheel Estate.* It pulls people in.

At *Marketing Times,* the staff must constantly monitor certain subjects in newspapers and magazines. We popularized the movement by saying: "When in doubt, clip it out." It worked. Productivity increased.

Slogans are valuable in making *yourself* memorable. A social-page reporter asked Pearl Mesta, the greatest Washington hostess since Dolley Madison, the secret of captivating so many rich and famous people.

"It's all in the greetings and good-byes," Mesta said. "As each guest arrives, I met him or her with 'At *last* you're here!' As each leaves I expressed regrets with: 'I'm *sorry* you have to leave so *soon!*' "

Simple? Yes, power speech usually *is.* But if it's so easy, why didn't you think of it? Don't worry, though, you can always adapt it. Dedicated power speakers do.

Phrase-Making in World Affairs

Victor Hugo said: "No army can withstand the strength of an idea whose time has come." And if that idea is suitably and memorably packaged, it can move millions.

Recognizing this, world leaders spend a great deal of staff sweat coming up with globe-shaking wordage. After the hard digging is done, golden phrases emerge calmly in speech, as if by natural eloquence or divine inspiration.

Governments try to dominate public discussion of foreign policy via phrases and slogans. Editors and broadcasters help popularize these labels—the shorthand that helps make reporting easier.

In explaining why he assumed unusual powers during the Civil War, Lincoln said: "The dogmas of the quiet past are inadequate to the stormy present."

Dwight D. Eisenhower and John Foster Dulles proclaimed a fear of *falling dominoes* in Southeast Asia. John F. Kennedy talked about a *missile gap*. Richard Nixon and Henry Kissinger discussed *the new influentials*—Brazil, Nigeria, Saudi Arabia, Iran—and hoped they might act as America's *regional surrogates*.

Jimmy Carter and Zbigniew Brzezinski, surveying the Persian Gulf, Middle East, and Southwest Asia, were concerned about *arcs of crisis*. And since the Iranian revolution, policymakers have been concerned about *Islamic resurgence*. Ronald Reagan and Caspar Weinberger want to close *the window of vulnerability*. And *détente* and *linkage* remain a description of United States–Soviet relations. Israel and Lebanon agreed on an agenda for peace negotiations after Israel decided that *normalization* by some other name could work as well.

"Man is a tool-using animal," said Thomas Carlyle. "Without tools he is nothing, with tools he is all." Slogans are the tools of the power speaker. With slogans that work, you can rule the world.

Slogans in National Persuasion

In national causes, slogans—when they are right—cure (or cause) gallstones throughout the Republic. Long before the current anti-smoking movement, Horace Greeley sloganized: "Fire on one end, fool on the other." No anti-smoking polemic has lasted half so well since.

Memorable presidential administrations have ridden off into the sunset on slogans: Teddy Roosevelt's Square Deal, Wilson's New Freedom, FDR's New Deal, Harry Truman's Fair Deal, JFK's New Frontier. The less-memorable tenures of Eisenhower, Ford, Carter? No slogans.

Calvin Coolidge's laconic New England phrase-making helped his political infighting. In a smoke-filled room over a proposed candidate for Congress, one pol said: "But Mr. President, that man's an SOB." "Well," said Calvin the Silent, "there're lots of sons-of-bitches in the country. And they ought to be represented."

To date, Reagan has not produced an overall slogan. Not that his minions haven't tried. Creating a presidential word-label that people make part of the language occurs about as often as drawing four of a kind in poker. But when it does happen, it's great.

Word-Magic in Instructing and Inspiring

The typical airline passenger has great need for memorable reassurance. Yet nowhere is phrase-making in greater poverty. All the more memorable when a steward says (as one did on my friend Walter Hogan's flight): "Ladies and gentlemen, we're coming into New York, New York—the city so spectacular they had to name it twice. Look at that skyline and just remember: Each of those light bulbs was screwed in by hand!"

Refreshing and rare! That power speaker foments thousands of dollars worth of goodwill each time he gets on the intercom. His inventiveness should inspire all the droners who read dully from routine airline sheets.

Power speech is available to all. But most people don't pick up on it. When you do, welcome to the Movers & Shakers Club.

A good inspirer isn't afraid to perpetuate his own legend—even if others are doing the work. Savings and loan tycoon Bart Lytton had worked earlier as a Hollywood screenwriter for Ernst Lubitsch. The famed director called a story conference.

"What's needed here," he told the writers and production assistants, "is a typical Lubitsch touch. Please see to it." He then left the room. He had just delegated continuation of his own legend.

In the theater, the director can tell the actors what to do. But to be effective, he must *inspire* performance via adroit phrase-making. When actor Herbert Beerbohm Tree arrived in New York to join the already elaborate rehearsals for *Henry VIII*, he approved cheerfully enough of everything until he came to the collection of the queen's ladies-in-waiting. He looked at them in pained and prolonged dissatisfaction: "Ladies," said Tree, plaintively peering through his monocle, "just a little more virginity, if you don't mind."

On the gridiron, in instructing human sherman tanks with numbered jerseys, Vince Lombardi was a past master. "Winning isn't everything," Lombardi said. "It's the only thing." (Green Bay tackle Forest Gregg described Lombardi's democratic viewpoint: "He treats us all alike—like dogs.")

On winning, Jesse Unruh, the California pol kingmaker, amended: "Winning isn't everything. But losing isn't anything."

Getting compliance in the office requires memorable phrase-making. My friend John Peterson, a Los Angeles engineering office manager, wanted employees to stop overusing copying machines. He posted notices, with no results.

He called a meeting and wheeled in sloganeering. Said Petersen:

> Some people are absolute nuts about copies. They make copies and send them all over the place. It clogs up everything. The copying machine is a mixed blessing. When you need copies, it's good. When you don't need them, many make them anyhow. *The only difference between men and boys is the price of their toys.* Excess copying is an enemy of productivity.

It worked. As reminder, Petersen posted this part-slogan near the machine: "The only difference between men and boys. . . ." Excess copying was reduced drastically.

A foreman in a decorative-accessories plant wanted to improve vertical communication within the company. He called a meeting of first-line supervisors and said:

> Many organizations have a good rule: The boss *can* and *does* talk to any person. It reminds me of the question: "Where does an 800-pound gorilla sit in a restaurant?" The answer: "Any place he likes." But if the boss talks to you two levels down, go to your superior immediately afterward and repeat what *he* said and what *you* said. Keep off personalities. Talk about methodology.

Humor helped make the point.

In instructing and inspiring—both roles of the power speaker—you cannot force-feed a person. You *can* help the person *discover* for himself or herself. Slogans and phrase-making will aid that discovery.

Sloganeering in the Executive Suite

Good phrase-making starts at the top and filters down. It starts back in business school. Richard West, when dean of Dartmouth's famous Amos Tuck School (he now heads the N.Y.U. Business School), got future CEOs off on the right foot by describing his own function.

"Business schools are like bottling plants," says West. "The product is about 90 percent complete before we ever get it. We put it in a bottle and label it. The price is merely a function of what the market will pay."

Henry Ford II kept corner-office wordology going by commenting on the qualities of a top manager: "Asking 'Who ought to be boss?' is like asking, 'Who ought to be the tenor in the male quartet?' Obviously, the man who can sing tenor."

Bill MacDonald, earthy leader in the mobile-home field, once lectured a group of plant supervisors on over-correcting employees:

> Back in the barnstorming pilot days before World War II, fliers who stunted biplanes at county fairs did all their own maintenance work. One pilot asked his policies for deciding what needed fixing, said: "If it doesn't work, get a bigger hammer and hit it. If it does work, don't _____ with it." There's a good people-management lesson here.

Casey Stengel, unorthodox in personnel management as in all else, sloganized as he ruminated. Once, sitting on the bench with outfielder Bob Cerv, Ol' Case said: "Don't look now but one of us has just been transferred to Kansas City."

No executive ever fired an employee more obliquely.

Ray A. Kroc, who made McDonald's symbolize America in the 1980s, believed in persistence—and employed this slogan to get submanagers to be persistent about persistence:

> Nothing in the world can take the place of persistence.
> Talent will not; nothing is more common than unsuccessful men with talent.
> Genius will not; unrewarded genius is almost a proverb.
> Education will not; the world is full of educated derelicts.
> Persistence and determination alone are omnipotent.

Kroc had been inspired by an earlier apostle of never giving up. A young reporter once asked Thomas Edison how it felt to have failed 10,000 times with the electric light.

"Young man, since you are just starting out in life," Edison said, "I'll tell you something of benefit. I have not failed 10,000 times. I have successfully found 10,000 ways that will not work."

Edison performed more than 14,000 experiments before perfecting the incandescent lamp.

Granted, the positive thinker doesn't give up easily. But at times you must know when to stop battering against the stone wall. Remember this slogan:

> Everyone said it couldn't be done
> And the odds were so great, who wouldn't?
> But I tackled the job that couldn't be done,
> And what do you know—it couldn't.

The effective manager knows when to reassign his time to more do-able goals. Time does run out. Your goal: a project that produces actionable results. Said Winston Churchill: *"Perfectionism* is spelled P-A-R-A-L-Y-S-I-S."

Use adapatations of these slogans in managing your work, your employees, and your boss.

Sloganeering Self-Management

In this do-it-yourself era, you're naturally concerned about how speech inspires self-management. Jo Foxworth, New York ad agency head, understands this. Witness her biblical-style advice to women careerists. "Save thy sex appeal for after five," she advises, "even though thy C-cup runneth over."

Unforgettable. No wonder Foxworth is in such demand as a speaker.

On self-management of investments, Mark Twain remarked: "October is a peculiarly dangerous month to speculate in stocks. Others are November, December, January, February, March, April, May, June, July, August and September."

Will Rogers, the cowboy sage, saw it differently: "Buy some good stock and hold it. Wait for it to go up and then sell it. If it don't go up, don't buy it."

Harold J. Cummings, former chairman of Minnesota Mutual Life Insurance Co., is a phrase-maker on self-management:

- If you would move the world, you must first move yourself.
- Your *pull* will be measured by your *push.*
- Does that chip on your shoulder prove there is wood up above?
- Courage is not the absence of fear. It is the conquest of it.
- No steam engine ever ran on lukewarm water.
- A bee's stinger is scarcely an eighth of an inch. All of the rest you feel is enthusiasm.
- If you mean to leave footprints on the sands of time, wear work shoes![22]

And graffiti is often an inspiration to the phrase-seeking power speaker:

- Don't sweat the small stuff.
  P.S.: It's all small stuff.

- Don't spend a dollar's worth of energy to produce a dime's worth of result.
- Why pay for hatred? A little dislike will usually do the job.

Phrasing Your Exit

Dedicated phrasers prepare smash exit lines, like the one Sir Walter Raleigh delivered at the Tower of London just before the headsman's ax fell: "It's a sharp medicine but it cures all ills."

Shakespeare supplied his own epitaph:

> Good frend for Jesus sake forbeare,
> To digg the dust encloased heare:
> Blese be ye man yt spares thes stones.
> And curst be he yt moves my bones.

But in following slogans and in exhorting others to do so, don't take a long walk down a short pier. Remember the dictum of Émile Coué, the French psychotherapist: "Every day in every way, I'm getting better and better." That movement, John Bremner tells us, was taken seriously by a bowlegged man who followed the slogan too far and became knock-kneed.

WRAPPING IT UP

Sloganeering—either by originating choice phrases or by collecting and adapting them—is an irreplaceable attribute of the power speaker (and, by extension, of the successful leader of men and women).

The most traceable slogans are employed in business. The dollar value of *American Express—don't leave home without it* is beyond calculation.

Effective slogans and apt phrase-making have helped raise funds, re-elect presidents, avert nuclear war. An idea whose time has come—when adroitly presented via smash wordage—will move mountains.

In instructing and inspiring employees, peers, or bosses, the right phrase can make the difference between success and failure.

Sloganeering can help you manage your own work and can enhance the way you instruct others on self-management. But don't follow any slogan out the window.

12

Keep Their Attention: Be an Expert Storyteller

My speaking colleague Tom Johnston stood at the podium at a seminar for educators held at the Sheraton Center in Manhattan, waiting patiently for the delegates to quiet down. Then without preamble he told this story:

> A mother was having difficulty in getting her son up for school. He pulled the covers over his head.
> "I'm not going to school," he said. "I'm not ever going again."
> "Are you sick?" his mother asked.
> "No," he answered, "I'm sick of school. They hate me. They call me names. They make fun of me. Why should I go?"
> "I can give you two good reasons," the mother replied. "The first is you're 42 years old. And the second is *you're the school principal.*"

The audience roared, then settled down in earnest. After all, this speaker *knew* about education. Johnston capitalized on that empathy by quickly adding:

> Now if we could all pull the covers over our heads in the morning, rather than facing our problems, there'd be no need for seminars. But since we cannot, let's get down to business and face up to the three knottiest problems in education today.

He then started his speech.

Was Tom Johnston lucky to happen on that story? Did a guardian angel present it to him just before he went on? No. It came from his extensive story collection and was carefully selected to suit the group. He rehearsed it diligently ahead of time to get the emphasis just right.

That which appeared artless was, in fact, planned, practiced, and most deliberate. Hal Holbrook, extremely popular on the platform as Mark Twain, said: "It takes two weeks to prepare a good ad-lib speech." Commenting in *Nation's Business*, Peter Hannaford, former communications adviser to President Reagan, said:

> It can take years. I have been with Ronald Reagan countless times when he gave impromptu remarks to an audience. Those comments were not composed out of thin air. In most cases, he was relying on his excellent memory for anecdotes, well-turned phrases, and examples to illustrate his points. His remarks thus had a pace and conviction that brought immediate and positive audience response.

Such is the rule of power speech. Collect stories from magazines, newspapers, books, and other speakers. Adapt them to your needs, then they become yours.

Draw on this inventory for "impromptu" needs.

Where to Find and How to Tell Stories

As you start your story hunt, look for anecdotes that fire your thinking and stimulate your imagination—vignettes that reveal human nature or the way the world works as you perceive it. Jot them down in your story journal. Say them aloud as part of your oral reading exercises.

As you collect stories, you will automatically develop good listening skills, and you will discover the principles of good storytelling. As you add to your repertoire, make adjustments and amendments that suit your style.

Stories you collect and retell in your own words become vehicles for ice-breaking at luncheons, formal meetings, or social gatherings. The adroit storyteller is always in demand.

To be a memorable storyteller, set your narrative in a specific time, place, and situation. Make sure your characters *want* something specific. Let the conflict develop out of a clash of objectives. A good story is a mini-stage play: Protagonist vs. Antagonist results in Resolution. Make something happen. Conditions at the punch line must be different from those at the beginning. Insist that your main character learn something from the unfolding of the events.

Use *visual* words. Help your audience see what's going on. Get a smash opening. The first 10 words are worth the next 10,000. Work for a perfect punch line. The last thing said is the first thing remembered. Make storytelling fun. When you have a good time, your audience will, too.

Update classic stories. John Randolph, House floor leader for Thomas Jefferson, once flayed a colleague thusly: "His mind is like a parcel of land, poor to begin with and rendered more barren by too intensive cultivation."

In 1919, almost 90 years after Randolph died, Senator Thaddeus Caraway of Arkansas scored Massachusetts senator Henry Cabot Lodge: "I have long heard of the reputation for wisdom and wit of the senator from Massachusetts, but his speech today has convinced me that his mind is like the land of his native state, barren by nature and impoverished by cultivation." Senator Caraway got credit for spontaneous wit. Yet Caraway had stored the Randolph story away until needed.

Draw on your story inventory to add light touches to your speeches. An apt line will spark creativity, inspiring you to refine, rephrase, redesign a comment to fit specific audiences and occasions. By the time you finish revising it, the story will be yours.

Once you've collected and selected appropriate stories for your speech, you're ready to rehearse. Learn to tell anecdotes in a direct and animated manner. Paint word pictures of situations and players. Never start by saying, "That reminds me of a story," or, "Let me illustrate my point with an anecdote I find amusing." Simply begin: "Last month the mayor of a Nevada town was startled to learn . . ."

In telling a story, never telegraph your punch line. Imply your point, but don't state it outright; give the listener a sense of participation.

What Makes a Good Anecdote?

Stories are invaluable for opening and closing speeches, sprinkling through presentations, brightening conversation. Your listeners will recall a clever story long after they forget other speech details. An anecdote, aptly chosen and skillfully presented, will stick in the memory as a reminder of your main point.

To be good, anecdotes must:

- Be suitable to the context. They're never dragged in for their own sake.

- Arouse curiosity and concern over the outcome.
- Make the point quickly. Attention wanders during a tiresome narrative.
- Have a clear point to make. No story that must be explained is effective.
- Add interest by using names, places, dates.
- Be in good taste. If you are in doubt about a story, then don't use it.
- Be artfully presented. Rehearse before you tell.

The Power Speaker's Starter Set

Here are candidates for your story starter set, arranged by topic with suggested tie-ins to the subject:

Topic: When Things Go Wrong

Tie-in: A sense of humor about yourself and your follies is a valuable asset. When things get out of hand, think about this analysis from a retired dean of management named Murphy:

- If anything can go wrong, invariably it will, and at the worst possible time.
- Everything you decide to do costs more than you first estimated, and every activity takes more time than you have.
- Whatever you set out to do, something else must be done first.
- If you tinker with something long enough, eventually it will break.
- By making something absolutely clear, somebody will be confused.
- You can fool some of the people all of the time and all of the people some of the time, and that's sufficient.
- Nothing is impossible for the person who doesn't have to do it.
- Anytime things appear to be going better, you have overlooked something.
- Once a job is fouled up, anything done to improve it makes it worse.
- Every discovered gain is more than offset by some undiscovered loss.
- Never tell anyone your troubles. Half the people don't care. The other half are glad you're finally getting what's coming to you!

Topic: Striving for Perfection

Tie-in: We must all work to get better. Only the amateur disdains rehearsal.

A young reporter was assigned to interview cellist Pablo Casals on Casals' ninetieth birthday. Anxious to make a good impression, the reporter arrived at Casals' home two hours early. Five hours later, he was still waiting—while beautiful cello sounds came drifting through the room. When Casals finally came out, the young man said: "I've been waiting for five hours! What were you doing all this time?"

"Practicing," said Casals with a contented sigh.

"Practicing?" said the reporter. "You are the best cellist in the world. Why do you have to practice five hours a day?"

"Simple," replied the master. "I want to get better."

Topic: Delegating Work

Tie-in: One of our supervisors told me the other day: "I'd rather do the job myself. Then I know it will be done right." But there're not enough hours in the day for that. Delegation is vital. Consider this story from the eighteenth chapter of the book of Exodus:

> Jethro, Moses' father-in-law, saw Moses staggering under the problem of delegation. All by himself, Moses was trying to perform the impossible task of judging and supervising his people. Jethro came to Moses and said:
>
> "The thing you are doing is not good. You will surely wear away, both you and these people who are with you; for this thing is too heavy for you; you are not able to perform it by yourself."
>
> Jethro then counseled Moses on how to solve the problem: "Select able men to be rulers of thousands, and rulers of hundreds, rulers of fifties and rulers of tens. Let them judge the people at all seasons. Every great matter they shall bring to you, every small matter they shall judge themselves. It will be easier for you. They will bear the burden with you."
>
> Moses listened to his father-in-law. He chose able men out of all Israel and made them heads over the people and they judged the people. The hard cases they brought to Moses, but every small matter they judged themselves.

Topic: First Things First

Tie-in: In order to advance in a career, you have to get your first job. That initial effort is what sets everything else in motion.

Someone once asked Senator Alben W. Barkley, "What does it take to make a great senator?"

"First," said Barkley, "you've got to get elected."

Topic: Finishing on Time

Tie-in: No matter how much time you allow, some people will miss the delivery date. Some say God created the world in six days—but promised it in four.

A woman cleaning her parents' attic discovered a tattered shoe-repair ticket dated 68 years ago. She took the ticket to the shop. The repairman carefully inspected it, went to the back, and returned saying: "Your shoes will be ready Tuesday."

Topic: The Motivating Power of Bargains

Tie-in: We spend our lives trying to find something for nothing. We never really succeed, because there is no free lunch. But does that keep us from trying again and again? Not at all. The desire to get something for free is basic. A fantastic bargain has powerful appeal—even if it's something you don't need.

A man once got a call about an unusual bargain in elephant sandwiches. An entire carload was suddenly available. Quality was A-1—they were the best elephant sandwiches on earth.

"But I'm a vegetarian," the man told the caller. "I eat no meat. Even if I did, I don't believe in killing off endangered species. On top of that, I'm on a liquid diet. Doctor's orders. There's no way you could possibly sell me any elephant sandwiches."

The caller remained calm. "I forgot to tell you," he said. "These elephant sandwiches are only 25 cents apiece."

The buyer changed his tune. "Now you're talking my language," he said.

Topic: Tapping Human Potential

Tie-in: Regardless of age, we all have inherent potential for accomplishment yet to be fulfilled.

A minister once asked a lad, "Sonny, who made you?" And the boy replied, "To tell you the truth sir, I ain't done yet."

In Tampa, Florida, a teen-age boy jacked up his car and crawled under to tinker with the oil pan. Suddenly, the jack slipped and the car crashed down, pinning the youth. His cries brought his mother and father.

The father reasoned he couldn't pick up a 3,500 lb. car so he reached for the jack. But the mother grabbed hold of the rear bumper, lifted the car and her son rolled free. The woman was 49 years old, in ill health, and weighed 123 pounds. What she did was a physical impossibility, but as she later said: "I only knew I had to save my boy."

People perform incredible feats under hypnosis in times of crises, demonstrating that we all have tremendous unfulfilled potential mentally. William James claimed people used only 10 percent of their brain power. In seminars on human potential, scientists have found that the equivalent of the human brain would be a 5 billion digit computer that can handle seven computer programs simultaneously—technology so powerful it'd take the Mississippi River to cool it!

Topic: Being Close to Target

Tie-in: Being close pays off in only two areas: pitching horseshoes and dancing. Close is a way to describe failure, it's when you *almost* care enough to want the very best.

Marvin's mother called from the other room: "Marvin, are you spitting in the goldfish bowl?" Marvin answered: "No, but I'm coming pretty close."

Topic: Following Advice

Tie-in: You've heard a lot of advice here tonight. Most classic advice can be boiled down to a few simple principles. For example, novelist Nelson Algren received this advice from a prison inmate:

Never eat in a restaurant called Mom's.
Never play cards with a man called Doc.
Never sleep with a woman who has more troubles than you do.

Topic: Providing Accurate Estimates

Tie-In: We must have precise estimates from this division.

Once Colonel Willard F. Rockwell, founder of Rockwell International, was talking to his regional sales manager. "How many can you sell?" the Colonel asked.

"A hell of a lot," said the regional manager.

"How many?" the Colonel persisted.

"Well," said the R.M., "I wouldn't want to put a number on it, but I'm sure we can sell a hell of a lot."

Colonel Rockwell exploded. "Goddamn it, Carl, a handful of wet cow turd isn't very much if you want to fertilize a 40-acre field, but if someone shoves it in your face, it's a hell of a lot."

Topic: Need for Entrepreneurship

Tie-in: Today we need the unconventional man and woman in corporate circles. Many of today's CEOs couldn't pass their own companies' personnel-screening procedures. Let's encourage the unusual person who doesn't fit the mold. Here's the résumé of a man who wouldn't get past most personnel departments today:

Incident	Age
Failed in business	22
Ran for legislature, defeated	23
Failed in business again	24
Elected to legislature	25
Sweetheart died	26
Suffered nervous breakdown	27
Defeated for speaker of legislature	29
Defeated elector	31
Defeated for Congress	34
Elected to Congress	37
Defeated for Congress	39
Defeated for Senate	46
Defeated for vice president	47
Defeated for Senate	49
Elected president of the United States	51

That's the résumé of Abraham Lincoln.

Topic: Need to Communicate with Colleagues

Tie-in: When a manager says nothing, goes into an office, and sulks, he's displeased with a subordinate. Silent treatment communicates the manager's own inadequacy in dealing with the problem. Don't sulk—communicate.

> Don't be like Archie Bunker. Archie complained to the parish priest that his Italian neighbors were taking Edith to too many functions at the local Catholic church.
> "If Edith seems interested," said the priest, "maybe that's telling you something. Why don't you try to communicate with her?"
> "Why should I try to communicate with huh?" Archie said. "Jeez, we live in da same house dere."

When you live in the same house, communication is *particularly* important.

Collect Quotable Quotes

Anecdotes taken from inventory, dusted off, and updated are extremely useful. At times, however, you need to *build* an anecdote on the spot. The best raw material: quotations.

Collect quotations. Keep only quotes that appeal to you. Here are starters. Make your favorites part of your inventory:

He uses statistics as a drunken man uses lampposts—for support rather than illumination.

Andrew Lang

Those who cannot remember the past are condemned to repeat it.

George Santayana

What do you give a man who has everything? Penicillin!

Jerry Lester

The last time I saw him, he was walking down lover's lane holding his own hand.

Fred Allen (about Jack Benny)

A billion here, a billion there—pretty soon we'll be talking about real money.

Senator Everett Dirksen

Every man sees in his relatives a series of grotesque caricatures of himself.

H. L. Mencken

Ever wrestle with a pig? You both get dirty and the pig loves it!

Anonymous

The trouble with being punctual is that nobody's there to appreciate it.

Anonymous

Experience: what you get when you didn't get what you wanted.

Anonymous

Always do right. This will gratify some people and astonish the rest.

Mark Twain

The man who has no more problems to solve is out of the game.

Elbert Hubbard

The only difference between stumbling blocks and stepping-stones is the way we use them.

Anonymous

It is a funny thing about life. If you refuse to accept anything but the best, you very often get it.

W. Somerset Maugham

I am easily satisfied with the very best.

Winston Churchill, in describing the level of quality he expected.

If you are going to soar with eagles in the morning, you can't hoot with the owls all night.

Anonymous

Dr. Samuel Johnson characterized second marriages as a triumph of hope over experience.

Politics is the art of obtaining money from the rich and votes from the poor, on the pretext of protecting each from the other.

Traditional

In politics, merit is rewarded by the possessor being raised, like a target, to a position to be fired at.

Christian Bovee

Every time we have an election, we get in worse men, and the country keeps right on going. History has proved one thing: You can't ruin this country even with politics.

Will Rogers

When you are down and out, something always turns up—and it is usually the noses of your friends.

Orson Welles

Going to church doesn't make a man a Christian any more than going into a garage makes a man an automobile.

Billy Sunday

I'm opposed to millionaires, but it would be dangerous to offer me the position.

Mark Twain

One of the best ways to measure people is to watch the way they behave when something free is offered.

Ann Landers

I'm in hock for over a million. What am I supposed to do, switch to nickel cigars?

                                                                    Michael Todd

I have no time to be in a hurry.

                                                                    John Wesley

Be a Permanent Collector

Once you get started acquiring stories and quotations, collecting will become part of your life as a power speaker.

Look for material everywhere. Adapt it to your own needs. A good story is worth a thousand textbooks. The lively storyteller can touch the mind and the heart, melt the ice and cool the fires of resistance, and build empathy and receptivity.

WRAPPING IT UP

Anecdotes are the vital difference between boredom and enlightenment. You can pile fact on fact to build the strongest argument in the world, but people will quickly forget it unless that argument is accompanied by lively illustrations. Stories are windows into arguments. They allow your audience to "see" and remember.

It is impossible to overemphasize the value of anecdotes. You simply can't get along without them. Your speech is a series of statements and facts. Each must be illustrated by an anecdote. Speeches and conversation without illustrations are deadly and dull.

Put yourself into the story. Color it with real feelings. Make it important for yourself and meaningful to your listeners. Look for reactions from your immediate audience. Adapt each story to the here and now.

Never tell a good story the same way twice. Give stories "the illusion of the first time" by practicing them aloud.

Good illustrations are all around you waiting to be collected. Develop a simple, usable system for finding and classifying materials.

Stories entertain, inform, or inspire. Thus you make people listen and act—every power speaker's goal.

PART IV

Fine-Tuning Your Speech

13

Your Voice: Improving Your Basic Instrument

In high school Jack Chase was plagued by stuttering. Bright and ambitious, he was determined to lick the problem—he wasn't about to be held back. "Your brain works faster than your tongue," a sympathetic teacher told Chase. "You've got to build in some *deliberate* pauses in your speech."

Jack slowed down, placing planned blocks in his sentences. He attended Fairleigh Dickinson's Reading and Study Institute, where instructors taught him to read aloud with a Beethoven Symphony on the phonograph—"to give structure to speech." He was assigned as homework an activity that many perform as a hobby: singing in the shower. He progressed so well at school that he became an instructor in the evening classes.

Today Chase heads up Chase Marketing and Sales, Hampton, Virginia. He recruits, trains, and supervises sales reps for companies selling consumer products to retailers. Not only is perfect speech required for his own work, he *instructs* other salesfolk on *what* to say and *how* to say it. Further, he is a bishop in the Mormon Church. He presides masterfully over large and small meetings several days each week. There's no trace of stutter in his standard American speech.

"What people don't know," Chase says, "is that the stutter is always lurking in the background—trying to get out. I'm particularly vulnerable when I'm tired. I must always keep it under control." But people who overcome a speech impediment often end up with excellent speech—Demosthenes and Churchill are two well-known examples.

That's quite a lesson in what determination can do to drastically improve a voice problem! Compare Jack Chase's dedication to George Gloom's fatalism: "I'm just that way. Nothing can be done about it."

In 90 percent of voice problems, something *can* be done. Whether it *will* be done is up to you. If you are afflicted with a mechanical speech problem, such as a stutter, stammer, or lisp, get professional help. Good instruction, along with dedication and practice under direction, can transform you.

Lauren Bacall, as Betty Perske in a Bronx high school, had a thin voice not unlike many of her colleagues. When she became a fashion model, who cared how she sounded? But when she went to Hollywood to appear in *To Have and Have Not* with Humphrey Bogart, she ran headlong into a voice problem. Her thin, reedy Betty Perske sound just wouldn't do.

Director Howard Hawks sent Bacall out to the canyons to yell. Under his tutelage, she developed the husky throaty sound that made her famous. Triumph of therapy over problem. As the poet Lord Byron said:

> The devil hath not, in all his quiver's choice,
> An arrow for the heart like a sweet voice.

Nasality, Shrieks, Monotones

Maybe you have a nasal sound. Actually, nasal is a misnomer. By *not* talking through the nose—thus losing the desired resonance that comes from throwing your voice through the upper head passages—you get a sound called nasal.

To test yourself for nasality, clasp your nose between thumb and forefinger (to close your nostrils) and say, "Woe, oh woe, oh woe, oh woe!" The sound should come *entirely* from your mouth. If you buzz, even on those *o* vowels, you are a nose talker.

An actor playing a complaining character sometimes adopts nasal speech. When exaggerated, it's funny. Carol Burnett's cohort, Vicki Lawrence, uses nasality effectively portraying Mama on TV.

But for normal speech, you cannot be lovable at first listen if you talk through your nose—whining, lifeless, negative. Your voice comes out through your nose if your mouth does not open enough. When you look into the mirror and say, "Hi, you wonderful, lovable creature!" you should see a half-inch strip of darkness between your teeth.

If your teeth are jammed together like corn on a cob (or if your lips are virtually closed like a ventriloquist's), you almost certainly speak nasally. If you want to be persuasive at work or seductive after hours, get your resonance from your stomach and in the upper cavities of the head, not your nose.

Think of your vocal cords as guitar strings. Pluck a string in the open air without the resonating box. You get noise, but not a sastisfactory sound. Just a *plunk*.

Your vocal cords work the same way. To get power and projection and richness, you must resonate sound through the cavities of chest and head—preferably both. Without reverberation in these caverns, you get a timid, weak, uninteresting sound. With the right force and maximum resonance, you can sound like Richard Burton reading "Under Milk Wood" by Dylan Thomas (providing, of course, that's what you're reciting).

When you achieve good resonance, you possess an orotund quality—full, rich tones usually delivered at a slow rate. Clergymen employ orotundity in reading scriptures with holiness, awe, profound respect. As Aldous Huxley said: "A good voice can transform the most conventional of sermons into something like a divine revelation."

To produce orotund sounds, exercise your resonating chambers to the fullest. Stress vowel sounds particularly. Your lips form a natural megaphone.

The orotund quality can be extremely effective when properly used, but when substituted for sincere feeling, it turns into bombast—a problem Richard Nixon never overcame. Many old-style orators, still heard occasionally at political conventions, make matter-of-fact statements in orotund.

Are you guilty of speaking in a monotone? A few years back, a movie performer named Virginia O'Brien made a brief splash as a deadpan monotonist. After the novelty wore off, the fickle fans went on to idolize others. She strutted and fretted off the stage. Monotony doesn't wear well.

Enthusiasm, which is knowledge on fire, is the enemy of monotone. When you emphasize the right words, you can produce inflection. Speak enthusiastically. It's catching! Enthusiasm moves the world.

When enthusiasm is out of place, make certain you at least avoid sameness. After centuries of experiment, the Chinese evolved the ultimate torture: a victim in solitary, in the dark, listening to slowly dripping water. In time, the prisoner can be bored to death. If you speak in a monotone, you are torturing your listeners.

Throwing Your Voice to the Last Row

Another kind of torture is not being able to hear a speaker. A clubwoman got up to speak. Only the first few rows could hear her. "She might as well have stayed home," one backbencher whispered loudly. More women heard the critic than the speaker—who suffered from lack of projection.

Projection is packaging sound in the cavities of your head and chest and throwing it out "so they can hear it in the cheap seats," as theater folk used to say.

This means speaking from the diaphragm—not the throat only. If you have trouble making yourself heard, get professional help. Ever wonder why the old-time carny barker held a cane against his lower chest with both hands? It aided him in voice projection.

If you shout for a living—as commodities traders do—you'd better shout from the diaphragm. If you don't, you soon won't be able to talk at all. (Pit trading has never been gentle. In 1984, a corn futures trader bit a rival's earlobe. The trader needed stitches.)

In a recent newspaper article, Chicago voice coach William Rush stated that most traders require three to five sessions to learn proper voice projection. From Rush's office in Chicago's Lyric Opera building, two baritones can be heard singing a strange song: "65s at a half. 65s at a half. Six on 60. Six on 60. Three bid 70s. Three bid 70s." Besides showing them how to make their bids or offers carry over other voices, Rush also trains traders to keep their voices from rising in anxiety over a weak trading position and thus tipping off their bellowing rivals.

Do his techniques work? Jim Downs, a Rush student and a trader for three and a half years, says yes. "One day a broker wanted to buy December 160 calls at $2," he says. "I was about halfway across the pit, but I'm the one he heard. I sold him 25."

The Tape Recorder: Your Valuable Ally

Often not *what* you say but *how* you say it makes a difference in establishing your reputation and image. To find out whether you speak in a modulated, expressive voice and have good diction, use a tape recorder. When you hear yourself on tape for the first time, you'll shudder and exclaim: "Is that me? I don't sound like that."

Maybe you *wish* you didn't! Maybe you *hope* you won't always sound that way. Maybe you *will* sound better in the future. But for now, believe it, old sport. The tape doesn't lie.

Taping yourself is the first step. Only by being conscious of what needs changing can you improve. Make a note of what changes are needed and try again. After repeated playbacks, you'll start making adjustments in speed, volume, pitch, and tonal quality. If improvement is blocked by tension (from tight mouth or throat muscles or nerves), you may need to consult a speech therapist.

A tape recorder, the best investment you'll ever make, is a workhorse. Use it to review ideas aloud, to edit and practice speeches and presentations, to rehearse interviews, to record your voice on the telephone. By listening and refining, you'll soon be able to come across the way you want to come across.

As you play the tape, ask yourself these questions:

> Voice too high?
> Speaking too fast?
> Voice too low?
> Too monotonous?
> Enough pauses?
> Words hard to pronounce?
> Meaning conveyed?

Read famous speeches aloud and tape yourself whenever you can. (See Chapter 10, "Adding Eloquence to Your Speech," for selections to read aloud.) Oral reading slows your speech and forces you to mouth each word exactly.

Reading aloud enriches your life and triggers a deeper part of yourself. It awakens your built-in capacity for adding emotion, attitude, and rhythm to words. Every time you listen to how you sound, you get a clearer picture of how others hear you.

Avoid the catch phrases, the slick slogans, the current jargon—they usually represent the worst choice of words. Managers known for using buzzwords often become the butt of jokes (behind their backs). Keep your speech fresh, alive, immediate.

Reading aloud is valuable exercise for the professional communicator. No matter how good a speaker you already are, you can improve by reading aloud. Try it for six weeks. Then compare an early tape with your most recent one. You'll be astounded at the improvement in confidence, poise, impact.

As you read, you'll discover you're beginning to emphasize your arguments with hand gestures. Let this happen. Your reflex gestures will pay dividends when you're on your feet in public.

In sound and gesture, you're building reflexes that recur to your credit when you speak your mind under pressure.

The Pause that Refreshes

Reading aloud helps develop a good sense of when *not* to read aloud— that is, when to insert the strategic pause. A well-timed block of silence can be more powerful than sound.

Mortimer Levitt, founder of the Custom Shop shirtmakers, has devised an astoundingly simple way of improving diction. His formula: Place a comma between *each* word. Says Levitt:

> If, I, place, an, invisible, comma, after, each, word, and, an, invisible, semicolon; after, some; words, my speech, has, presence.[23]

Try it. You'll see an improvement almost immediately. The inaudible comma makes each word stand by itself—no matter what your pace.

You can extend this exercise further by marking up a speech or presentation script. If a word is underlined, say *beat* to yourself after the word. If the word is circled, say *beat beat* after the word. A dash going upward means rising inflection. A dash going down means drop your voice (usually needed at the end of a sentence of summation).

Now mark your script for one beat and two beats. Mark upward and downward inflections. Read the first sentence slowly. Then (beat), attack the second sentence at a faster pace and higher volume. What you're doing is *orchestrating* the spoken word. No conductor steps up to the podium without building in highs, lows, pauses, attacks. Neither should you.

Vary your pitch, volume, and pace. You've given the passage new color, provided it with rhythm effective for the ear. Do this throughout your entire speech or presentation and you're on your way to making a memorable impact.

Listen to John Houseman on investment commercials, Charles Kuralt on CBS's *Sunday Morning*, Tom Brokaw on *NBC Network News*. Although their voices are unmistakably their own, each has one quality in common: *Each, word, stands, by, itself.* That's the professional's secret.

This also explains why actors and announcers sound so different from the people who call in to talk shows. On one TV call-in show, a woman delivered a 204-word message—and 32 of those words were *ah*. She was pausing all right, but she was filling the pause with garbage. No wonder the host just said: "Thank you for sharing. Now we must move on."

Do you add *ahs* and *yunnos* where silence would be golden? Only your tape recorder knows for sure. Speakers who are afraid of dead air bring forth a steady stream of garbage. Don't be afraid to stop to collect your thoughts. A strategic silence is far better than any *ah, uh,* or *yunno*.

Much of the art of speaking lies in timing. The story told by A to tumultuous applause meets with a stony silence when told by B. The words are the same. But if the pauses are wrong, the effect is quite different. Punctuate your speech with pauses to let your ideas sink in.

First read a speech passage aloud without any pauses. Then read it again and insert the pauses. You'll hear the difference at once. A pause, properly used, heightens the dramatic effect. It helps make the meaning clearer.

Now let the pendulum swing the other way. Read the same passage aloud again, giving each word the same stress and the same emphasis—with pauses of the same length between each word. Now you've gone too far in the other direction. The message does not come through. You sound like a robot in a sci-fi movie.

For impact, pause a few moments after each important point. Let the audience chew and digest. Don't lower your eyes during the pause. Continue to look at the audience. Some speakers count up to five for important pauses.

Refining Your Voice

For better or worse, your voice reveals who you are. Listeners form an immediate impression from how you sound—friendly or cold, honest or false, strong or weak. This impression is subjective and often subconscious. Listeners are hard-pressed to explain why they like one sound and distrust another. But the judgments take place every day.

You must improve the impression you make by improving your voice in the following areas:

Volume

You normally use three levels of voice—low, conversational, and loud. Experienced speakers use six levels—from a stage whisper to a stentorian bellow.

Key your volume to content. Use considerable volume on ideas needing emphasis and employ low volume for somber content. The sound of authority is slightly loud but relaxed, without shouting. Between a shout and a whisper, variations of loudness showcase your words.

With practice, you can project to the balcony—even if you're whispering. (Watch actors do this the next time you attend the professional theater.)

Actors can speak louder without changing their pitch or voice quality. They project without being harsh or strident.

Elizabeth Taylor's good screen characterization in *Who's Afraid of Virginia Woolf?* was marred considerably by shrieking in the higher register. Ditto her stage performance in *The Little Foxes.* As a movie-trained actress, she never learned the stage actor's technique of projecting from the diaphragm. This shows when her character needs to turn up the high volume (as the characters she plays often *do*).

To check your own progress, practice with a friend standing across the room to advise you whether you're projecting or shouting. Too little volume sounds as if you're afraid to be authoritative. The always-loud voice signals *insecurity* (an effort to compensate for inferiority feelings).

Power speakers keep their voices under control. Save high volume for when you need it. (Using only high volume is monotonous.) Some supervisors demonstrate power over subordinates by speaking so softly everyone is forced to lean forward in a reverent position to hear. (This works when you use it sparingly and appropriately. All emphasis is no emphasis.)

Control your voice. Don't allow your voice to say *fatigued* when you're fresh, *weak* when you're strong, *frustrated* when you want it to say *confident*.

Tension, the enemy of voice control, produces high-pitched, too-fast, too-loud sounds. Tension produces physiological changes in the vocal cords that add a squeakiness to the voice. When a busy employee is interrupted by the phone and forgets to switch gears, he often projects *impatience*. The caller judges the company as impatient. This can be a damning indictment.

Rate

Although Americans speak at different speeds in different places (urbanites faster, southerners slower), power speakers generally produce words at a slightly slower-than-average rate for their area. The effective speaker makes each word stand out, which takes slightly longer. Also, the power speaker wants to give speech a serious cachet.

A baseball pitcher forces the batter to stay alert by changing pace. Do the same to your audience. Vary your speed to keep your listeners challenged.

Ever get impatient with a slower-than-molasses speaker? The speaker might have been ill at ease, too. You might have sounded to him like a 33 rpm record spinning at 45. Each person thinks he or she speaks at a normal rate. If you speak at the listener's rate, you will be perceived as trustworthy. On TV's *Dallas*, J. R. Ewing is a fast talker in a world of slow talkers. Your gut response: I don't trust this man.

The average speaker delivers 125 to 200 words per minute. But audiences can comprehend language much faster. Adapt your pace to the audience, the situation, the content. For example: The personnel manager presenting new insurance alternatives to employees must alter delivery so all present can evaluate each point. Keep fast-paced speech in reserve to impart urgency when you need it. Don't overdo. Again, all emphasis is no emphasis.

Inflection

Ronald Reagan is a master of vocal inflection. It gives warmth and vibrance to what he says and plays a large part in his popularity.

Inflection is change in intonation and pitch that shades meaning. When you ask a question, you use an upward inflection. The same words, with a different inflection, indicate a statement of fact. Rising inflection on non-questions characterizes southern speech.

Pitch

Pitch is the level of your voice (soprano, alto, tenor, bass). Western society prefers a low-pitched voice for both men and women. As broadcasters demonstrate conclusively, a low voice conveys assurance and relaxed authority. High-pitched voices sound immature, strident, hysterical.

Without a recording, you will never realize that a high-pitched voice could be your problem; that's what happened to me. In high school, my voice had never changed into deeper adult tones. I didn't know that until Elizabeth Welch, an influential speech teacher, recorded my voice. Then I realized I sounded like a pre-pubescent girl.

I did relaxation exercises. (Make yourself limp like a rag doll, so limp you fall on the floor, then lie on your back and repeat, in the lowest tones you can produce: "Out of the cradle, endlessly rocking, the nightingale's voice is a musical shuttle!") That produced open vocal cords because of less tension and encouraged lower tones.

These exercises, plus a general awareness, coupled with re-recordings to check progress, did it. Four recordings later, I sounded like a different person. Because I sounded different, I *was* different. A lower voice changed my life.

Many women reach 21 and older and still talk in a childish treble. Actors mimic babyish voices in comedy (Fanny Brice did with her Baby Snooks character). Most women can't afford to sound like Baby Snooks all the time. As philosopher Brendan Francis said: "Men will always delight in a woman whose voice is lined with velvet." And, he should have added, vice versa.

Once you reach a good, low, basic pitch, speak at that level in most situations—to give the impression you're in control and not buffeted about by emotion. Reserve variations in pitch for situations when you need emotional overtones to win a point. Over-use of pitch variations makes you sound melodramatic.

Your voice generally gets higher in pitch under stress. As you gain speaking experience, you are more relaxed, nervousness decreases, and pitch drops. Cordelia in Shakespeare's *King Lear* was an experienced speaker. Said Lear: "Her voice was ever soft, gentle and low—an excellent thing in woman!"

Demosthenes developed his voice by going to the seashore and speaking over the roar of waves—with his mouth full of pebbles. Congressman Brooks Hays of Arkansas described how he used marbles in a public speaking course: "At the beginning of the course, each student was given a mouthful of marbles. After each practice speech, we were allowed to reduce the number by one marble. After we lost all our marbles, we became accomplished public speakers."

Flexibility

Notice how good announcers and actors, lawyers, preachers, and persuasive salespeople vary their voices. That makes their words mean more. When you couch words in a flexible voice, your meaning grows.

Work for a range from about three notes below your natural pitch to three notes above. On the telephone or radio, you need a seven-note range, because your listeners can't see your facial expressions and gestures. Voice must do it all.

The power speaker who can inspire others to top performance has a marked advantage. Influential people usually have persuasive voices. About Theodore Roosevelt, critic H. L. Mencken—normally no praiser of presidents—said: "He was excited about what he did. He had the ability to get others excited about his actions, too." In short, Roosevelt had an inspiring voice.

WRAPPING IT UP

You are judged by your voice. We tend to avoid voices that grate on our nerves. Voices can soothe, irritate, intimidate, discourage, or inspire.

Listen to your own voice critically on tape. Decide if your pitch is too high. To correct this fault, consciously relax your vocal cords and force your voice down to a lower pitch. Practice the exercises regularly. In time, your low pitch will become second nature.

To get pleasing, colorful vocal delivery, you must blend volume variation with changes in the *rate* of speaking, ample *pauses,* and skillful use of *inflection.* As you gain experience, this becomes largely subconscious. Your voice will automatically respond to the demands of each situation.

To improve diction, place an invisible comma between each word— it works.

Use pauses in silence. Don't fill dead air with garbage words.

An ideal speaker produces volume to fill a room, in low tones that caress the eardrums, at a pace that's interesting without being incomprehensible. Work for resonance in chest and head cavities. Learn to speak from the diaphragm. Get a good, low pitch that's yours. But be prepared to go three notes above and below it when you seek special effects.

The voice is the dial we use to tune in on other personalities. When your voice is clear and well broadcast, you're easy to listen to. The persuasive voice gets the right kind of results. It quiets frayed nerves, convinces hesitant minds, uplifts dejected spirits, turns away anger, commands respect, changes negative attitudes, and increases your popularity.

14

The Dynamic Techniques of Verbal Persuasion

Bob Jones and George Halloran worked together in the shipping department. Both wanted the promotion when their boss retired. Bob had the edge in knowing the work. But George made up a presentation about new methods and gave it to the general manager.

"George knows where the department is going," the general manager explained to the executive committee. "And he can articulate it. Bob may know the work but never opens his mouth. George is our best bet for the promotion."

Bob did the work better. But George got the better job. Score another victory for persuasive speech.

You, too, can use power speech to persuade—to gain power over others. Remember those exotic ad headlines in pulp detective magazines: Five Easy Ways to Gain Power Over Your Fellow Man. Ah yes! We all want to make others do our bidding.

Society pays a premium to people who develop persuasion power. The profession of personal salesmanship, in fact, emerged to serve this need. And salesfolk, the good ones, wield much of their power through speech.

The Darvin Theory

Bob Darvin, the founder and moving force behind the Scandinavian Design furniture store chain, based in Natick, Massachusetts, knows power speech inside out—what you should and shouldn't say to persuade.

"Never say, 'May I help you?' to a customer," Darvin says. "If you do, the only answer is, 'No, I'm just looking'—even from people sincerely interested in buying."

Instead, Darvin's salesfolk approach the prospect with: "Have you seen the way this chair leg is molded into the body of the chair? It's our proof that it comes to us from Denmark." Whether the prospect has or not, it starts a conversation. And a stimulating conversation is the first important step to persuasion.

By eliminating "May I help you" and using "Look at this," Darvin outsells his competitors as year chases year.[24]

Defusing Explosive Words

Knowing what to say is important. Knowing how to avoid explosive words is sometimes even more valuable. Be aware of these potential grenades and don't touch them with a ten-foot sapper's stick.

- *Contract.* Never talk about a contract when you're the persuader. Talk about *our understanding*. It's just as legal. And it switches the power back to you. Wondering if the teenager has authority to buy? Don't ask outright. Say: "Isn't it nice to have your own money!" And watch the reaction.

- *Signing.* Your persuadee should never "sign" anything. Ask him to "O.K. the understanding" or to "initial our project."

- *Objections.* Your persuadee's objections are really *points* that must be *handled*, says Robert Ringer in *Selling Through Intimidation*.

- *Subscribe.* People doing telephone sales for a Chicago newspaper are able to sign up hundreds of subscribers by eliminating the word *subscribing* from their vocabularies.

Housewife: I don't want to subscribe.
Caller: No, ma'am, we aren't doing that. We just want you to start getting the newspaper at home rather than *down at the corner*. [Emphasize *down at the corner* and she thinks you know the *specific* corner. Actually, you have no idea where she gets it.]

Housewife: Well, fine. As long as I don't have to *subscribe.*
Caller: No, just start getting the newspaper at home. That's all.

Choosing words that go down easily gives you power. Use these powerful persuasion expressions:

- "I want to make certain I understand how you feel."
- "May I ask why you feel that way?"
- "I would like very much for you to give us the go-ahead. We're in a position to do a good job for you."
- "In addition to that, is there any other reason for not moving forward on this matter now?"
- "Let's move forward on this basis."

These expressions—confidence-builders and resistance-chasers—boost your persuasion power.

Everyone must persuade. No matter what your job, you must convince someone—your boss, employees, stockholders, or suppliers. To do this, you need power words and phrases, words that change moods from *no* to *yes.* Making your persuadee yes-minded is golden.

Value of the "Yes"-Response

If the buyer gets into the habit of saying *yes* all along, saying *yes* when you ask the important closing questions is natural enough. If on the other hand, you allow the customer to develop a *no* outlook, you can lose the sale on attitude alone.

Use positive questions to generate a "yes" response:

"You like the pattern, don't you?"
"Yes."

"Perhaps you're wondering just what this attachment does?"
"Yes, I have been."

"Would this go well with the drapes in your dining room?"
"Yes, it would."

By asking yes-generating questions, you can build a series of favorable responses.

Let's say you're a travel agent. You soon learn to avoid turn-off words like *if.* You never say: "*If* you take this trip to London, you'll get a free trip to Henry VIII's Hampton Court."

Which is a much better word. Say: "*Which* of these free trips would you prefer when you go to London? Shall I make out your ticket for June or July?"

In one case, your listener is wondering if she's going at all. In the other, she's choosing between two ways to go. Use *which*, not *if*.

Remember the power speaker's S.O.S.—something or something. Avoid S.O.N.—something or nothing.

In influencing others, certain words have proved extraordinarily powerful. Great trial lawyers collect and use these words. Professional performers teach legalists relaxation exercises and sensory-awareness techniques and then progress to improvisations and basic scene studies.

"The courtroom is like a theater," said Kathleen Swann, an actress in Manhattan who offers a speech course to attorneys. "Throughout history, the great trial lawyers have also been great actors."

Under Swann's direction, lawyers practice relaxation exercises. They flex their feet, roll their heads from side to side, and shake the "tension" out of their hands.

"Can't you, won't you, don't you," they intone, working on sustaining their voices and using inflection, rather than allowing their voices to drop off at the end of a sentence.

Attorneys who win know the power of proper speech. In *The Touch of Treason*, author Sol Stein reports on prosecutor Roberts' opening address to the jury at a murder trial:

> "Ladies and gentlemen," Roberts said—he wanted to be sure the press caught every word—"there are two kinds of crimes. Those that may attract our momentary sympathy—like crimes of passion—and those that produce a profound sense of *revulsion*, as in this case when a great man with a unique capability is killed by one of his own closest students, who *pretended* to love and admire him.
>
> "The people will prove Professor Martin Fuller died not of natural causes or an accident, but as the result of the willful intent of another person, that person being the defendant, Edward Sturbridge, also known under the *alias* Edward Porter."

In his opening, Roberts had used *revulsion*, designed to create a crime that was not in the statute books, a crime worse than murder, a crime that had just been invented. And in the same first breath, Roberts had pulled a rug from under the defendant's case: *pretended* to love and admire him. The jury now had *revulsion* and *pretended* and *alias* implanted in their heads.

Such persuasive words are not unusual. They are, in fact, simple, everyday words. But power speakers find them invaluable.

Always Ask *Why*

Why is an excellent persuasive connector. Without it the power speaker's work would be much harder—sometimes impossible. When you're the buyer, *why* is hard to answer without committing yourself. Yet it's inoffensive. Children are forever asking *why* of parents. We're used to it. Great persuaders use *why* whenever the convincing gets on shaky ground.

Suppose your customer says: "I don't think this is exactly what I want." Your best reply: "Why?"

Suppose she says, "Oh, I don't know—I just don't think I want it." Smile and ask *Why?* Repeat the word, with charm, to draw out the real reason she's hesitating.

During any persuasion, moments occur when the persuadee hesitates. You ask: *"Why do you ponder, Mr. Rinker?"*

Or: *"Why do you think that is true?"*

Or: *"Why do you want to wait until after April 15, when the price will undoubtedly advance before that time?"*

Don't forget that little word *why*—one of the most powerful words in the rich American language.

A Chicago sales trainer carries the use of *why* to a higher degree. He calls it The Bounce-Back. You use *why* on your opponent after she throws her *why* at you.

Even against an original *why*, the most powerful defense is often another *why*. Suppose you ask a buyer for an order. The buyer counters: "Why should I buy these goods now?" Use the bounce-back: *"Why do you ask, 'Why should I place an order now?' "*

Let's Use *Let's*

Lyndon B. Johnson, one of history's most devastating users of one-on-one speech, coupled his famous "laying on of the hands" with the biblical quote: "Come, let us reason together."

Generally, his persuadees found this meant, "Let's do it Lyndon's way," but often they didn't realize it until later (such was the power of his speech). LBJ was a master of *let's*.

"Let's is highly useful," one ace salesman explained, "because it's a cooperative word. It's a you-and-I-together word. 'Let's do so and so' and they don't feel coerced. They think it's as much their own idea as yours."

Besides, psychologically the seller and buyer working *together* is an effective atmosphere for moving toward your objective.

To prove the power of *let's* in personnel management, say to your employee: *"Let's* see why this project will work better if you finish the the inventory today." See how much more effective and acceptable it is than the dogmatic statement: "John, I want you to finish the inventory today." The idea is the same. But *let's* makes it infinitely more palatable.

The ace salesman, whose earnings are in six figures, continued: "I often say to a prospect, as a strong, powerful close: 'Let's arrange to try this in your own home.' "

Build phrases around *let's*. It's much more effective than the same ideas expressed in almost any other way.

The Magic of *How*

You're standing in the supermarket checkout line, passing the time by reading the cover headlines on magazines in the rack:

- How to Lose 80 Pounds.
- How to Make Frothy Desserts for Pennies.
- How to Solve Mother-in-Law Problems.

These headlines, composed by experts in mass motivation, carry a power speech lesson: Use *how* whenever you can. It's pure power. *How* arouses curiosity, a dominant characteristic of the mind.

One effective in-store demonstrator always starts his presentation with: "I'm going to show you how this will save you money." This is infinitely better than: "You will save money if you install this."

If a saleswoman tells you she's going to show you *how* a new food blender works, your curiosity is immediately aroused. You must hear the rest. Pepper your speech with *how*. Everyone wants to know *how* to do something.

Listen and Translate

Ace persuaders are also excellent listeners and translators. Often what people mean is light years away from what they say. In a newspaper letter to the editor, Nancy Clark Reynolds, a Washington insider, offers these translations of what Potomac biggies say to lobbyists—followed by what they mean. The contrast is startling:

> "It's good to see you again." *(Why are we having the fourth meeting in seven days on this issue?)*
> "Of course I remember meeting your client at that reception in 1978." *(If they put me on a rack, I wouldn't be able to remember him.)*
> "I understand you talked to my staff assistant about this issue." *(You have not convinced my staff, and there is no way you're gonna convince me either.)*
> "On the face of it, your argument sounds good, but of course I want to read your materials first." *(I don't know what the hell you're talking about.)*

We all need translation in dealing with one another. If you are trying to persuade teenagers (God help you!), you'll need to translate this conversation:

> If you're a *rent,* you are naturally a *squid* to your teenager, but it doesn't have to be *tamale time.* So *kick back, chill out,* and *mellow up,* because it's *rad, really ruff.*
> *Translation:* If you're a parent, naturally you're out of it, but don't be embarrassed. Relax, take it easy, and calm down, because it's cool, really cool.

Caution: No language is more ephemeral. By the time you learn one teen translation, you've missed the next two waves.

Right and *Truth*

"The truth is such and such," the senator says. *Truth* immediately gets attention. Being for truth puts you on the side of the angels. *Truth* is a strong word. It stands for a quality we all respect. "Here are the findings about the situation, Mr. Roberts," a researcher says. Everyone in the room listens.

Robert D. Esseks, a Harvard Law graduate, used words with universal appeal in selling a leasing service to business executives. *Right* was one of his workhorse words. In leasing, the interest rate is, of necessity, arrived at through much back-and-forth negotiation. Yet the prospect often asks: "What's the rate?" at the beginning. Esseks always said: "Whatever's *right!*" The prospect invariably relaxed. After all, isn't every buyer interested in the *right* price? Esseks closed dozens of leasing contracts at the right price.

William E. Bolster, an advertising agency executive, also uses the word *right.* When a client threatens to cut budget, Bolster tells him seriously: "That isn't *right*." The client reconsiders. After all, if it's not *right*, who wants to do it?

Use *truth* and *right* to strengthen your speech.

Simple vs. Ornate Persuasion

"Use the language of the people," speech pundits cry. Well, yes, that's often good counsel to the persuader. But not always. Suit your rhetoric to the need.

Simple words are usually, but not always, the best. The Gettysburg Address, for example, is not the simplest language. "Four score and seven" is not as simple as "eighty-seven," "brought forth" is more old-fashioned than "established," and "dedicated to the proposition" sounds clumsy.

Yet the overall effect of that great oration lies in its gloomy magnificence. It was just what that occasion demanded. The Union had won a victory at Gettysburg. But people were horrified at the enormous price. And thousands were numb with grief.

The brevity of Lincoln's address was also a masterstroke. The crowd had already listened for two hours to Edward Everett, the greatest orator of an age that could absorb a lot of oratory. Even so, the audience must have been jaded when the learned rhetorician gave way to the former backwoodsman.

Lincoln's brevity was refreshing. And his words immortal.

The Declaration of Independence, if reduced to common vulgate, would have been wrapping fish the next day—as H. L. Mencken pointed out in this "People's Translation": "When things get so balled up that the people of a country have to cut loose from some other country and go on their own hook, without asking no permission from nobody, excepting maybe God Almighty, then they ought to let everybody know why they done it, so that everybody can see that they're on the level, and not trying to put nothing over on nobody."

To boil it down: Persuasion must be geared to the audience. Sometimes this requires ornate language. When it does, don't be afraid to lay it on.

Connote, Not Denote

Every word has two meanings. The dictionary meaning is *denotation:* A dog is a quadruped of the canine species. The second meaning, *connota-*

tion, is that peculiar and personal interpretation based on your own experience. Dog means your dog, a neighbor's dog, a dog you owned, a dog that recently bit you. You give *dog* your own inner meaning.

In power speech, connotation is far more important than denotation.

If you tell a customer to "sign here," the connotation is formal, legal, formidable, binding, fearful. We've all been warned about signing contracts, wills, waivers. Connotation frightens the buyer.

On the other hand, if you suggest that the customer give you his or her name and address, the customer will readily and willingly do so. There are no fearful connotations about name and address. People supply that all the time.

The cigar-chomping straw-hat-era salesman browbeat customers: "Put your John Hancock right on the dotted line." But customers, by not signing in droves, made such methods obsolete. Today we use pleasing but powerful phrases:

- "Just your name and address, please."
- "Would you mind looking this over, and if it's correct, O.K. it on the last line?"
- "Please write your name and address the way you want it to appear on our records."

Joseph Conrad, the novelist, had a keen respect for the fine shades of word meanings. A friend suggested that Conrad write an autobiography. Conrad refused. He didn't believe he had anything to say in a life story.

Then his friend insisted: "You know, you really *must*."

"It was not an argument, but I submitted at once," said Conrad, who continued:

> *If one must!* You perceive the force of a word. He who wants to persuade should put his trust *not* in the right arguments but in the right *word*. The power of sound has always been greater than the power of sense.
>
> On the other hand, you cannot fail to see the power of mere words, such words as *glory,* for instance, or *pity.* Shouted with perseverance, with ardor, with conviction, these two by their sound alone have set whole nations in motion and upheaved the dry hard ground on which rests the whole social fabric.
>
> Of course, the accent must be attended to. The right accent. That's very important. Don't talk to me of your Archimedes lever. Give me the *right* word and the *right* accent and I will move the world!

One hard-bitten executive, a respecter of words, lacked Conrad's finesse. But what he said may be practical long after Conrad's fine words are forgotten: "Worship words, you fellows. If you ever stop using 'em right, you stop eating. Remember that."

Preparation: Key to Persuasion

I once arranged for the president of a Boston retail chain to speak to a marketing convention in the South. An ego-involved man, he wouldn't rehearse—and much to my sorrow, he was a flop.

The hardest work for any convention manager is getting amateur speakers to rehearse before going onstage. They often say: "Oh, I'm not worried. I'll just get up and wing it. It'll be all right." All right for them maybe; but they always seem to be insensitive to audience torture.

Ace persuaders, on the other hand, never *stop* rehearsing. The director of a long-running Broadway show invariably calls for rehearsal every few months to "take out all the improvements the cast has been sneaking in."

The pro knows he needs rehearsal. The cloddish amateur disdains it. During the New Orleans World's Fair, I saw a polished emcee at work outside a concession. He was in complete charge for each instant during his presentation. He made the crowd do exactly what he wanted it to do. It was masterful power speech.

During a lull, I asked him how many times a day he gave his presentation.

"Five times an hour, 12 hours a day."

"Sixty times a day?"

"That's right."

"Have you been giving it long?"

"Four months."

Each time he gave the talk—without ever changing a word or altering an accent, since both were perfect—he signed 20 attendees. He gave it 6,000 times; it contained exactly 237 words.

"I didn't write the talk," he said. "The audience did. I tried telling them and watched results. Whenever I'd think of an improvement, I'd try that. Some worked. Some didn't. Whenever I found a word or phrase that increased sales, I added it. In time, I got a presentation that really brought them in. That's what I wanted.

"Every word in that talk is important. I wouldn't change one word for $500. I couldn't afford to. I'd lose money."

Peter Jacobi, professor of journalism at the University of Indiana, in his book *Writing with Style*, stated that preparation and enthusiasm are the difference between persuasive platform speakers and sleep inducers.

A pharmaceuticals executive delivered a speech to his local Rotary Club this way:

> It's a pleasure and a privilege to be here today to speak with you and tell you, uh, about what I do, uh. My job, uh, is to promote the activities of our region's largest drug company, a distinguished one, uh, Coldstream Pharmaceuticals, Incorporated. And it's, uh, a wonderful job, one that I've done, uh, for about ten years now, I guess. It's an exciting job, with different things, uh, happening every day. I'm, uh, never bored.

But by now, the audience *is* bored and drifting fast. The speaker is without energy, without conviction, without fire. He hasn't prepared.

Jacobi recommends that the speaker tackle group persuasion this way:

> The druggist is the heart of a community. Sometimes he's a heartbeat away from disaster.
> He is first aid and relief. Shelves of magazines. He's sun shields and beauty creams and bubble gum. The druggist provides directions and dreams.
> We could not exist without him. He could not exist without my company, Coldstream Pharmaceuticals, which supplies potions and lotions that folks need and want.
> We'd all find it much harder to exist without the pioneering research that leads Coldstream toward new health solutions.
> Just the other day, we unveiled a medicine that will stop a cough caused by cold congestion. And let me tell you more about it, first, by recalling some of the events that led up to this. . . .[25]

The audience is right there with this speaker. He's prepared. No, he doesn't sound like Richard Burton. But we're listening because we can learn something. He's also going to entertain us by re-creating an exciting event. We're listening because he's involved in what he's saying.

Sure, voice, tone and pace, volume, and rhythm are important. And avoid reading as reading rather than reading as talking. But if you feel the message, and if you've thought out content until you're comfortable (as with an informal chat with a friend), you're going to avoid the worst pitfalls. You'll become a performer who can turn a strong message into audience involvement.

Good group persuasion starts with an idea. Then you turn it into effective language. Then it becomes performance. Preparation and emotional content are the keys.

Don't Use *Write* Words! Use *Talk* Words!

Edward J. Hegarty, a New York sales consultant, believes the right word used in the right way can persuade the world. But get the *right* word. Here's how Hegarty builds a presentation.

List the physical features of your product. Translate each into a short statement of fact, emphasizing value to the prospect. Arrange statements in logical sequence. When you write them down, don't use *write* words—use *talk* words!

Say *do* rather than *accomplish, find out* rather than *ascertain, go with* instead of *accompany, buy* instead of *purchase, use* rather than *utilize*.

Cut every word you can. Telegraph, don't write. Deliver your carefully prepared words like the old *Gangbusters* radio show—bang, bang, bang! Your job is to bowl your listeners over, keep them awake, keep them with you. According to Hegarty:

> You can hardly overuse questions, those great testers of attention. Interface your presentation with questions. If you suspect you're losing the prospect's interest, bring out a question to regain it.
>
> When you have the complete presentation worked out to your satisfaction, start giving it, time and time again, until you're delivering it with the poise and confidence of an actor. After all, you are a skilled business actor, a skilled persuader using words.

Structure is valuable in persuasion. There are two ways to advance your argument:

> 1. Lead off with your strongest point, followed by your weakest argument, and close with the next-to-strongest argument.
> 2. Begin with a strong argument, but not the best one. Follow with a weaker argument. Close out with the strongest argument of all. Be brief, be forceful, do not drag in extraneous ideas. Don't let attention lag.

WRAPPING IT UP

The ability to persuade is the ability to succeed—in business, management, selling, the law, and countless other lines of work.

Avoid explosive words that sidetrack the issue. Learn to use power phrases that stimulate action. Powerful words are *let's, why, how, right, truth,* among others.

Always give your persuadee a choice between something and something else—never between something and nothing.

Preparation is the key to persuasion. You cannot bore and persuade at the same time.

Great persuaders are ace listeners and translators. Listen to what people say and understand what they mean, which is often quite different.

15

Using Speech to Attack and Defend

Ben Franklin saw the colonial innkeeper as a versatile character—raconteur, one-man post office, human newspaper, commentator on politics, gossipmonger, busybody, and (in today's terms) a real ear-bender. (The closest twentieth-century parallels: a small-town barber or a big-city cabbie.) But sometimes the weary eighteenth-century traveler (riding a springless stagecoach over corduroy roads) didn't want all—or *any*—of the innkeeper's "services." Franklin, for one, yearned for peace and quiet by the fire.

So he spoke on the offensive. When he first entered a roadside inn, Franklin immediately sought out Ye Olde Host. According to legend, he said:

> My name is Benjamin Franklin. I was born in Boston. I am a printer by profession, and am traveling to Philadelphia. I shall have to return at such and such a time, and I have no news. Now, what can you give me for dinner?

Speaking on the offensive often saves you time, patience, and purse. Sometimes you can speak on the offensive so deftly that you reduce the possibility of a fracas.

Suppose you're dealing with a person who'll swear black is white once you identify it as black. Start out with what you *don't* believe. Suggest that your opponent cannot possibly do what you want him to do. Or that your objective isn't his sort of thing. Soon he'll be vehemently presenting *your* case as *his*.

You'll need to be on the offensive when speaking with clerks, waiters, and lower-level bureaucrats. Since they often dislike their jobs, they get their kicks by making things difficult. They pretend they're doing you a favor. Never bully those people—that reveals your fear and lack of assurance. Instead be calm and courteous and proceed on the assumption that your slightest wish will be met.

Never allow a waiter to say: "I'm busy right now." Start off by saying: "When you get a moment, I'd like . . ." You've acknowledged that he *may* be busy. But your tone indicates that you expect prompt attention. This is also effective with bureaucratic clerks.

Ask (Within Reason) to Get

A large crowd of us were waiting at Newark airport for the regular Port Authority bus. We had another five minutes to go (if you trust the posted schedule—which you shouldn't). A special bus pulled up to discharge a charter group. When the people were out, I asked the driver: "Going into Manhattan?" "Sure," he said. I got in. The others waited for the regular bus. Ask and get: a basic principle of on-the-offensive speech. ("Ask and it shall be given to you"—Matthew 7:7.) Other applications:

1. You're late for your flight. But there's a long line ahead of you at the check-in counter. Don't just move up gradually until you miss your flight. March to the head of the line, politely explain that you have only minutes to make your plane, and say: "Would you be gracious enough to allow me to go ahead?" Almost always, they'll oblige. Courtly aggressiveness wins again.

2. A truck is blocking your car in the middle of a side street. Politely explain to the truck driver that you have a pressing time problem and "I'd appreciate it if you'd pull over and let me pass." This almost always produces better results than blowing your horn and making threatening gestures. When it doesn't, conspicuously write down the driver's license number. Tell him you're about to call the police and his employer.

3. You want to switch lanes on a busy city street. Don't try to bully your way in. This touches off determination to stop you. Instead, politely signal with your hand, catch the eye of the driver in the other lane, smile, and say: "Thank you very much."

4. When your restaurant reservation is not honored even though you arrived on time, give the restaurant ten minutes leeway. Then ask for the manager or the owner. Say: "I've kept my part of the bargain. Now you must keep yours."

5. Do not automatically tip a certain percentage or the way "everybody does." Base your tipping on the service and pleasantness. To tip for airline personnel, send letters to the airline commenting on courteous and helpful service. When people are, for no reason, downright rude, fire off a negative letter to the home office. Explain your intentions in both cases.

I first encountered the power of Ask to Get when I worked at a Kinney shoe store. We carried socks and shoe polish behind the register. Some customers asked for socks or polish when they were purchasing shoes.

Then one day an enterprising regional manager (he was new and didn't know all the reasons why things won't work) said: "From now on, we're going to *ask* each customer to buy socks and polish. Just ask. Nothing more."

Each retail salesperson started doing just that. No sales talk. No product benefit. Just: "Would you like to pick out a pair of socks? Would you like black (or brown) polish for those shoes?"

Now as professional salesfolk know, that's not an ideal selling presentation—far from it. But sales of socks and polish jumped 50 percent. Did it cost anything? No. Did it take extra time? No. But it sure sold the product.

Ask and Get is a not-so-secret weapon available to all. People will often do something if you ask them to. So ask!

Coping with Disaster

At times, you're on the defensive because you're trying to cope with natural disaster. Often humor is your best choice. Sales trainer Paul Micali once made a dramatic point at a meeting. You could have heard a pin drop. Then the meeting room door swung open and a shrill waitress screamed: "Anyone here driving the blue Chevrolet? It's blocking the entrance!"

A hush. The train of thought: broken. Micali had to mend the breach. "I told the audience she was training to be an opera star," Micali says. Laughter. Disaster defused.

Robert Orben, former White House humor writer, had a microphone go dead during a speech. When it was turned back on, Orben said: "I'm glad you fixed that. For a while there I was beginning to feel like Marcel Marceau."

Humor also helps when you're just plain wrong. When I met my client Ted Demmon for lunch, he was 45 minutes late and I was fuming. When he turned up, Demmon said jauntily: "Isn't dating me a problem?" Well, you can't laugh and cry at the same time. I laughed.

I was equally hot after trying repeatedly to reach Walter Johnson, New York marketing counsel, on a project of mutual benefit. I called five times. No callback. Finally, I got him on the line.

"We've both been trying to reach one another all day," he said. "And we've both been having trouble. But isn't it good that we've made the connection?" There was no denying the sentiment. It hadn't really been that way, but defensive diplomacy scored again.

Even a professional disturber of the peace knows when to admit defeat. H. L. Mencken, a lifelong agnostic, was once asked: "What would happen, in the Great Beyond, if you meet up with the 12 apostles?" Said the sage of Baltimore: "I will say: 'Gentlemen, I was wrong.'"

Often outright admission of being wrong is the best defense. Suppose your company's best customer calls to report an outrageous foul-up in a shipment. Concede before you contend. Agree, if possible, with what the customer says.

- "I can understand why you are upset . . ."
- "I know exactly how you feel. I'd feel the same way if I were in your shoes . . ."

Is this insincere? Not at all. If you really were the other person, you would feel the same way he does.

When the customer sees you're on his side, not fighting him, he'll feel differently. He might even start to worry that he's overdone it. Complained too loudly. Been unreasonable. Possibly cost someone his job. Complainers sometimes back down and apologize if you quietly and sincerely admit to the problem. All they wanted was an audience, some attention, a little recognition.

When the problem is more severe, never make light of it. Problems and errors are not a laughing matter. When they occur, this is not the time to bring in whistles and funny hats.

Keep cool. If your customer becomes unreasonable and says uncomplimentary things, stay calm and listen. Let the customer blow off steam. Don't argue. He's mad. He's itching for a fight. Silence is your only line of defense. Then when the storm blows over, say:

- "I don't blame you one bit for feeling as you do Mr. Smith. I would personally be just as mad."

- "There's simply no excuse for it to have happened. I would be just as upset as you."
- "I'm going to get to the bottom of this thing right away. I give you my word—I'll get it straightened out."
- "Now don't you worry about this anymore. Just leave it for me to handle. This thing is ridiculous!"

Be a good listener, but never run down your company. If he says you work for a lousy outfit, don't agree. Just remind him you'll fix the error.

In answering complaints, it helps to restate the objection—in question form:

- "In other words, what you are asking is . . . ?"
- "What you are telling me is that . . . ?"
- "If I understand you correctly, you're saying that . . . ?"
- "Are you saying . . . ?"

This softens the problem. It brings the complaint out into the open where you both can look it over. You exhibit interest, respect, and attention and reinforce the fact that you're trying to help. By restating an objection, you show that you understand the problem. (There's no point in addressing a non-existent objection. You might be creating a new one!)

When You're Walking on Eggs

In delicate business situations, what you say can have a major impact on your career.

You're assistant plant manager, and the president wants his son Pomroy to get hands-on experience. He calls you in and says: "Because of your levelheadedness and experience, you're the ideal person to supervise him." Hmmm. Flattery will get you everywhere.

To start off, hold two or three good discussions with the president. Find out how he sees Pomroy's shortcomings (around home and other places). You need an evaluation of Pomroy's pluses and minuses early on.

Pomroy doesn't *have* to do what you tell him. You know it and he knows it. The boss's son is about as knotty a problem as you'll encounter. But if you've got the right kind of top man, he'll want you to instruct the boy on the straight and narrow. Tell him what he does right *and* wrong.

Obviously you can't yell at him. A light touch is best. Chide him a little—to wit: "Do you feel sensitive about what your dad would say in this case?" It's a difficult situation. But defensive power speech can handle it.

Suppose you're an ambitious careerist but are holding down a good job now. You get a call from a headhunter. Right away, you're walking on eggs.

Be cautious. If the headhunter asks if you want a job, the answer is: "No. I'm happy where I am. Management treats me fine. I have no interest in moving."

You don't know who the headhunter represents—he may be hired by your boss. Displaying interest on the telephone is not a good idea.

Usually, however, the headhunter inquiring will request a meeting. "We've been told, Mr. Manager, that you are one of the most knowledge-able people in your industry. We'd like to explore your knowledge of candidates who might fill a given position."

That approach allows you to say to your boss later: "XYZ Head-hunters have contacted me as a source. But as I sat down and talked to them, it turned out they were really interested in talking to me, which I had not suspected."

Don't be coy and fail to tell your boss about the meeting. He'll find out about it, sooner or later, and you'll be in the soup.

Consultant Ned Klumph of Cherry Hill, New Jersey, says you can walk on eggs doing your current job, too.

1. In a staff meeting, your boss is explaining an organization change. You have difficulty understanding. She snaps, "You seem to need a lot of explanations. Do you think because I'm a woman my ideas aren't logical?"

Your best reply: "I apologize for taking so much time. I want to support your program, as I always do, but I just don't seem to see the *best* way to do that. Perhaps we had better discuss it later in your office."

2. A supervisor has just informed you that essential elements of an important job have broken down. The department can't meet a sched-uled delivery to a most valued customer. At that moment, your spouse telephones—your child has been suspended from school for fighting.

Say to your spouse: "Keep him home until I get there. I'll leave early after I tackle a current panic."

To your supervisor, say: "Give me all the *facts* and we'll take steps to *correct the situation.* Let's set a *firm, new* date with the customer. Make sure we meet with customer relations, sales, and production so we'll have an *honest* status and delivery report."

3. You are trying to concentrate on a report that's due shortly. You overhear an argument between two employees outside your office. George enters your office very upset: "If you don't do something about that woman. . . ."

Make it clear that you'll tolerate no further public arguments. Then ask both parties in to discuss their apparent "problem." Make it quick, take no sides, *get it resolved!*

4. After you have explained the importance of completing particular assignments on time, work continues as usual—no improvement. Call a special staff meeting and say: "The blackboard shows key assignments with scheduled completion dates. Let's find out what roadblocks we're hitting."

The Communispond Test

Take this test, created by Communispond, a New York communications firm, to check your defensive-speech acumen. Pick the power speaker's answer:

1. Your boss's immediate supervisor asks you to lunch. When you return, you sense your boss is curious. Do you

   a. Give your boss a detailed description of the lunch?
   b. Avoid telling your boss anything?
   c. Mention the lunch casually—as though it really had no significance?

2. You're in the middle of an important meeting with your boss—there's a long-distance business call for you. Do you

   a. Ask the boss's secretary to say you're out of the office?
   b. Accept the call and take as much time as it needs?
   c. Tell the person you're in a meeting and ask when you may call back?

3. You're conducting a staff meeting on new sales procedures. One employee keeps interrupting with questions not germane to the subject. Do you

   a. Request all employees to hold their questions until you've finished?
   b. Accept the interruptions?
   c. Tell the employee that interruptions are out of order?

4. A staff member comes to you to complain about the work habits of another. Do you say

   a. "We'll have to discuss that later—there's too much else to do now"?

   b. "I'll be glad to talk with both of you—together, not separately"?

   c. "What's the problem . . . let's discuss it now"?

5. Your employees' Christmas party is underway when you arrive. Everybody seems well into the season's spirits—too well, in fact. Do you

   a. Try to be a "good guy" and join in the fun?

   b. Leave immediately?

   c. Tell the person in charge that the party is out of hand and suggest it be ended as soon as possible?

6. For the fourth consecutive Friday, a staff member asks to leave early. Do you say

   a. "I can't keep giving you permission like this—others will resent it"?

   b. "Not today—there may be a staff meeting at 4 o'clock"?

   c. "You're important to us—I need you to put in a full day, especially on Friday"?

7. You've been hired from outside the company as director of a large department. You know several staff members thought they should have had the position. On the first day, do you

   a. Initiate individual conversations with those persons about the situation?

   b. Ignore the problem and hope it'll go away?

   c. Be aware of the problem but concentrate on your job and on getting to know everyone?

8. An employee says to you, "I shouldn't tell you this, but have you heard _____?" Do you say

   a. "I don't want to hear any office gossip"?

   b. "I'm interested only if it concerns our business"?

   c. "What's the latest—let me in on it"?

9. Your boss, in a customer meeting, makes an inaccurate statement. Do you

   a. Point out the mistake later to your boss—and expect him to correct the statement?

    b. Correct your boss in front of the customer?

    c. Try to handle it yourself with the customer—at another time?

Question	Answer	Statement
1.	a.	Never forget who your boss is—and where your loyalty lies. If you tell him nothing or if you tell him casually, you plant seeds of mistrust.
2.	c.	Honesty and courtesy are the best policies. It's never right to lie. And it's never smart to waste you boss's time.
3.	a.	Controlling the meeting starts with your setting the ground rules—*up front*. Conceding to one person's self-interest is neither productive nor fair.
4.	c.	It's best to nip problems in the bud—procrastination is a sin. And you must first talk with one employee to determine if there's a need to talk with two.
5.	c.	Place the responsibility where it belongs. To be a "good guy" or to leave immediately is *not* facing up to the problem.
6.	c.	Project a positive thought as you make your position clear. Blaming others is passing the buck; hiding behind a possible meeting is a sign of weakness.
7.	c.	Let sleeping dogs lie, particularly on your first day. To ignore the problem is foolish; to initiate conversations is a greater folly.
8.	b.	Keep the conversation on a business level. It's your responsibility to stop office gossip, not encourage it.
9.	a.	This action is prudent and professional. You don't want to embarrass your boss and customer. Nor do you want to be in an awkward position afterward.

Answering Objections

Complaints occur after the fact. Objections occur when your persuadee is balking. Sonny Harris, president of the Window Man, Durham, North Carolina, uses these answers to objections in setting up home demos for replacement windows:

I can't afford it now; call me later. Mrs. Jones, replacement windows are expensive and I agree with you. However, we are having a special promotion on these windows and before the prices change, we would like to come to your home and show you and Mr. Jones what our new Sontronic window looks like and let you know how much we can save you at this time.

My husband and I are never home together. We're having this special for a very few days only. If you can see us at any time of the day or night or on Saturday or Sunday, we can save you several hundreds of dollars while the sale is in progress. If you are really interested in windows for your home, now is the time to save money! What time does your husband come home? 5:00 or 6:00 P.M.?

We never buy anything over the phone. I don't blame you, Mrs. Jones. I wouldn't buy anything over the phone either. However, what I would like to do is have our representative stop by, without any cost or obligation. If we can get together at this time, our representative will be able to save you a great deal of money. What time does your husband get home? Could we stop by at 6:30, or would 8:00 P.M. be better?

In answering objections, it pays to know when objections are only excuses. My friend George Wringer turns the spotlight on excuses.

Prospect: I'll have to ask my dad!

Winger: All right, I tell you what. I'll go see my dad, too. While you're asking if it's O.K. to buy, I'll ask if it's O.K. for me to sell. Of course, you realize neither of us need go through this. We can just . . .

Frontal Attack

In a verbal war, the best approach at times is frontal assault. You're not trying to soothe an ally. You're determined to demolish an enemy—or, at least, to tell it straight and avoid any misunderstanding.

With this as your mission, the right words can decapitate. When *Washington Post* editor Ben Bradlee called Accuracy in Media's Reed

Irvine a "miserable, carping retromingent vigilante," he was using a direct attack. It was all the more deadly because the victim had to look up *retromingent* to find it meant "backward-urinating." (Irvine riposted by enlarging the comment and placing it on his office wall as a trophy.)

Using obscure words that, upon examination, are worse than they first appear is a technique of the seasoned verbal infighter. Pretending to be honored by invective and displaying it to the world is a good defense. Many latecomers to the incidents will sympathize with the victim and cluck-cluck the aggressor's intemperance.

But if the attack is vigorous and your reply tepid, you lose. Poor Clement Atlee's replies to Winston Churchill's attacks have not survived. But Churchill's original volleys are classics:

- "Atlee is a sheep in sheep's clothing."
- "He's a modest man with much to be modest about."
- "Atlee's automobile pulled up to Number 10 Downing Street— and nobody got out."

Some say all's fair in love and war, and Churchill saw politics as total war. His mission: to demolish his opponent. Launching grenades is one part of war—dodging return fire is the other. At a dinner party, Lady Nancy Astor, the American-turned-British M.P., said to Churchill: "Winston, if you were my husband, I'd poison your soup." "Madam," said Churchill, "if you were my wife, I'd eat it."

On another occasion, a fellow M.P. said to Lady Astor: "I just don't know what to make of Winston." The witty Nancy purred: "How about a nice rug?"

Since Churchill wasn't in earshot, that was one up for Lady Astor. As a strong adversary in verbal barrage, Churchill probably failed to get underdog sympathy.

Nor did Tallulah Bankhead get the sympathy vote when Broadway press agent Richard Maney said: "A day away from Tallulah is like a month in the country." But she hardly needed it—that was like attacking the Statue of Liberty with a pea-shooter.

Sheridan Whiteside, the title character in *The Man Who Came to Dinner,* unleashed artillery on his nurse—after she cautioned him about the ill effects of eating candy.

"Madam," Whiteside said, "my great-aunt Jennifer ate a whole box of candy every day of her life. She lived to be 102, and when she'd been dead *three* days, she looked better than you do now."

But as Whiteside's real-life roman à clef, Alexander Woolcott, well knew, those who dish it out sometimes get hit with custard pies.

One of Ben Franklin's enemies said: "Franklin loves the truth so much he is most sparing in its use."

Generally when an amateur takes on a professional in verbal joust, the odds-makers favor the pro. (Damon Runyon, who studied such matters, said: "The race may not always go to the swift, nor the battle to the strong, but that's the way to bet.") William S. Gilbert met a friend on the street shortly after Gilbert and Sullivan's *Ruddigore* had opened:

"How's *Bloodygore* doing?" the friend asked—joshing Gilbert for steering so close to the taboo word *bloody*.

"It's *Ruddigore*," said Gilbert with an establishment sniff.

"Same thing," said the friend.

"Not at all," shot back Gilbert, his ire rising. "If I tell you that I admire your *ruddy* countenance, which I do, it's not the same as saying I appreciate your *bloody* cheek, which I don't."

Politicians, in the *Sturm und Drang* of low-road assassination, often circulate *bon mots* on the rumor circuit. If such bombs are funny ("Mondale's had a charisma bypass"), the effect is lasting. Witness Disraeli's comment about an opponent: "He has committed every crime that doesn't require courage."

Harry Truman consigned an enemy to anonimity by labeling him "a revolving S.O.B. He's a[n] S.O.B. any way you look at him."

Of course, pols on the hustings are politicians. But in the hallowed halls of Congress or Parliament, they are statesmen—and they must temper one-on-one vitriol. To ensure temperance, both legislative bodies ban members from using certain abusive words to identify one another.

Fascist was recently banned in Parliament. Other no-no's: *blackguard, cad, coward, young pup, guttersnipe, hooligan, jackass, murderer, rat, stool pigeon, swine, traitor, villain.*

In Congress, you may not villify via *dupe* or *demagogue*.

In 1937, Senator Tom Connally of Texas lit into Senator Champ Clark of Missouri with, "I protest against the Senate being made a sewer by the vaporings of the Senator from Missouri," and he was shut up for that. Thirteen years later, as presiding officer, Connally slapped down Indiana's William Jenner for unfairly blasting Maryland's Millard Tydings for, "the most scandalous and brazen whitewash of a treasonable conspiracy in our history, who would continue to cover up these termites and vermin who, even as I speak, are gnawing at the foundations of our freedom."

Senator Homer Capehart was once savaged as, "a rancid tub of ignorance," which was considered then (and would be considered now) beyond the pale.

So if you watch congressional proceedings and find the interchange dull, be aware of what serious restrictions the members operate under.

Authors who insult their fellows have always considered kicking and eye-gouging fair game. About Chesterfield's letters to his son, Dr. Samuel Johnson said: "They teach the morals of a whore and the manners of a dancing master."

Not content with that, Dr. Johnson went on to call Horace Walpole "a babbling old woman," adding that "prejudice and bigotry, and pride and presumption, and arrogance and pedantry are the bags that brew his ink."

Thomas Carlyle, in turn, called Emerson a "gap-toothed and hoary-headed ape . . . who now in his dotage spits and chatters from a dirtier perch of his own finding and fouling."

Oscar Wilde said of George Meredith: "As a writer, he has mastered everything except language; as a novelist, he can do everything except tell a story; as an artist, he is everything except articulate."

Sinclair Lewis, a good hater, dropped this depth charge on Bernard De Voto, a prominent critic of the 1930s: "I denounce Mr. Bernard De Voto as a fool and a tedious and egotistical fool, as a liar and a pompous and boresome liar."

So much for authors' antics—they're usually in good fun. Drama critics, on the other hand, are paid for delivering frontal attacks on undeserving producers and performers (that's the backstage view). Or, they act as early warning devices for an innocent public (that's the critic's view).

Either way, both brickbats and rapiers are often at the ready. Said Robert Benchley: "It was one of those plays in which the actors *unfortunately* enunciated very clearly." Walter Winchell topped it with: "The title of *Wake Up and Live* ought to be changed to *Wake Up and Leave*."

Heywood Broun made short work of a comedy: "The play opened at 8:40 sharp and closed at 10:40 dull." Walter Kerr was even defter in reviewing *I Am a Camera:* "No Leica." Of short-lived *Moose Murders,* theater critic Frank Rich said:

> From now on, there will always be two groups of theatergoers in this world: those who have seen *Moose Murders* and those who have not. Those of us who witnessed the play will undoubtedly hold periodic reunions in the noble tradition of survivors of the Titanic.
>
> The 10 actors trapped in this enterprise, a minority of them of professional caliber, will not be singled out. I'm tempted to upbraid the author, director and producers of *Moose Murders,* but surely the American Society for the Prevention of Cruelty to Animals will be after them soon enough.

Performers often take the hide off one another just to sharpen their verbal equipment. Oscar Levant, upon learning of the illness of an acquaintance, said: "I hope it's nothing trivial." And Noel Coward said: "Miss Erickson looked more peculiar than ever this morning. Is her spiritualism getting worse?"

These are masters of personal assault at work.

Managing the Polite Put-Down

Suppose your opponent is your dinner guest, and, wrong though he is, you're not really mad. If you want to keep his friendship but cannot let him get away with drivel, the philosopher Mortimer Adler suggests you select from these replies:

- "I think you hold that position because you are uninformed about certain facts or reasons that have a critical bearing on it." (Then be prepared to point out information you think the other lacks that, if possessed, would result in a change of mind.)
- "I think you hold that position because you are misinformed about matters that are critically relevant." (Then be prepared to indicate the mistakes she has made that, if corrected, would lead her to abandon the position.)
- "I think you are well informed and have a firm grasp of the evidence and reasons that support your position, but you have drawn the wrong conclusions because of mistakes in reasoning." (Then be ready to point out those errors of logic that, if corrected, would lead to a different conclusion.)

In other calm situations, try using the *"no" sandwich,* a negative sandwiched between two cushioning statements. The first layer acknowledges what the other person wants. It demonstrates that you have listened and understand. The second layer is your refusal. The third layer is something you *will* do to ease the sting. Here's an example:

1. I understand you want to borrow my car because yours won't start.
2. But I do not let others drive my car.
3. I have some extra time and will be happy to drive you to your appointment.

Or, try this tactful way to close a discussion:

1. I understand that you want me to agree with you.

2. But I see the issue from a different point of view.
3. I hope we can disagree and still be friends.

Calm responses are sometimes sugarcoated arsenic. A well-known bore was seated opposite James McNeill Whistler at a dinner party. During a lull in the conversation, he leaned toward the artist and said, "You know, Mr. Whistler, I passed your house this morning." "Thank you," said Whistler quietly. "Thank you very much."

Outrageous statements can be put down with a calm tone. When Margaret Fuller proclaimed, "I accept the universe," Thomas Carlyle said: "By God, she'd better."

When the Hearst newspaper empire was growing, assistant city editor Jake Dressler (a tall man, fiercely mustachioed, with a bass voice) exploded over the delinquency of reporter Blinker Murphy. "You're fired!" Dressler bellowed across the room. Murphy, with a trace of brogue, said: "That's all ver-ry well, but you cannot fire me." "The hell I can't!" Dressler roared.

The staff watched. Murphy and Dressler moved into the antique-furnished office of William Randolph Hearst. Each gave his own version. Hearst nodded.

"Mr. Murphy," he said hesitantly, "it has always been my understanding that it was the right of the editor to discharge a man if he felt it necessary. Do you have any reason for suggesting that we make an exception?"

"I have, Mr. Hearst," Murphy replied. "The reason is that *I refuse to be fired.*"

Hearst gazed impassively. Then he turned to Dressler, lifting his hands.

"In the circumstances, Mr. Dressler," he said, smiling, "I don't see what we can do about this."[26]

Replying to Attack

Answering attacks is constantly required to hold your own in a competitive society.

John Randolph of Roanoke, floor leader in the House of Representatives starting in 1801, returned fire so vigorously that other pols usually shrank from debating him. An exception: one Philomen Beecher, congressman from Ohio. Randolph at first tolerated Beecher's interruptions of "Previous question, Mr. Speaker." But when this happened a number of times, Randolph launched a verbal grenade: "Mr.

Speaker," Randolph said, "in the Netherlands, a man of small capacity, with bits of wood and leather, will in a few minutes construct a toy that will, with the pressure of a finger and thumb, cry 'Cuckoo, cuckoo!' With less ingenuity, and with inferior material, the people of Ohio have made a toy that will, without much pressure, say 'Previous question, Mr. Speaker!' "

Amid gales of laughter, Philomen Beecher slunk out of the chamber and off history's stage.

The persuasive power of some veteran congressmen is awesome. One freshman congressman was called into House Speaker Tip O'Neill's chambers for The Treatment—chapter and verse on how to vote on an upcoming bill. When he emerged, he announced his switch in vote.

"Did you see the light?" a friend asked.

"No, indeed, I felt the heat," the converted congressman said.

Giving as good as you get—or better—is the goal of many ambitious politicians. They get a lot of practice. Abraham Lincoln ran for Congress against Peter Cartwright, a hellfire-and-damnation evangelist who charged that Lincoln was godless. Both candidates attended a revival meeting. "All who desire to give their hearts to God and go to heaven will stand," shouted Cartwright. Many stood. "All who do not wish to go to hell will stand." Everybody but Lincoln stood.

"I observe that everybody but Mr. Lincoln indicated he did not want to go to hell. May I inquire of you, Mr. Lincoln, where are you going?"

"Brother Cartwright asks me directly where I am going," Lincoln said. "I desire to reply with equal directness: I am going to Congress."

Old Abe was following a precedent set by Davy Crockett ten years earlier. When Crockett arrived in Nacogdoches, Texas, he announced: "I am told that when a stranger like myself arrives here, the first inquiry is—what brought him here? I was for some years a member of Congress. In my last canvass, I told my people that if they saw fit to reelect me, I would serve them as faithful as I had done; but if not, they might go to hell, and I would go to Texas. I was beaten, and here I am."

But in 1912, William Randolph Hearst and William Jennings Bryan—the would-be kingmaker and the would-be king—were on the outs with one another. Bryan's enemies accused him of fraternizing with the opposition. Bryan admitted this. "I have even shaken hands with Mr. Hearst," he said. "In fact, a man in politics is required to shake hands with almost everybody—without requiring a certificate of character."

Hearst returned the attack. "Mr. Bryan must be mistaken," he said. "I am rather particular about the people I shake hands with. The only time I have noticed Mr. Bryan's hand was when it was extended for campaign contributions."[27]

Veteran political mudslingers called it a draw as far as the debate's content was concerned. But vocally, Bryan's famous delivery outgunned Hearst's thin, high-pitched voice (a serious handicap to a man who wanted to go to the White House).

Sometimes the less-renowned jouster walks away with the prize. H. L. Mencken lost few contests, but poet Maxwell Bodenhein came up the clear winner when he said: "H. L. Mencken suffers from the hallucination that he is H. L. Mencken. There is no cure for a disease of that magnitude."

Benjamin Disraeli and William Gladstone were rivals—with debating points more often going to Disraeli.

Gladstone: My opponent will either perish on the gallows or will die from a loathsome social disease.

Disraeli: That depends on whether I embrace my opponent's policies or his mistress.

Walter H. Johnson, Jr., speaking to the Graduate School of Sales Management and Marketing, told about the ultimate verbal revenge:

> In England, there is an organization which meets each year and awards a prize to the three men who've done an outstanding job as citizens and fathers. This is always done on the eve of Father's Day.
>
> This year the meeting was in London's Dorchester Hotel. Some of you know that hotel. It has a wonderful ballroom that seats 1,200 people. The toastmaster got up and said: "Ladies and Gentlemen I'm terribly pleased to introduce to you our first man to be honored tonight—Leigh Mallory. Leigh Mallory, will you please come to the platform."
>
> Leigh Mallory got up and said, "Leigh Mallory here, brigadier, married, two sons, both barristers." There was a strong round of applause because to be a brigadier and to have two sons as barristers is quite an achievement.
>
> The second man got up and said, "Smythe Willoughby here, brigadier, two sons, both Harley Street physicians." Another wonderful round of applause. In England's social structure, to be a Harley Street physician is a prestigious achievement.
>
> The third man got up and said, "Aye, sir, Jack Watson here, sergeant major, unmarried, two sons, both brigadiers."

WRAPPING IT UP

Language is a weapon for both attack and defense. To use it effectively, know when to choose the rapier and when the baseball bat.

Speaking on the offensive to anticipate problems or to avoid tedium will save time, money, wear and tear. With bores or hecklers, control the conversation. Never let your opponent gain control. Never give clerks and waiters a chance to tell you they're busy. Tell them you know they're busy but then state *your* needs.

Avoid unpleasantness in declining a request by (1) restating what your antagonist wants, (2) pointing out that you *won't* do that, and (3) stating what you *will* do. End of petition.

If you're the petitioner, don't be afraid to ask! Many people are left standing on life's street corners because they didn't ask. Ask to get.

When you run into a disaster, humor helps. If you receive a legitimate complaint, restate it in your own words—it shows sincerity, defuses the complainer's argument. Often an outright admission of error—"We were wrong"—is an excellent defense.

When you're walking on eggs, be careful of what you say—each word goes on the record.

Ridicule is valuable. Most attacks fail when the aggressor ends up looking silly. When your enemy hits you with a mudball, reshape it and fling it back. Then your enemy will be, as Shakespeare said, "hoist by his own petard." If you throw rocks, be prepared to dodge return fire. Prepare adroit wordage in advance—and then get credit as an ad-lib devastator.

To defend yourself in polite society, point out that your opponent would feel differently if he or she had at hand all the facts or had the opportunity to see the consequences of such action.

Adapt ammunition from the classic vituperators. Even when your tested quips are used for purposes other than attack or defense, they add color and verve to your speech.

16

Keep Them Laughing: You Can Be Funny—Most of the Time

"My topic is serious," the proper executive said. "I cannot pretend to include humor. It's not a funny subject." Well, neither is nuclear arms control. Or the national budget. Or flood relief. Yet President Reagan sees fit to use humor in speeches on subjects of national concern.

So can you—for these reasons:

Humor Helps You Get Your Points Across

Said Bob Hope:

Humor's not limited to the professional comedian. It's a powerful tool available to everyone who ever will give a speech. Everyone can have a one-liner or two for listeners—that includes the new president of the PTA, a business executive addressing the employees. Yes, there's even a joke or two in Washington. You should know that—you voted for some of them.

Humor is the welcome mat between a speaker and his audience. A short joke, a quick laugh, breaks the ice between you and that sea of strangers. When they laugh they're immediately on your side. The laughter makes them your friends. It's the most powerful ammunition you can carry. David could have saved himself a lot of trouble if he'd just told Goliath the one about the giant farmer's daughter.[28]

Humor Aids Learning

Says Gene Perret, professional comedy writer:

Playwrights have used this principle for centuries. It's called comic relief. They realize that serious, heavy drama can be wearisome work for an audience. So, they interject lighter moments to refresh the audience. The author wants them bright and sharp again so they can better perceive and appreciate the drama still to come.[29]

Comic relief also works in leavening chunks of learning. Use it in employee indoctrinations, says Jane Evans, executive vice president of the $650 million General Mills fashion apparel and accessories division, who adds: "A little shared laughter can make everyone more comfortable, get rid of underlying tensions, and so make a meeting progress faster."

But she warns that "humor should never be directed at another person, and it is equally important not to make yourself the center of the laughter. The idea is to focus humor on the problem, so that you can quickly create an atmosphere that is both relaxed and businesslike."

Humor helps you get and hold executive posts. William Gould, executive vice president of the Association of Executive Search Consultants, explains why: "What companies are seeking is someone who can see issues clearly. If a person can laugh, particularly at himself, he can probably step back and get the right perspective."

Humor Builds Leadership

If you ask people who they think highly of, chances are it's someone who uses humor effectively. Jokesmith Robert Orben claims anyone can be funny, and while shyness is no barrier, the style must be compatible with the speaker. "A Don Knotts executive can't get away with Don Rickles humor," he says.

In making a flipchart presentation to a prospective client, I once found—to my horror—that a yellow reminder note from a colleague had somehow remained on the glassine sheet facing the audience.

I picked it off, explained that it was a behind-the-scenes note, and read it aloud to the audience: "Don't you think you should work in a comment here about the need for TV news film?" The audience roared.

"Well, you've heard my instructions," I ad-libbed. "I happen to agree. The reason why we must not forget TV news film as a technique is . . ."

After this break, the audience was relaxed and on our side. That unplanned episode worked so well that since then I sometimes deliberately plant those notes in other presentations and feign surprise when I come across them.

Humor Spells Control

If you can get others to laugh, you're much more likely to get your own way.

In business settings, a person who uses humor tends to wield more influence over a group's decision. "Think of anyone you know who's funny," Orben suggests, "and you'll find they almost always have a lot of power in a group."

Your capacity for humor develops between the ages of one and two, stated Paul McGhee, a Texas Tech psychologist, in a newspaper article. Some people develop a terrific sense of humor, while others remain poker-faced. Studies starting at age two reveal that pre-school clowns, always trying to provoke laughter in others, are the most physically and verbally aggressive kids in class.

"When you tell jokes, you're taking the floor, demanding attention," McGhee says. "These kids discover that while others don't like aggressive behavior, it's acceptable if you're funny. How can you dislike someone who makes you laugh?"

And there's evidence that a yen for cutting up continues through life. "Timid kids don't become the humorous adults," McGhee says.

Insurance Against Egg-Laying

Humor is an enormous benefit to the power speaker, whether he's talking to one or to 1,000 people, but it carries risk. No one is funny *all* the time. Johnny Carson carefully rehearses lines to fall back on when the jokes don't work. He knows some won't pan out, despite his expensive writers, world-famous delivery, and much-imitated mugging. So he plans on being funny about jokes that flop.

In business speaking situations, you can count on something going wrong. The mike's too high, the mike's too low. Or you turn to thank so-

and-so and he's not there. If you address it with a joke, you gain control of your audience. And if you don't address it, everyone else will address it behind your back.

When you use humor in speech, you risk laying an egg. Take out an insurance policy in advance to make upside potential outweigh downside peril. The policy has a number of clauses:

- *Never program yourself to fail.* In using humor on the platform, don't say: "I understand it is appropriate to tell a story, so I found just the right one to introduce our subject tonight." (Even a funny story won't be funny under this handicap.)

- *Re-use your stories if they're good.* If you discover a joke that always hits the mark, don't put it aside because a few listeners have heard it. A good story wears well. At the same time, don't persist with truly stale and weary jokes.

- *For outdoor audiences, test humor carefully.* Humor somehow evaporates in wide-open spaces.

- *For small groups, select your humor even more carefully.* To get a laugh from small audiences (10 to 15 persons) is sometimes impossible. Have a substitute plan if your humor fails to take root.

- *Don't telegraph the punch line.* The inept storyteller goes on with a joke after the audience has anticipated it.

- *Don't step on your punch line.* Your fear that people won't laugh often prompts you to move on too quickly. Give it a chance.

- *Don't squirm if a joke fails.* Save it if you can, but don't make matters worse by trying to dredge up laughter that won't come. If the story makes a point, it really doesn't matter if your listeners laugh or not.

In one-on-one conversations, never say, "Did you hear the story about. . . ." It prompts the listener to think: "No, thank God, I didn't. I'm just sorry I must hear it now." Or: "Yes, I was bored by it before, and now, O Lord, I'm destined for boredom again!"

Shopping for Laughs

In searching for jokes to invigorate your speech or conversation, heed the counsel of Houston's John Wolfe, professional speaker:

- *The joke must make a point.* Your primary job is to convey a message. Don't use *Playboy's* latest thigh-slapper unless you can make it fit. Remember, you want integrated, not isolated, humor.

- *It must be funny.* In Gilbert and Sullivan's *Yeomen of the Guard,* jester Jack Point says: "They'll forgive you as long as you're funny." There's nothing worse than an un-funny joke.

And the longer the joke, the funnier it must be. If a one-liner doesn't go over, keep right on going. But after a big buildup, if your punch line brings only vacant stares, the silence can be deadly! So use surefire gags. Listen to your audience. Test humor in advance. If your audience doesn't react, it isn't funny!

■ *Keep it clean.* In a back-room poker game, anything goes. But don't offend an audience.

Admittedly, today even daytime television is full of double entendre. Slightly risqué humor rarely bothers anyone. But between risqué and just plain vulgar there's a huge difference.

If you decide to use outside help in adding humor to your speech, make your own decisions about what you want to say. Then work closely with your writer. Let the preparation be a mutual enterprise. Make sure the speech reflects your thoughts and personality.

When a ghostwriter working for Samuel Goldwyn fell ill, his aides arranged a substitute ghost. Goldwyn, reading the latest manuscript, expressed dismay: "This," he said, "is not up to my usual standard."

Mix Humor with Message

To be effective, let your audience laugh while they listen. But they don't want to laugh all the time. They also want a message. The speaker delivers a message—humor is a means to that end. The comedian's job is pure entertainment.

But even Bob Hope and Red Skelton close shows on a serious note—a charity appeal, for example.

As to type and amount of humor, it depends on your audience. If you're discussing embalming trends, any humor might be out of place. Your own personality is another factor. If you're blessed with an inborn gift to make people laugh, you're rare. Most of us must work at it.

Humor defines issues. John Kennedy, rather than shy away from potentially embarrassing issues, attacked them with wit. When a reporter asked (at a post-election press conference) why the vote was so close, Kennedy replied, "I didn't want my Daddy to pay for a landslide."

He also silenced criticism of his appointment of Robert Kennedy as attorney general with: "I wanted him to get some experience before he hangs up his shingle."

Being Funny with Style

A new inmate was eating his first meal in the state penitentiary. Suddenly someone yelled "36!" Howls of laughter. Then someone shouted

"79!" Again the convicts went crazy, rolling on the floor. The new inmate asked his mate what was happening. He replied: "The numbers signify jokes. We've been here so long we just tell 'em by number."

A few days after, the greenhorn haltingly called out a number. Nothing. Not even a hint of laughter. He asked his cellmate what happened. The inmate replied, "Some people can tell 'em; some can't!"

Of course, *you* want to get beyond that stage—quite a bit beyond. Here are ways to make your jokes funnier in the telling:

- *Keep it short.* Leave out all the excess garbage. Don't narrate a gag—tell it! Don't say: "It seems there were these two guys in a bar. And well, you know, things were kinda busy that evening. It was Saturday night, or something like that. See, this cat comes in. Or maybe it was a dog. Let's see if I can remember. . . ." Would you laugh at that? Neither will your audience!

- *Know it word for word.* This requires preparation and rehearsal. Deliver it smoothly and with precision. (Bill Gove, a famous motivator, calls this overlearning—meaning make each story a reflex package.) And when you rehearse, also rehearse the pauses. Usually your most important pause comes just before the punch line.

In emphasizing the importance of time, say: "Things *do* take time. I remember in Vietnam, they gave us little pills to stop us from thinking about girls. Now (pause) I'm finding out (pause) *they're just beginning to work!*"

- *Leave something to imagination.* Let your listeners think they're clever. In a classic Jack Benny skit, a robber stops Benny on the street and demands: "Your money or your life!" Long pause. The robber repeats: "*I said* your money or your life!" Whereupon Benny finally answers, "I'm *t-h-i-n-k-i-n-g* it over!"

Artful pauses allow listeners to figure the joke out on their own.

- *Use workhorse humor.* Use funny stories that make a point. Then, if the audience laughs, you've entertained. But even if you don't get a laugh, you've still made your point. If the point is pertinent, you haven't lost anything, and you've gained a building block in your argument.

Suppose you're talking to supervisors about humility. Tell this story:

> Near the end of World War II, at the Yalta conference, Churchill, Stalin, and Roosevelt were relaxing after one of their formal meetings.
> Churchill lit a long cigar, puffed contentedly, and said: "History will show that I, more than any other man, shaped the destiny of mankind for the first half of this century."
> Stalin, lighting his big black pipe, responded: "Nyet, God Almighty Himself has told me, Josef Stalin, that I have been chosen to rule the world."

FDR looked across the table at Stalin and indignantly replied: "Now, Joe, I never told you any such thing."

Usually a laugh-getter, this story will stand by itself even if it doesn't strike the audience as uproarious.

Similarly, at an investment club seminar, you can quote comedian Joe E. Lewis: "I've been rich and I've been poor. Believe me, rich is better." Even if they don't roll in the aisles, they are certain to get the message.

- *Let the audience laugh at you.* They'll like you better for it. Jack Benny was a master at this. So is Bob Hope.

To tell jokes funny—and not just tell funny jokes—let yourself be the goat. Self-deprecation is the most powerful humor of all. My friend George Hall proved this when he opened a speech with: "When I gave this speech to my secretary to be typed, I asked her to eliminate anything that was dull. So in conclusion. . . ."

A play on humble beginnings is always good. Sam Levinson said: "We never locked the door at night—we figured if a burglar came in, maybe he'd leave something."

Abraham Lincoln's opposition candidate spoke first. Time and again during the debate, he referred to Lincoln as two-faced. When Old Abe's turn came, he said: "Friends, I ask you, if I were two-faced, would I be wearing this one?"

- *Keep 'em laughing.* Laughter is like applause: The longer it runs, the better it gets. Rehearse what to *say* and *do* after the joke, too.

Some speakers deadpan it Bill Cosby–style. For most of us, this is not the best approach. Don't frown after every gag; that says to the audience: "That joke wasn't very funny, was it?" Also avoid the nervous chuckle.

Do what Bob Hope does: Simply stand there and smile, for however long the laugh lasts. This communicates two-way humor between you and the audience.

Some performers, like Sam Levinson, laugh out loud during and sometimes following a joke. They do it because they're genuinely enjoying themselves. But the best way to build the laugh following a joke is to repeat the straight line.

- *A joke doesn't have to be new.* Will Rogers' lines, presented by James Whitmore in his smash one-man shows, are as clever today as years ago. And look what Hal Holbrook did with Mark Twain!

If a joke makes a point, if it's funny and clean, and if you tell it well, use it. More than 90 percent of your listeners won't have heard the oldest joke in the world.

Humor's Basic Building Blocks

In choosing jokes for your inventory or in learning to deliver them with style, begin by understanding the basic ingredients of humor.

■ *The surprise factor.* Dorothy Parker, on attending a Halloween party, was told: "People in the next room are ducking for apples."

"Change one letter in that sentence and you'll have the story of my life," she riposted.

Woody Allen mixes trivial and profound to gain surprises. "Why does man kill? He kills for food. And not only for food. Frequently there must be a beverage."

■ *Overstating the truth.* A speaker before a veterans' group got his address off to a rousing start by saying: "We all recall the Army. It's like going to Boy Scout camp—but *without* adult supervision."

Woody Allen says: "I'll say one thing for bisexuality—it doubles your chances for a date on Saturday night." Well, yes. Come to think of it, that's true.

Back in the days of vaudeville, comedian Fred Allen recalled playing a town so far back in the woods the assistant manager of the hotel was a bear!

These are exaggerations, but the truth shows through. That makes them funny.

■ *Understating the truth.* Understatement is also funny, but sometimes it's harder to deliver effectively. The motorist asked the Maine character: "Have you lived here all your life?" Said the Down Easter, carefully whittling a piece of wood: "Not yet."

■ *The joke's on the audience.* James N. Eberhart, operations auditor for the southwestern region of General Waterworks Company (Pine Bluff, Arkansas), uses these job descriptions to loosen up an executive audience:

> *Sales Manager:* Knows very little about many things and keeps learning less and less about more and more until he knows pratically nothing about everything.
> *Engineer:* Knows a great deal about very little and goes along learning more and more about less and less until finally he knows practically everything about nothing.
> *Accountant:* Starts out knowing everything about everything but ends up knowing nothing about everything—because of his unfortunate association with engineers and sales managers.

Your listeners will love jokes tailored to their fields, as I found out in telling this story to a group at a medical convention:

A fellow went to an analyst to report feelings of inferiority. After six months of therapy, the doctor said: "We've found the trouble. You really *are* inferior."

Or, pick a member of the audience to spotlight: "I'm not saying Charlie is a dud. But whenever we get a response to one of our ads that say, 'No salesman will call,' we send Charlie."

• *The joke's on rivals.* Most groups have that number one rival. General Electric has Westinghouse. McDonald's has Burger King. Army has Navy. A friendly put-down of the competition gets an amplified response.

Robert Orben suggests this story: "I had a wonderful thing happen today. A cop was chasing a pickpocket yelling, 'Stop thief!' And three of my competitors turned around. [Pause for laugh.]

"I'm only kidding. We have very fine, upstanding competitors. The reason they're upstanding is they just had their furniture repossessed."

• *Kid local programs.* Travel agent Michael Cummings reports great success with this opener to employee groups: "I've been asked by management to make this announcement. Please stop putting suggestions in the employee suggestion box. The handle is broken and it won't flush."

• *Go after national institutions.* Said Will Rogers: "Well, I see Congress reconvened this week. I was *afraid* they was going to do that!" Or:

> A farmer once took his ten-year-old daughter to the nation's capital. As they entered the gallery of the Senate, the chaplain was starting his prayer.
> "Does the chaplain pray for the Senate, Daddy?" asked the little girl.
> "No," chuckled the farmer. "He comes in, looks at the Senators, and then prays for the country."

WRAPPING IT UP

People like to laugh while they listen. But they also want to hear a message. For better humor: Make it fit, make it funny, keep it clean. Humor breathes life into a presentation or speech. Good stories support points, act as transitions, build audience rapport.

Never read a story. Memorize the story line, but don't recite it word for word. Tell stories with feeling. Breathe life into each one. Let your feelings show, and don't worry about captivating listeners.

Test material on friends and acquaintances in lunch conversations, on the family over dinner, on guests at a party. Gauge from the response whether people enjoy it or not. Cautiously add workable humor to your inventory. Try again with material that doesn't work. If it still falters, drop it.

Don't just tell funny jokes. Tell jokes funny. The laugh depends on you. Know what to say and do following a gag. Keep them laughing after the joke is over. Every audience can be won over. With some, you just have to work harder, that's all. Your jokes should come as close to the truth as possible.

You gradually build up humor content with little jeopardy. Over months, you'll discover certain gags work for you and others don't. With practice, you can soon be funny—most of the time.

Epilogue: Power Speech in Real Life

The techniques of power speech, discussed in considerable detail in this book, show you the fast route to business and personal success in real life. Now let's complete our visit together with two stories from life—one I experienced personally and one *you* experienced.

Let's take mine first.

Spring in the Rocky Mountains is an inspiring place. Here Agamemnon, Inc. set up its first dealer meeting. Retailers arrived from all over. The resort hotel was first-rate. The company president, general manager, and sales manager spent weeks putting together a three-day training and information program—including films, speeches, and product instruction.

In addition to the company officials slated as speakers, the programmers also arranged for two outside speakers—a consultant who had just sold Agamemnon an engineering study and a former trade association executive who was in the process of making a career change.

George Hinney, the consultant, was scheduled to speak Friday evening after dinner. Ransome Barber, the trade association man, was on the platform Saturday after dinner. Both men had known about the speech for 30 days.

On Friday, the dealers galloped through a tightly scheduled day of inspiration and exhortation, sales training films, product knowledge seminars. At 5:30 P.M., with a slightly wilted look, they all headed for the company-sponsored cocktail party in the lobby—with speaker George Hinney leading the pack. He had had several drinks before dinner ("helps settle my mind") and then another drink during dinner. During

221

a short film, Hinney "progressed" to this stage: He decided he was clever and full of droll insight.

After his intro, he rose to speak—without notes—and committed the following major sins:

- He panned the movie (just-seen) as "not being really on target."
- He made derogatory remarks about consumers that buy Agamemnon's products.
- He couldn't remember statistics from his study. (That study was the reason he was on the program.)
- He concluded by panning the entire free market system (of which all his listeners were proud participants).

Company officials were aghast. ("If I'd had a gun, I would have shot him," the general manager said.)

Hinney still didn't sit down. He asked for questions. Since the audience hadn't understood what he had said, several delegates raised their hands. The meeting coordinator hopped in the breach and suggested that delegates see the speaker on a one-on-one basis afterwards. Finally, the "speaker" was silenced.

The audience, puzzled, had been on a high all day. Now it was confused. ("What was he trying to do?" "Was he drunk?" "Why so flippant about our business?" "I didn't understand.")

Chalk up one gigantic disaster that demonstrates the value of power speech—in reverse. (The power works both ways.)

George Hinney didn't stay for the rest of the meeting. He sneaked out the side door. He had originally hoped to get more research work from Agamemnon. Clearly, that was now impossible.

No one in the audience would recommend him for future speaking dates. Since speaking is an important entrée to new research work, he lost new business. The consultant that recommended him to handle Agamemnon's research work won't recommend him again.

He lost enough ground to set his consulting business back two years. All because (1) he didn't prepare his speech and (2) he tapped into Dutch Courage at the bar. A highly qualified man in his work got a big round goose egg from an important roomful of retailers and from an ex-client.

Ransome Barber, slated to speak on Saturday night, arrived early on Friday to attend other sessions. He talked to delegates to try to understand their problems. He drank only club soda. ("I never drink when I'm speaking.")

On Saturday night, Barber took an outline to the podium with him.

It was a skeleton he had prepared well ahead, but had changed and localized as he sat in on sessions. He opened with a story about a town not far from the convention site. This got his listener's attention.

He mixed inspiration and instruction with humor. He employed broad arm and hand gestures. He told stories about himself to illustrate points. It was fire and brimstone, sandwiched into poetry and propelled by eloquence. He ended with a flourish—and right on time.

The audience rose and gave him a standing ovation. Barber was a rousing success. The company president immediately engaged Barber to speak at another meeting. Several audience members made notes about recommending him to other groups. The acclaim aided Barber considerably in his career change.

That's *my* experience. Now let's talk about *your* experience—the hostage crisis in Lebanon in the summer of 1985.

You were there. TV brought you the story minute by minute. Lebanese Shiites seized TWA flight 847, took American passengers hostage, and murdered a Navy man on board. The hostages were not freed until 17 days later.

During this complex period, an amazingly simple process occurred that demonstrated the effectiveness of power speech. One hostage, Allyn B. Conwell, a salesman from Houston, emerged as the spokesman for the group—and was accepted as such by the hostages held full-term. (Later he was put under fire for showing too much sympathy for his captors.)

How did he do it? *Not* by experience. No one in the hostage group had been skyjacked before. They entered the event equally unschooled. *Not* by influence. The isolated group, a mini-society just created, installed its leader because he articulated their problems. He asked for the responsibility of talking for the group. As the released TWA captain, John L. Trestrake, said: "Our spokesman [Conwell] is very eloquent. He says it very well for all of us."

Conwell, a sincere person, communicated his sincerity at a press conference held upon the release of the hostages.

> I want to commend all the people that I've had the pleasure of being the spokesman for.
> I have an extremely high regard for these individuals. They've all in their way exhibited their strength. They've all maintained their dignity. They've all kept very cool heads throughout this ordeal. No one tried anything foolish. They've acted in a professional manner—a mature manner. And I'm extremely proud of every man in this room. We without exception, the hostages (who were unfortunately separated from the crew), want to express our deepest thanks for the manner in which the

crew performed throughout this ordeal, particularly referring to the three days on the airplane.

These men did one hell of a lot to keep us all together. I know we all had our heads bent down between our knees, and if everyone was as frightened as I was, it was a unique course of fear going on in that plane. But the manner in which the crew, the entire crew, behaved and conducted themselves and guided us through the ordeal is one that I give my deepest appreciation.

I'm sorry. We're all very tired. We've had a long day already. We've got a longer night ahead of us. We're going to close for now. We appreciate your questions. We appreciate your professional demeanor. And it's good to be here. It's good to see every one of you. Thank you very much.

Let's hear it for power speech, the quality that propelled Allyn B. Conwell to instant celebrity. You'll hear more from him in the years ahead.

With this kind of force to push you forward, it's not surprising that power speech *is* the quickest route to business and personal success!

Notes

Chapter 1

1. Bergen Evans, *The Word-a-Day Vocabulary Builder* (New York: Ballantine, 1981), pp. 4-5.

Chapter 3

2. As quoted in Dorothy Sarnoff, *Make the Most of Your Best* (New York: Holt, Rinehart and Winston, 1983), p. 53.
3. As quoted in Philip J. Koeper, *How to Talk Your Way to Success in Selling* (Englewood Cliffs, N.J.: Parker Publishing, 1983), p. 133.
4. As quoted in C. B. Roth and Roy Alexander, *Secrets of Closing Sales* (Englewood Cliffs, N.J.: Prentice-Hall, 1983), p. 35.

Chapter 4

5. William Manchester, *The Last Lion* (Boston: Little Brown, 1983), p. 30.
6. As quoted in Charles B. Roth and Roy Alexander, *Secrets of Closing Sales* (Englewood Cliffs, N.J.: Prentice-Hall, 1983), pp. 212-213.
7. Ibid., p. 34.

Chapter 5

8. Dr. Joseph Mancuso, "Picking the Best Corporate Name," *Marketing Times* (January-February 1980), pp. 47-49.

Chapter 6

9. As quoted in Charles B. Roth and Roy Alexander, *Secrets of Closing Sales* (Englewood Cliffs, N.J.: Prentice-Hall, 1983), pp. 196-198.
10. Roth and Alexander, *Closing Sales*, p. 61.

Chapter 7

11. As quoted in James F. Bender, *How to Talk Well* (New York: McGraw-Hill, 1949), pp. 146-147.
12. W. R. Espy, *The Almanac of Words at Play* (New York: Crown, 1980).
13. Peter Hockstein, "How to Turn American into Gobbledygook," *Marketing Times* (September-October 1979), p. 35.

Chapter 8

14. As quoted in Charles B. Roth and Roy Alexander, *Secrets of Closing Sales* (Englewood Cliffs, N.J.: Prentice-Hall, 1983), p. 67.

Chapter 9

15. Ed Daytrik, "A Turn with the Greatest," *It's a Hell of a Life* (New York: Times Books, 1984), p. 185.
16. As quoted in James A. Newman and Roy Alexander, *Climbing the Corporate Matterhorn* (New York: Wiley, 1985), pp. 62-64.

Chapter 10

17. Paul Dickson, *Words* (New York: Delacorte Press, 1982), pp. 213, 237.
18. Gary Provost, *Writer's Digest* (February 1983), pp. 21-23.
19. As quoted in David Ogilvy, *Ogilvy Advertising* (New York: Crown, 1983), p. 200.
20. Sir Winston Churchill, *The American Civil War* (first published in *A History of the English Speaking Peoples: The Great Democracies*, Apollo edition), (New York: Dodd, Mead, 1958), pp. 110-111.
21. Lance Patterson, "Daniel Webster," *American History Illustrated* (February 1963), p. 22.

Chapter 11

22. Harold J. Cummings, "Rx for Tomorrow: 13 Ways to Manage Your Life and Mind," *Marketing Times* (March-April 1979), p. 7.

Chapter 13

23. Mortimer Levitt, "The Right Impression Is Just Plain Common Sense," *Marketing Times* (November-December 1982), p. 42.

Chapter 14

24. Judy George, "Retailing the Way Others *Don't* Do It," *Marketing Times* (September-October 1979), p. 22.
25. Peter P. Jacobi, *Writing with Style* (Chicago: The Regan Company, 1982).

Chapter 15

26. W. A. Swanberg, *Citizen Hearst* (New York: Charles Scribner's Sons, 1984), p. 83.
27. Ibid., p. 231.

Chapter 16

28. Bob Hope, in Foreword to Gene Perret, *How to Hold Your Audience with Humor* (Cincinnati: Writer's Digest Books, 1984).
29. Gene Perret, *How to Hold Your Audience with Humor.*

Index